Linking
Theory TO Practice

CASE STUDIES FOR WORKING WITH COLLEGE STUDENTS

Edited by

Frances K. Stage, Ph.D.
Dept. of Educational Leadership and Policy Studies
Indiana University at Bloomington

Michael Dannells, Ph.D.
Dept. of Counseling and Educational Psychology
Kansas State University

Brunner-Routledge

New York • Hove

Published in 2000 by
Brunner-Routledge
270 Madison Avenue
New York, NY 10016
www.brunner-routledge.com

10   9   8   7   6   5   4   3

Library of Congress Cataloging-in-Publication Data
    Linking theory to practice : case studies for working with college students / edited by
       Frances K. Stage, Michael Dannells—2nd ed.
       Stage's name appears as principal author on the earlier edtition.
          p. cm.
       Includes bibliographical references and index.
       ISBN 1-56032-865-7 (alk. paper))
       1. Student affairs services—United States—Case Studies. 2. College students personnel
       administrators—Training of—United States. I. Stage, Frances K. II. Dannells, Michael.
       LB2342.9 .L56 2000
       378.9´946—dc21   99-057551

ISBN 1-56032-865-7 (paper)

LINKING THEORY
TO PRACTICE

Contents

Preface

This book is a new edition of the original *Linking Theory to Practice: Case Studies for Working with College Students*. We think this book, with 26 new, updated cases, will be as useful to up and coming student affairs professionals as the former book was. The first three chapters have been updated and we have included reviews of newer theories to reflect the changing student affairs profession. Additionally, on the advice of reviewers, we have added an index to the case studies. Faculty and workshop facilitators can use the index to quickly identify cases covering issues and institutional characteristics that are of interest to them. Students are cautioned however, that we only identified the three most salient and obvious issues for each case. More subissues likely exist and will need to be identified and analyzed for a thorough case analysis. Once again, we expect a future demand for even newer case studies reflecting broader campus issues that we have yet to envision. Therefore we again solicit your comments now on this book as well as suggestions for cases to be included in a future volume.

We intend for this book be used to supplement other reading materials within student affairs preparation courses. It might also be used as material for workshops for student affairs professionals and paraprofessionals. While we included a cursory overview of theories that guide student affairs practice, it is impractical and impossible to comprehensively cover the theories involved. Other material that covers these important topics, especially those referenced in the first three chapters, should be used in conjunction with this book.

The book is organized into two major sections. The first three chapters set the stage, so to speak, for case study analysis. Chapter 1 presents an extensive argument for the use of case studies in linking theoretical study with practice. Chapter 2 provides an overview of four topical areas that comprise the study of college student affairs: student development, college environments, organizational theory, and the changing college student body. Chapter 3 introduces an algorithm to be followed in conducting case study analysis. A sample case study is presented along with a detailed analysis to be used as a guide for the facilitator as well as the student in using the remainder of the book.

The second part of the book contains the cases. The cases themselves are divided into the remaining six chapters based on areas of work within student affairs: organization and administration, advising and counseling, residence life, student activities, academic issues, and legal and judicial matters. One of the first things the reader may notice is the lack of discreteness of cases organized into these arbitrary chapters. Cases in advising and counseling sometimes overlap into academic issues. Residence life and student activities problems sometimes look similar. Most cases have a legal component to consider. This is the reality of today's complex college campus.

The case study authors present a challenging array of problems to be tackled. Cases include setting, characters, and a statement of the events of the case. A few cases also have a list of facts. In each case, professionals are faced with an array of short- as well as long-term issues. Topics of cases within sections vary across such current issues as racial diversity, campus violence, alcohol abuse, and student activism. The campus environments vary as well; cases occur at large research universities, community college campuses, historically black institutions, and residential liberal arts colleges. The professionals involved in the dilemmas described range from vice presidents for student affairs to fresh student affairs hires in their first weeks on a job.

The authors of the cases in this book have collective experience, by a conservative estimate, of over 250 years. We are fortunate to have their expertise to help with such an important aspect of student affairs preparation—the application of the learnings of the classroom to practical reality. Finally, we would like to thank Joyce Regester for her help with this project.

Fran Stage and Mike Dannells

Contributors

Editors' Biographies

Frances K. Stage is professor of Educational Leadership and Policy Studies at Indiana University, Bloomington. She holds Bachelor's and Master's degrees in mathematics from the University of Miami and Drexel University respectively and a Ph.D. in Higher Education from Arizona State University. Stage teaches graduate courses in learning theory and research design. Her research focus is on learning in college mathematics classrooms and on students' progress in the math/science pipeline. She has won the Association for the Study of Higher Education's "Promising Scholar" award, Indiana University's "Outstanding Young Researcher" award, the ACPA's "Annuit Coeptis" award, a National Science Foundation/AERA Research Fellowship for the 1999/2000 academic year and is currently vice president of the American Educational Research Association for Postsecondary Education. Stage has numerous books, chapters, and articles focusing on college students and the methods for studying them and is the lead author of *Creating Learning Centered Classrooms: What Does a Learning Theory Have to Say?*

Michael Dannells is professor and department chair of Counseling and Educational Psychology and coordinator of the college student personnel program in the College of Education at Kansas State University. He earned his B.S. from Bradley University and his Ph.D. in College Student Development from the University of Iowa. He has worked in a variety of student affairs offices, including dean of students, residence life, and admissions and new student services. He is past director for Commissions of the American College Personnel Association. He also served as chair of the Commission on Professional Preparation. He has researched and written numerous journal articles and book chapters on a range of topics in student affairs, particularly in the area of student discipline and judicial affairs. He is the author of *From Discipline to Development: Rethinking Student Conduct in Higher Education* (ASHE-ERIC, 1997).

Authors' Biographies

Marilyn J. Amey is associate professor in the Higher, Adult, and Lifelong Education program at Michigan State University. Amey held several administrative positions in Student Affairs and has conducted research on college students, collegiate contexts, administration/governance, leadership, and faculty and taught courses at Penn State University, the University of Kansas, and MSU.

Guadalupe Anaya is assistant professor of the Educational Leadership and Policy Studies Department at Indiana University. She has a Ph.D. in Higher Education from the University of California, Los Angeles. She has conducted many evaluation studies of college student programs and has extensive experience working with undergraduate students and student organizations. Anaya conducts research on student learning and development, the validity of alternate indicators of learning, and the educational experiences and achievement of African American and Latina/o students.

Aaron D. Anderson is currently working as a graduate research assistant and studying for his Ph.D. at the Center for the Study of Higher and Postsecondary Education at the University of Michigan. Having been employed for the past several years at the University of California at Berkeley, Aaron is a seasoned student affairs professional. His most recent areas of foci are on team, leadership, and organizational development as well as change and transformation in higher education institutions.

M. Christopher Brown is assistant professor of Higher Education at the University of Illinois at Urbana-Champaign. He is the author of *The Quest to Define Collegiate Desegregation* and an editor of *Organization and Governance in Higher Education: An ASHE Reader* (Fifth edition). His teaching and research focus is on equity and educational opportunity. He is currently working on a monograph on affirmative action initiatives in higher education.

Scott C. Brown received his bachelor's degree in English at the University of California, Irvine, his Master's degree in College Student Personnel Administration/Counseling and Counselor Education at Indiana University, and his Ph.D. in College Student Personnel Administration at the University of Maryland. He has worked at Dartmouth College and on Semester at Sea. He has written and presented on issues related to enhancing learning environments and serving a community of diverse student learners.

Anne S. Butler, Ph.D., currently works as director of the Center of Excellence for the Study of Kentucky African Americans at Kentucky State University in Frankfort, KY. Previously she held a split appointment at Kansas State University serving as assistant professor of Counseling and Educational Psychology and director for Women's Studies.

M. Lillian Casillas is interpreter and administrator for the education department in the Indiana State Museum and Historic Sites. She earned an M.S. in Student Affairs Administration from Indiana University. Lillian served as program coordinator for the Office of Women's Affairs and for Latino Affairs at Indiana University. She has served as a counselor for International Programs in Mexico and Spain. Lillian has extensive experience working with undergraduate students and Latina/o student organizations. She currently designs and conducts museum outreach programs for Indiana schools and community groups.

Jeanett Castellanos, an educator and administrator, holds a Master's in Counseling Psychology and a Ph.D. in Higher Education Administration from Washington State University. She completed a summer postdoctoral fellowship at Indiana University and is currently working at the University of California, Irvine.

Sally Hood Cisar is associate instructor in Language Education at Indiana University completing her third year of doctoral work in language education with a focus on foreign language and reading. She has taught a required reading methods course for the last two years and is also currently teaching a Master's level course through distance education. Part of Cisar's work is with the state department of education's foreign language consultant and several foreign language teachers. They are collaborating on a project that will provide teachers with an instructional component in the state proficiency guide. She spent eight years teaching French in the rural southern part of Indiana.

Michael D. Coomes is associate professor of Higher Education at Bowling Green State University. Coomes earned his B.A. in History from Western Washington State University and his Ed.D. from Indiana University-Bloomington. He is a member of the American College Personnel Association, the National Association of Student Personnel Administrators, and the Association for the Study of Higher Education. His scholarly activities focus on federal education policy, student financial aid, and the first year experience.

Janice Dawson-Threat is assistant professor of Higher Education and Student Affairs at the University of Missouri-Columbia. She teaches History of Higher Ed., Race, Gender, & Ethnicity in Higher Ed., Student Development Theory, and Student Affairs Administration. Her research explores the relationship between academic experiences in higher education and the process of identity formation for American college students. She recently published, "Enhancing in-class academic experiences for African American men" in the New Directions for Student Services series entitled *Helping African American Men Succeed in College.*

Robert DeBard is associate professor in the Department of Higher Education and Student Affairs at Bowling Green State University. His more than 20 years of administrative experience includes being the campus executive officer and dean of Firelands College of BGSU, and dean of the School of General Studies at Old Dominion University. He holds his doctorate in Higher Education from Indiana University.

W. Houston Dougharty is associate dean for student services and director of counseling, health, and wellness at the University of Puget Sound. He earned his B.A. from Puget Sound, and M.Ed. from Western Washington University, and an M.A. from UC-Santa Barbara, where he is a Ph.D. candidate. He was formerly associate dean of students at Iowa State.

Katie Branch Douglas is assistant professor of the Department of Human Development and Family Studies at the University of Rhode Island. She has held positions in women's services, financial aid, residence life, and multicultural affairs. Her research interests include college student development and learning, person-environment interactions, student retention, and multicultural issues.

John P. Downey currently serves as associate director of the Advisement Services Center at the University at Albany. His career shift to academic affairs comes after many years of working in Student Affairs at both public and private colleges. He received his Ph.D. in 1994 from Indiana University, where he studied Educational Leadership and Policy Studies.

Michael Elmore, with an M.A. and M.Ed. from the University of Virginia, has 18 years experience in the field of Student Life. He has served at the director level on three different campuses. Currently, he is working on his Ph.D. in Cultural Foundations and is the director of Student Activities at Syracuse University.

Cathy McHugh Engstrom is assistant professor of Higher Education at Syracuse University. She spent 14 years in student affairs administration in such areas as residence life, student activities, Greek life, and a dean of students' office. Her research interests lie in collaboration and student learning and diversity. She is currently conducting a major research study about how women senior student affairs administrators construct their experiences.

Teresa L. Hall is currently director of Student Activities at Towson University in Maryland. She has had additional professional experience in residence life, new student orientation, judicial affairs, and leadership development. Prior to her position at Towson, Hall served as associate director of Student Activities and the Coordinator of the Master's Program in Higher Education and Student Affairs at Indiana University.

Florence A. Hamrick is assistant professor of Higher Education at Iowa State University, where she teaches courses in higher education and research methods. Her research centers on traditionally underrepresented groups in higher education. She earned her Ph.D. from Indiana University, her Master's degree from Ohio State University, and her baccalaureate degree from the University of North Carolina at Chapel Hill.

David W. Hardy is an attorney in private practice, specializing in alternative dispute resolution with an emphasis in business, employment, and domestic relations mediation. He was associate director of the Office of Organizations and Activities at the University of Kansas, where he is completing doctoral research on gay college student identity development.

Peggy Jennings is associate dean of Educational Services at Dickinson College in Carlisle, PA, where she oversees the Office of Residential Life, New Student Orientation, and the college's judicial system, and serves as dean for the freshman class. She has also served in a variety of positions at small liberal arts colleges including director of Residence Life at Salve Regina University, Newport, RI, and coordinator of Counseling Services and director of Developmental Studies at Bethany College, Bethany, WV.

Adrianna Kezar is assistant professor at the George Washington University, teaching organizational theory, leadership, and history of higher education. Kezar is also director of the ERIC Clearinghouse on Higher Education. She holds a Ph.D. and M.A. in Higher Education Administration from the University of Michigan and a B.A. from the University of California, Los Angeles. Her scholarship focuses on higher education leadership, diversity issues, organizational theory, systems change, and administration.

Jillian Kinzie is a research associate and Ph.D. candidate in Higher Education at Indiana University-Bloomington. Previously, she served as assistant dean in an interdisciplinary residential college and as an administrator in student affairs. She earned her M.Ed. in Postsecondary Education in 1988 and B.A. in Psychology in 1986 from Cleveland State University. Kinzie's research interests include theories of teaching and learning, women in math and science, feminist pedagogy, and retention issues for underrepresented students. She is a coauthor of *The Learning-Centered Classroom: What Does Learning Theory Have to Say?*

Susan R. Komives is College Student personnel Graduate Program coordinator at the University of Maryland. Susan was vice president for Student Development at the University of Tampa and Stephens College. She served as ACPA president in 1982–1983 and is co-chair of the ACPA Senior Scholars. Susan and Doug Woodard are co-editors of *Student Services: A Handbook for the Profession* (Jossey Bass, 1996) and with Nance Lucas and Tim McMahon she is co-author of *Exploring Leadership: For College Students Who Want to Make a Difference.*

Jane L. Lambert is director of Undergraduate Programs at Indiana University's

Kelley School of Business at Indianapolis. She is also a faculty member in Accounting and a Ph.D. candidate in Higher Education from Indiana University School of Education. Lambert's research interest is in academic and social integration at urban universities.

Gail Londergan has been involved in nonprofit project and service management since 1980, including experience in the areas of library automation, database services, marketing, human resources, development, and public relations. For the past ten years she has worked at Indiana University, Bloomington in academic advising. Her Ph.D., from IU, is in information science with a minor in public management. Her research interest is creativity.

Cheryl D. Lovell is assistant professor of Education and Coordinator of M.A. Programs in Higher Education and Adult Studies at the University of Denver. Her research areas are in postsecondary public policy and college student development. In the area of student development, she has investigated the role of involvement in campus life as an indicator of student growth and learning. She serves as NASPA's chair of the Public Policy Division.

Kerry A. McCaig is director of the Learning Resources Center at Arapahoe Community College in Littleton, Colorado. Her research has focused on self-regulatory learning processes and academic achievement of high-risk students in higher education.

Glenda Droogsma Musoba is a research associate and Ph.D. student at Indiana University, Bloomington in Educational Leadership and Policy Studies with an emphasis on higher education. Prior to that, her professional experience included several student affairs positions primarily in Dordt College in Sioux Center, Iowa and Reformed Bible College in Grand Rapids, Michigan.

Julie Nelson was a graduate student in the Educational Leadership and Policy Studies program at Iowa State University. Her commitment to diversity in higher education took various forms. She facilitated a support group for lesbian and bisexual women; directed Diversity Players, an educational theater group that used dramatic scenarios to teach students, faculty, and staff about various diversity issues across campus; and collaborated on a research project about women full professors in higher education.

Suzy Nelson is associate dean of Students for Fraternity and Sorority Affairs at Cornell University and has worked in Student Affairs for over 13 years. Her experience lies in student activities, residence life, Greek affairs, and leadership development. She has a Master's degree in college student personnel from Bowling Green State University and is pursuing her doctorate in Higher Education at Syracuse University.

Becky Ropers-Huilman is assistant professor in Higher Education and Women's and Gender Studies at Louisiana State University. Her scholarly interests include curriculum and college teaching, race and gender, educational leadership, and qualitative research. She has published articles in several forums, including the *National Women's Studies Association Journal,* the *International Journal for Qualitative Studies in Education,* and *Higher Education: Handbook of Theory and Research.* She has also published a book with Teachers College Press entitled *Feminist Teaching in Theory and Practice.*

Brian Ropers-Huilman has a B.S. in Electrical Engineering from the University of Wisconsin-Madison and has worked in the computer support industry for the past six years. His interests include high performance and research computing as well as Web enabled data, teaching, and learning. He currently works as a UNIX System Administrator for the High Performance Computing group at Louisiana State University.

Vicki J. Rosser is a doctoral candidate and graduate research assistant in the department of Educational Administration at the University of Hawaii at Manoa. Her research with Dr. Linda K. Johnsrud has examined the worklife issues and morale of midlevel administrators in higher education. Articles have appeared in the *Review of Higher Education* and *CUPA Journal.* Her dissertation has led her to study another midlevel administrative group—academic deans and their effective leadership.

Ruth V. Russell is professor of Recreation and Park Administration and associate dean for Academic Affairs at Indiana University, Bloomington. In the latter position, her responsibilities include the oversight of the University Division—the academic home of 12,000 undergraduate students. Her research is focused on leisure as a social/psychological and cultural phenomenon. Author of four text books in recreation and park management, she has taught world-wide.

Robert A. Schwartz is associate professor in the Higher Education program at Florida State University. His research has examined the access and participation of women minorities in higher education, the history of higher education, and students in higher education. He taught at Valdosta (GA) State University, the University of South Carolina, and worked in student affairs at the University of North Dakota.

Steven P. Thomas is program manager for the Illini Union Board of the Illini Union in the Division of Student Affairs at the University of Illinois at Urbana-Champaign. Previously, he was the coordinator of Campus of Difference and Multicultural Student Outreach in the Multicultural Student Center at the University of Toledo. As a diversity educator, he offers workshops and programs around the country.

Bill Tobin is a doctoral student in higher education. His research interests include student persistence, institutional research, and planning. He has a Master's in history and bachelor's in economics, both from Indiana State University.

Patricia M. Volp is dean of students at The College of William and Mary in Virginia. She is an adjunct instructor for George Washington University in the Higher Education Administration Doctoral Program. Volp formerly served as dean of students and associate professor at Southeast Missouri State University, dean of students at The College of Saint Teresa, and director of Student Voluntary Services at Ball State University.

Harriet Wilkins is associate professor of English and Technical Communications at Indiana University/Purdue University at Indianapolis. She has a joint appointment in the Department of English in the School of Liberal Arts (Indiana University) and the School of Engineering and Technology (Purdue) and is coordinator of the Technical Communications Program. She has served on numerous campus-wide student affairs committees. Previously she taught English as a Second Language at Louisiana State University and Meharry Medical College.

Part One

Theories, Practices, and Case-Study Analysis

Chapter 1

Theory in a Practical World

Frances K. Stage and Michael Dannells

Theories, particularly developmental theories, focusing on college students have grown in number and have become well defined in recent years (Evans, Forney, & Guido-Dibrito, 1998; Rodgers, 1983, 1989; Stage & Kuh, 1996; Strange, 1994; Terenzini, 1994). Nevertheless, many authors describe the difficulties of campus professionals' attempts to link theory and research to practice (Bloland, Stamatakos, & Rogers, 1994; Caple & Voss, 1983; Parker, 1977; Plato, 1978; Stage, 1994; Upcraft, 1994, 1998). This remains true despite an explosion of knowledge about student development, campus environments, organizations, and characteristics of diverse college students. While these are all requisite components in the education of student affairs workers (McEwen & Talbot, 1998; Miller, 1997), professionals also require practice applying this newly acquired knowledge to the reality of a college campus.

Student Affairs has moved from an apprenticeship type of profession to one with a strong educational base. In the past, individuals with a variety of educational backgrounds who liked the campus atmosphere and who liked working with students decided to enter the student affairs profession. Usually, they were given entry-level jobs in which they worked closely with administrators and learned the ropes. Under the protective environment the fledgling administrator was shielded from making serious professional errors and—perhaps with occasional minor slipups—was guided along under the watchful eyes of his or her mentor.

Today few student affairs divisions have the luxury of providing new employees with this kind of mentoring. At the start of the new millennium, there is

3

little evidence that such a luxury will return. Instead, the expectation is that new professionals, even at the lowest levels, will have the ability to work independently and solve complex issues knowledgeably and with skill and integrity. This expectation also follows from the fact that increasingly professionals in student affairs have graduated from a student affairs preparation program.

It is not unreasonable to conjecture that some of the difficulties in applying theory stem from difficulties inherent in studying concepts in the abstract atmosphere of the classroom or meeting room. Therefore, students affairs preparation programs typically include components of practical application. Internships, practica, and graduate assistantships all contribute to the increased sophistication of today's new professional. Nevertheless, there is only a limited amount of such experience that a student can gain. Additionally, such preprofessional experiences are necessarily limited to only one or two types of campuses. There is no guarantee that those campus settings will closely match that of the new job setting. Case study analysis can provide an additional and necessary method of linking the student affairs knowledge base with practicality across a broad range.

Additionally, within student affairs curricula, in sessions at professional association meetings, and in staff training, the focus is on developmental theories, campus environments, organizational theories, and student characteristics—usually one theory at a time. Interactions of a particular student at a certain stage of development for a given theory in a specific campus setting are considered. Rarely, however, are aspiring professionals given the opportunity to consider and choose from many theories, possibly in combination, within a general, more holistic and honest context. Later translation of those theories by practitioners in the work setting leaves gaps between theoretical intention and administrative action (Komives, 1998).

Finally, litigation concerning students on college campuses is growing. As U.S. citizens became more consumer oriented and more willing to litigate, so too became the college "consumer" as well as his or her parents. Now, approaching the new millennium, student affairs professionals often are involved in a legal defense of themselves and their colleges. Student affairs professionals must continually weigh decisions in light of the culpability of themselves and their institutions. Case-study analysis can provide a format for considering the legal implications surrounding campus decision issues.

Case-study analysis provides a means for consideration of the interactions between many elements of campus life and beyond. The broad perspective of a case study gives students and administrators a realistic opportunity to use theory in action before attempting to apply it in the work setting. In addition to considering students, the case-study analyst must take into account interrelationships between faculty, administrators, and community members in particular campus settings with specific histories, traditions, norms, and values. The idealism of the classroom is suspended while the analyst vicariously enters the college environment of the case study.

This chapter presents case-study analysis as a useful tool for connecting discrete theory and topics studied in student affairs classes to the aggregate reality of the college campus. This book is not intended to be used in lieu of other materials on college students, their growth and development, organizations, and campus environments. Rather, it is intended as a supplement to be used with other sources for education of those who work or who hope to work with college students. In the remainder of this chapter, some of the difficulties of applying theory in practice are discussed. Then, an argument is made for the use of case studies to link classroom learning with the realities of various campus settings.

DIFFICULTIES OF APPLYING THEORY IN PRACTICE

The usefulness of theory in working with college students has been questioned (Stage et al., 1992). Some authors assert that such theory may not be useful (Bloland, Stamatakos, & Rogers, 1994; Plato, 1978; Upcraft, 1994, 1998). Others suggest that theory is useful for administrative practice, but recognize gaps between the focus of those who produce theory and the needs of those who use it (Caple & Voss, 1983). Still others assert that even when theory addresses practical issues, difficulty might be encountered in altering one's practical behavior based on theoretical guidelines (Parker, 1977).

Parker (1977) discussed problems inherent in efforts to apply theory in practice. He described a paradox inherent in the creation of theory. In attempts to generalize, theorists must strip away the very idiosyncrasies that practitioners cannot ignore. By stripping away the idiosyncrasies, theorists and researchers remove the "humanness" from the situation. One thing we do know is that those who work with college students cannot ignore their human qualities.

A hypothetical example will illustrate how creation of theory and its resultant research can result in this paradox: Professors Hawes and Skaggs want to learn more about satisfaction and retention in the first year of college. They write a proposal and are awarded money to conduct a qualitative study of students at the end of their first year of college. The outcome of the research project is to be a theory of college student satisfaction.

They conduct two, hour-long interviews with 40 students. The format is open-ended with a handful of questions forming the basis for information gathering: "What were the most positive aspects of your year on campus?" "What were the most negative?" "If you could choose all over again, would you still choose this college?" "Would you tell a friend to come to school here?" "What would you change about this campus if you could?"

As a result of their study, Hawes and Skaggs have a wealth of information about college students. Consider elements gleaned from three interviews:

> *Bill was the first in his family to attend college. Early in the semester he had trouble with his roommate. He now has a new one and they get along fine. He thinks his family doesn't really understand how hard college is and how time-consuming the*

homework can be. He relies on his friends and resident assistant to give him support. He makes friends easily and particularly enjoys talking to faculty after class about things in which he is interested. Toward the end of the semester he started running out of money and got a job to cover expenses. His grades went down because he couldn't spend as much time as he needed studying.

Katharine is a basketball player majoring in physics. At the beginning of the year she had a hard time making ends meet but began working at the local community Girls' Club. A month after she came to school her ten year old cat died. She almost left college then. Sometimes she feels out of place in her classes full of men, especially when she has to go to lab right before practice and has her warm-up clothes on. First semester, she had a lab instructor who seemed to like her and who encouraged her to "stick it out" when she was thinking of quitting college. Though she enjoys basketball and has lots of close friends on the team, her athletic obligations take time from her studies. After a rocky start, she earned a higher GPA than she had expected first semester.

Chris is an ethnic minority student. Sometimes, especially at first, he felt lonely when he was in a class or at an event and he was the only African American student. He soon learned that other African American students were friendly, even if they didn't know him. He got in the habit of looking for them whenever he was in a new setting. After the first month of school Chris joined a service club. Now, when he is not studying, he is usually involved in community projects like working with kids at the Community Center. The advisor of the club was helpful to him when he needed someone to talk to and didn't want to worry his parents. He is thankful that his parents provide him with 100% financial support; he has other friends who struggle to pay their expenses. Sometimes, however, they expect him to go home on weekends for family occasions and special events at his church. Then he has trouble catching up with his work. He is proud of the fact that he earned a B+ average first semester.

In formulating their theory, the professors examined what they learned from these students and from 37 others. They looked for commonalities among the findings and carefully noted similarities in students' descriptions of that first year. Not surprisingly, they developed a theory that revolved around four elements: grades, finances, friends, and relationships with faculty and student affairs professionals.

The process in this research project is not dissimilar to the ways in which many theories of college student behaviors, experiences, and interactions are formulated. The researcher or theorist asks a variety of students to talk about the aspects of college life that were important to their satisfaction, intellectual growth, or other successes. In this case four common elements were mentioned by students over and over again and emerged to form the basis of a theory that would be generalized to all college students. Persons reading the report would agree that Hawes' and Skaggs's four elements were important to college success. However, readers also would have to agree that important elements of these individual students' college lives were missed.

The job of the theory builder and some kinds of researchers (like Hawes and Skaggs) is to ignore the finer details of students' lives. However, the student affairs professional's job typically is not to ignore these details. This discrepancy is a major cause of the gap between researchers and theorists and the practitioners.

In addition to the discrepancy described above, student affairs professionals must deal with relatively discrete bodies of knowledge (student development, campus environmental and organizational theories, and college student characteristics) derived almost exclusively from two disciplines—psychology and sociology. Differences in assumptions across the two disciplines also makes theory-based practice difficult. While these obstacles to applying theory in practice are formidable, they are not necessarily overwhelming. Case-study analysis provides one means for overcoming these difficulties.

A CASE FOR THE CASE STUDY

Despite a degree of familiarity with the basics of a particular theory, many student affairs professionals have difficulty in the translation of that theory to practice (Parker, 1977; Stage, 1983; Strange, 1983; Upcraft, 1994). Because of the proliferation of theories described earlier, little agreement occurs within the student affairs profession about which theories are most useful and, more importantly, about how to apply those theories in practice.

Process models present one means through which given theories can be translated into practice. Blocher (1987) defined a process model as a cognitive map that provides a direct and immediate guide for actions. It specifies what one should do in a given situation and should be evaluated in terms of outcomes. Finally, it should be polished continually and modified as experience provides more knowledge about its practical usefulness.

Several process models exist that guide student affairs administrators in implementation of theory (Cooper, 1972; Evans, 1987; Stonewater, 1988; Straub & Rodgers, 1978). For example, Stonewater (1988) described a process model using Perry's (1970) theory for a variety of residence hall issues. The theory can be used for judicial decisions, programming, student conflicts, and general advising of students. Most process models are good conceptual maps for applying theories in certain situations.

However, Perry's (1970) theory was developed through interviews with Harvard University students. It has been tested mostly on upper-middle-class, mainstream college students. Suppose you are the director of a residence hall serving physically disabled students in an inner-city setting. Which elements of Perry's theory or Stonewater's (1988) process model can you blend with knowledge about your students? As in the example above, many times process models based on just one specific theory are not quite right. The creators have made assumptions that don't fit every campus situation. Students with whom one is dealing may not be like those for whom the model was developed (they may be older, ethnic minorities, first generation college students, etc.). Variability in campus size, type, and culture can interfere with implementation of a model. Also, a preexisting process model may not be available for the theory of interest. In these cases, and many others, student affairs professionals need to create their own ways of proceeding. That is, those who work with college students must devise their own ways of applying a theory of their choice to a situation that arises from their specific professional situation.

One general process model often mentioned in the literature is the "Practice-to-Theory-to-Practice" (PTP) model of Knefelkamp, Golec, and Wells (as cited in Evans, Forney, & Guido-Dibrito, 1998; see also the reference to the Wells and Knefelkamp model in Upcraft, 1994). It involves eleven steps for relating theory to the practice of student affairs:

1 Identity concerns that need to be addressed.
2 Determine desired goals and outcomes.
3 Investigate theories that may be useful in understanding the issues and meeting the desired goals.
4 Analyze relevant student characteristics from the perspective of the theories.
5 Analyze characteristics of the environment associated with the issues from the perspective of the theories.
6 Identify potential sources of challenge and support, taking into account both student and environmental characteristics, recognizing factors that facilitate a balance.
7 Reexamine goals and outcomes in light of the theory-based analysis.
8 Design interventions using methods that encourage meeting the goals.
9 Implement the intervention.
10 Evaluate the outcomes of the intervention.
11 Redesign the intervention if necessary.

To these eleven steps, Upcraft (1994) proposed a twelfth (pp. 439–440): Revise or confirm the theory based on its utility in practice.

Case-study analysis and practice using process models can provide student affairs staff and those in professional preparation programs with experience in weighing such contextual considerations. Diverse characteristics of students along with other particulars such as characteristics of a specific institution, personalities, and considerations all play a role. Efforts to reach a decision take you, the analyst, from the abstract realm of the classroom or workshop to the concrete domain of reality.

BENEFITS OF CASE-STUDY ANALYSIS

Case-study analysis benefits student affairs administrators as well as students in professional programs in four ways: by providing challenges to conventional habits of administrative thought and action, promoting consideration of multiple perspective, promoting consideration of unique campus environments, and manipulating problems with realistic legal, institutional, and political constraints. Lessons learned along each of these dimensions provide an advantage to the professional who uses theory.

Challenging Habits of Administrative Thought and Action

Administrators cannot easily change their habits of action. Argyris (1976) called such habits, the underlying guides to professional behavior, "theories in use." Earlier in this chapter was a discussion of some of the difficulties of translating formal theories and newly acquired knowledge into theories in use or personal theories of action (see Parker, 1977). Another difficulty is simply habit.

For some administrators, habits of action become second nature. In a crisis situation they react almost without thinking in a manner that has served them well or adequately in the past. These administrators may not even recognize their behaviors as habits. Beyond that, changing them even when they desire to can be difficult (Argyris, 1976). Case-study analysis is an ideal way to begin to challenge and modify theories of action or, in the absence of theories of action, to cultivate positive ones.

An individual's consideration of a case, examined thoroughly alongside the analyses of others, reveals the value of flexibility in approaching issues. Through rehearsal, student affairs professionals develop the characteristics of a responsive administrator (one who listens to others and "reads" the environment) rather than developing into a reactive administrator.

For example, suppose in a case study an advisor to the student senate is presented with a decision issue. A Pro Life group of students has sought funding for their organization, and it appears that the request will be voted down. The Dean of Student's Office has received several calls from politicians and community members who are in favor of the organization. One parent threatened to sue the university if the organization is denied funding.

Perhaps the case-study analyst's own typical approach in advising student groups is "hands off" except to advise on institutional policy and procedural matters. The analyst, however, must weigh her or his typical response or habit of action (hands off) against the other reasonable alternatives from other analysts that might be more responsive to the campus environment.

Questions that may help challenge negative habits and create positive responses to issues include the following:

What is my first impulse on this issue?
What are the positive implications of that first impulse?
What are the negative implications of that first impulse?
Are any theories available that might apply to the situation?
How might knowledge of theory modify that first impulse?

By working through issues in several cases, the analyst will gain practice holding impulses or habits of action in check. As such, that habit or impulse will become just one of many options weighed for a more deliberate, less reactive style of administration.

Considering Multiple Perspectives

A student affairs professional advancing to increasingly responsible positions of administration experiences ever-expanding realms with which to be concerned. At the earliest levels, a student affairs administrator is most often concerned with students, a few subordinates, peers, and supervisors. Moving up the hierarchy, he or she experiences not just numerically more, but more complex relationships.

At the middle levels of administration, one moves further away from links with students, and becomes more focused on the student affairs division as well as peer administrators at other campuses. Supervisors remain important and, as a manager, the professional recognizes broader, campus-wide implications of administrative decisions. A chief student affairs officer must consider, in addition to students, not only a host of subordinates and institutional peers (the chief academic and business officers, academic deans, and those in other parallel positions), but also a cadre of regional and national chief student affairs officers. Finally, the president, board of trustees, and key politicians must not be forgotten.

The case study can give the analyst, as a beginning or mid-level administrator, practice thinking about these constituents and their sometimes contrasting influences. When the analyst eventually finds him- or herself in a position serving a wide variety of conflicting constituents, he or she will then be better prepared.

In addition to the changing relationships that bureaucratic advancement brings, with the multicultural nature of today's college campus, an important point is for administrators to be able to view issues from many perspectives. Case-study analysis can provide practice considering issues from the perspective of a minority student, a faculty member, a returning student, or a concerned citizen. With enough practice, taking the time to consider multiple perspectives can become second nature to any skilled administrator.

For example, in the sample case analysis presented in Chapter 3, analysts deliberate about issues surrounding racial conflict, a dean's priorities, students' differing political perspectives, and a president who is concerned about the university's image. Furthermore, analysts must decide how to work with a subordinate who makes public statements in direct opposition to her supervisor's public statements.

The case-study analyst becomes accustomed to seeking multiple views by asking the following key questions for every case:

Who are the actors in the case?
What roles do these actors play?
What is the view of each actor on the issues?

Which of the actors are also decision makers?
What would be each of their decisions?
Would some "invisible" actors be affected by the decision?
What would be their perspectives?

In working through issues of each case, an analyst will foster habits of an administrator who listens to others' voices. The case-study analyst will try to remove himself or herself temporarily from a limited perspective to consider others' views more fully. The analyst may also learn to shift from looking for answers to examining ideas (Wassermann, 1994). Finally, the analyst will gain practice listening to the weakest as well as the most powerful of those voices.

Considering a Wide Range of Campus Environments

While great diversity exists within the student and staff population on nearly every college campus, great diversity also exists across campus environments (Brazell, 1996). Lessons learned in a student affairs class or in an institutional training session typically reflect the environment of that campus setting. In studying theories or thinking of examples for application, professors tend to draw on their own limited repertoire of campus environments. Such provincialism can limit vision and stifle creativity.

Up until the last quarter of this century, many student affairs administrators could afford to be somewhat provincial. Institutions were relatively homogeneous and typically, administrators did not move from location to location. A thorough knowledge of one campus environment would be adequate to ensure success in administrative decisions. Now, however, the student affairs profession is more mobile. Administrators may move from large residential universities to commuter campuses to small liberal arts colleges as they progress in the profession.

Additionally, college environments are less homogeneous than they once were (Brazell, 1996; Stage & Manning, 1992). Many liberal arts colleges now offer professional programs such as nursing and teaching to draw people from their local communities and bolster enrollments. International students make up sizable portions of many colleges' student bodies. Some colleges engage in entrepreneurial efforts in conjunction with business or industry from their local communities. More frequently student affairs divisions are becoming heavily involved in fundraising. Case-study analysis can provide vicarious experiences in a variety of campus situations, giving student affairs professionals more flexibility in viewing their own campus settings. In essence, they contextualize problems and the abstract ideas and theories we bring to bear on those problems (Miller & Kantrov, 1998).

For example, suppose that you are an administrator at a small liberal arts college. Additionally, you attended a liberal arts college as an undergraduate. In a workshop utilizing case-study analysis you are asked to consider the problems of an urban commuter campus experiencing dwindling enrollments. As part of the analysis of the case you must consider the needs of commuter students as well as adult students who work full-time. This population may be invisible (existent, but not in great numbers) on your own campus. Hopefully, as a result of your work on the case, future administrative decisions you make might include consideration of the needs of these students. Of course, such change will not occur unless one is willing. Perhaps experience with case study work can provide the catalyst for professional growth.

Case-study analysis can force you, your facilitator, and your classmates out of the comfort of your own home campus environment and into one that presents new and greater challenges. You, as case-study analysts, are challenged within the supportive classroom environment in a way that fosters flexibility and creativity in everyday decision making.

Environmental questions that can help you broaden your institutional perspective include the following:

What is the history of the institution?
What is the history of student affairs at the institution?
What is the relationship of the student affairs officer to superiors? to subordinates? to faculty? to other stakeholders in the institution?
What is the relationship of the campus to the local community?

By working through a variety of campus settings presented in cases, the case-study analyst can develop flexibility. The analyst will gain vicarious experiences that can make him or her a more knowledgeable student affairs administrator. Finally, the practical knowledge can help analysts become more creative administrators in their present campus environment.

Considering a Variety of Legal, Institutional, and Political Constraints

The classroom or workshop environment tends to be idealistic. There, it is easy for armchair administrators to generate lists of shoulds and oughts when speculating about ways of administering. The reality of the college campus, however, presents a totally different situation.

In solving an actual campus problem, analysts must not forget to consider the legal implications of their actions. Additionally, decisions made must fit within established institutional processes and procedures. Finally, analysts may have difficulty as new professionals in envisioning and reconciling conflicts between a supervisor's desires and professional values.

Through analyzing case studies, one attends to descriptions of restrictions, limitations, and the facts of the case. This additional information presents a greater challenge for learning to apply classroom knowledge. Additionally, these details, delimited within a case, will help the analyst become accustomed to seeking similar information in dealing with issues on her or his own campus.

For example, suppose you are an administrator embroiled in a campus controversy. Students in a residence hall intend to show X-rated movies in order to raise money for intramural teams and social activities. The students and their law student advisor maintain that no one will be offended; it will not be a public showing since people must pay to get in. Others argue that university property should not be used to display pornographic materials. Someone notified the county sheriff who promised to check the situation out. As an administrator dealing with this issue, you should consult with the university's attorney. How do local standards for pornography affect your decision? Is such entrepreneurship encouraged at your institution? Have you briefed your superiors and the university president on this issue? What are their opinions?

Through analyzing case studies, idealism about a college campus can be tempered with reality. In an increasingly litigious society, it is important to consider the legal ramifications of any decisions made. One must not run afoul of institutional governance practices. Positive relationships with other campus constituents should be cultivated. Finally, politics must go beyond merely understanding the perspective of others.

Questions that can be used to identify constraints for a given institution include the following:

What is the mission of the institution in question?
What are the legal ramifications of possible solutions?
Are there particular aspects of institutional governance that must be considered?
Does the president (a trustee, a key politician) have any particular interest in this issue.
Could resolution of this issue cause bad press for the institution?

As the case-study analyst views a smorgasbord of case studies, he or she will see a variety of constraints affecting administrators' flexibility in decision making. The analyst will gain practice in balancing the ideals of the classroom with the realities of today's complex college environment. As a result, solutions to campus issues can be tempered in ways that meet multiple demands.

CONCLUSION

The case study can serve to blend the separate elements of student development, campus environments, organizational theory, and student diversity into ways of decision making on the college campus. Within a classroom or workshop one learns *what* an administrator should do, yet within the classroom one rarely learns *how* to do it. Through vicarious analysis of realistic cases, the administrator or future administrator can practice with the theoretical tools of the trade. While case analysis cannot replicate a sense of danger or urgency (no one will lose a job for a weak analysis of a case), it can provide useful practice for future administrative decision making. Sharing perspectives on a case in a workshop or classroom setting can provide not only a challenge but also a deepened and enriched learning experience.

REFERENCES

Argyris, C. (1976). Theories of action that inhibit individual learning. *American Psychologist, 31,* 638–654.

Blocher, D. H. (1987, October). On the uses and misuses of the term theory. *Journal of College Student Development, 66,* 67–68.

Bloland, P. A., Stamatakos, L. C., & Rogers, R. R. (1994). *Reform in student affairs: A critique of student development.* Greensboro, NC: ERIC Counseling Student Services Clearinghouse, School of Education, University of North Carolina at Greensboro.

Brazell, J. C. (1996). Diversification of postsecondary institutions. In S. R. Komives, D. B. Woodard, Jr., and Associates (Eds.), *Student services: A handbook for the profession,* 3rd ed. (pp. 43–63). San Francisco: Jossey-Bass.

Caple, R. B., & Voss, C. H. (1983). Communication between consumers and producers of student affairs research. *Journal of College Student Personnel, 24,* 38–42.

Cooper, A. C. (1972, July). *Student development services in higher education.* Report from the Commission on Professional Development, Council of Student Personnel Associates.

Evans, N. J. (1987). A framework for assisting student affairs staff in fostering moral development. *Journal of Counseling and Development, 66,* 191–194.

Evans, N. J., Forney, D. S., & Guido-Dibrito, F. (1998). *Student development in college: Theory, research, and practice.* San Francisco: Jossey-Bass.

Komives, S. R. (1998). Linking student affairs preparation and practice. In N. J. Evans & C. E. Phelps Tobin (Eds.), *State of the art preparation and practice in student affairs: Another look* (pp. 177–200). Lanham, MD: University Press of America.

McEwen, M. K., & Talbot, D. M. (1998). Designing the student affairs curriculum. In N. J. Evans & C. E. Phelps Tobin (Eds.), *State of the art preparation and practice in student affairs: Another look* (pp. 125–156). Lanham, MD: University Press of America.

Miller, B., & Kantrov, I. (1998). *A guide to facilitating cases in education.* Portsmouth, NH: Heenemann.

Miller, T. K. (Ed.). (1997). *The CAS book of professional standards for higher education.* Washington, DC: Council for the Advancement of Standards in Higher Education.

Parker, C. A. (1977). On modeling reality. *Journal of College Student Personnel, 18,* 419–425.

Perry, W. G. (1970). *Forms of intellectual and ethical development in the college years.* New York: Holtz, Rinehart, & Winston.

Plato, K. (1978). The shift to student development: An analysis of the patterns of change. *NASPA Journal, 15*(4), 32–36.

Rodgers, R. F. (1983). Using theory in practice. In T. K. Miller, R. B. Winston, & W. R. Mendenhall (Eds.), *Administration and leadership in student affairs.* Muncie, IN: Accelerated Development.

Rodgers, R. F. (1989). Student development. In U. Delworth & G. Hanson (Eds.), *Student services: A handbook for the profession.* San Francisco: Jossey-Bass.

Stage, F. K. (1991). Common elements of theory. *Journal of College Student Development, 32,* 56–61.

Stage, F. K. (1994). Fine tuning the instrument: Using process models for work with student development theory. *College Student Affairs Journal, 13*(2), 21–28.

Stage, F. K, & Kuh, G. D. (1996). Student development in the college years. In B. Clark & G. Neave (Eds.), *The encyclopedia of higher education,* CDRom. Oxford: Pergammon Press.

Stage, F. K., & Manning, K. (1992). *Enhancing a multicultural campus environment: A cultural brokering approach.* New Directions for Student Services, No. 60. San Francisco: Jossey-Bass.

Stage, F. K., Russell, R. V., Manning, K., Attinasi, L. C., Carnaghi, J. E., Nora, A., Schwartz, R. A., & Whitt, E. J. (1992). *Diverse methods for research and assessment of college students.* Alexandria, VA: ACPA.

Stonewater, B. B. (1988). Informal developmental assessment in the residence halls: A theory to practice model. *NASPA Journal, 25,* 267–273.

Strange, C. C. (1983). Human development theory and administrative practice in student affairs: Ships passing in the daylight? *NASPA Journal, 21*(1), 2–8.

Strange, C. C. (1994). Student development: The evolution and development of an essential idea. *Journal of College Student Personnel, 29,* 430–436.

Straub, C., & Rodgers, R. F. (1978). The student personnel worker as teacher: Fostering moral development in college women. *Journal of College Student Personnel, 29,* 430–436.

Terenzini, P. T. (1994). Good news and bad news: The implications for Strange's propositions for research. *Journal of College Student Development, 35,* 422–427.

Upcraft, M. L. (1994). The dilemmas of translating theory to practice. *Journal of College Student Development, 35,* 438–443.

Upcraft, M. L. (1998). Do graduate preparation programs really prepare practitioners? In N. J. Evans & C. E. Phelps Tobin (Eds.), *State of the art of preparation and practice in student affairs: Another look,* (pp. 225–237). Lanham, MD: University Press of America.

Wassermann, S. (1994). *Introduction to case method teaching: A guide to the galaxy.* New York: Teachers College Press.

Chapter 2

Theory and Practice in Student Affairs

Frances K. Stage, John P. Downey, and Michael Dannells

The changing dynamics and demographics of higher education have led student affairs professionals and scholars to develop a more comprehensive view of the students and campuses they serve. When the *Student Personnel Point of View* (a treatise on the ideals of the student affairs profession) was published in 1937, administrators had little or no knowledge of formal theories and research relating to student development, college environments and campus culture, college outcomes, organization and administrative practices, or issues of diversity on campus. Today it is difficult to imagine a book on student affairs that does not mention these areas as essential knowledge for any practitioner.

To help the reader respond to the cases in this book and apply the ideas that comprise our knowledge base, we have summarized pertinent theories and research informing the student affairs professional. Student development theory, college environments and campus culture, college outcomes, organization and administrative theory, and issues of diversity and multiculturalism are each reviewed briefly.

Student development theory today represents the cornerstone of our profession (Caple, 1987 a, b; Parker, 1977; Rodgers, 1989, 1991; Strange, 1994). Our focus on the out-of-class experience, in many ways the bread and butter of student affairs, becomes justifiable only when we can demonstrate the growth students experience as a direct result of that experience. Scholars have demonstrated student growth using developmental theories focusing on cognitive development (Perry, 1970), moral development (Gilligan, 1982; Kohlberg, 1981), and identity development (Chickering, 1969; Erikson, 1963). The recent focus on the *Student Learning Imperative* (American College Personnel Association, 1994) reinforces the importance of student development as a goal of student affairs, while encouraging us to move toward a closer working relationship with our academic allies. Understanding how students learn and grow as a result of their college experience may very well be the greatest contribution our profession can make to higher education.

While student development is the cornerstone of our profession, this development always occurs within a context. Early research exploring the context within which the student resides was referred to as environmental theory. While most student development theories are informed by psychology, environmental theory has traditionally been informed by sociology. The most recent studies of the campus context, however, have been informed by anthropology, as they have been concerned with the cultural context within which the student resides. Although the names and the disciplines informing their practice may be different, environmental theory and the study of campus culture are concerned with the same phenomena—the contextual conditions which foster student development.

Research on college outcomes or the impact of college on students, although similar to student development theory, is different enough to warrant its own section. Recent literature (Astin, 1993; Pascarella & Terenzini, 1991) has brought into focus the important areas of cognitive and affective growth and development that occur as a result of the college experience. This literature has built upon the seminal work of Feldman and Newcomb (1969) to include important information concerning the benefits accrued as a result of attending certain types of colleges and engaging in certain types of experiences.

Organization and administrative theories were perhaps the most significant body of research to the early 20th century practitioner. With the introduction of environmental and student development theory, coupled with unprecedented growth in higher education leading to increased specialization for administrators, this body of knowledge became less pertinent to the student affairs practitioner. However, student affairs administrators have begun to return to this literature as they find themselves fighting for limited resources, taking on increasing administrative responsibilities, and responding to an increasingly litigious society. Student affairs practitioners have once again been reminded they are administrators within complex and dynamic organizations.

Finally, perhaps the most important issue the profession is currently addressing is that of diversity and multiculturalism. The changing demographics of student populations over the past 30 years are mind-boggling (Blake, 1985; El-Khawas, 1996; Moore, 1990; Stage & Manning, 1992). Unfortunately, most of our student development theories do not reflect this diversity. Many scholars have begun to develop a growing body of research to define the characteristics of these groups and help student affairs professionals promote diversity as a tool for stu-

dent learning and development (Stage & Manning, 1992). Student affairs professionals who have a working knowledge of student characteristics and an ability to
promote the educational potential of diversity will be valuable resources to the
campus of the 21st century.

This chapter offers a brief overview of these areas of knowledge associated
with college student affairs administration. You are encouraged to return to these
pages and to seek the sources cited herein as you reflect on the cases in this book.

STUDENT DEVELOPMENT THEORY

Student development is an idea which has its roots in the progressive education
movement of the 1920s (Strange, 1994). In many respects, all theories of student
development can best be summarized with the two simple words first suggested
by Sanford (1962)—challenge and support. Without challenge, leading to dissonance, learning and growth cannot occur. Without support for the individual responding to these challenges, learning and growth may be stunted. Each theory
discussed below incorporates this simple idea in some manner. We have subdivided the theories into three categories: Psychosocial, cognitive structural, and
typology.

Psychosocial Theories

As its name implies, psychosocial theories are concerned with the psychological
and social development of students. Hence, they turn our attention to the development of one's identity and the relationship between self and society (Evans, Forney,
& Guido-DiBrito, 1998; Pascarella & Terenzini, 1991). According to psychosocial theories, development occurs throughout the life cycle as long as people successfully resolve the issues associated with the various stages. The stages and
related tasks are sequential and age related.

Student affairs scholars have drawn most widely from the psychosocial theory
of Erikson (1963). Chickering (1969) focused his work on the identity development stage of Erikson's theory to explain the development he observed in traditional age college students. The theory, which is perhaps the most respected in
student affairs, focuses on seven developmental issues—that Chickering referred
to as "vectors"—that students must resolve to progress to the next stage of development: *developing competence, managing emotions, developing autonomy, establishing identity, freeing interpersonal relationships, developing purpose,* and
developing integrity.

As a result of the increased diversity of college students, Chickering's seminal work was criticized for its lack of relevance to special populations. For instance, although both males and females were used as subjects in his study, recent
research suggests that the sequence of tasks differ somewhat for men and women
(Straub, 1987; Straub & Rodgers, 1986). Similarly, Branch-Simpson (1984; cited
in Rodgers, 1991) suggested that autonomy may not be as difficult to resolve for

black students as for white students. Recently, Chickering updated and revised his theory to reflect this and other scholarship (Chickering & Reisser, 1993).

Because of the importance of identity development in college students and the exclusion of minority students and other underrepresented or oppressed populations, such as women, adult/nontraditional students, and homosexual students as research subjects in earlier theories, some scholars have developed theories on these types of identity development.

Cross (1995) proposed an African American identity development that defines the concept of "Nigrescence" and describes a five-stage conversion experience. The five stages are: *preencounter*, in which the individual views their world through a "deracinated" frame and sees race as unimportant; *encounter*, in which the individual's identity is disrupted by repeated racist encounters leading to a sense of disequilibrium; *immersion-emersion*, "in which the individual discards remnants of the old identity and commits to personal change" (Evans et al., 1998, p. 75); *internalization*, wherein the conflict between the old identity and new worldview are resolved; and *internalization-commitment*, which is characterized by involvement in activities that address issues faced by African Americans and other minorities.

Phinney (1990) formulated a model of ethnic identity development centered on the idea that the self-concept of minority adolescents is impacted by what they learn from their family and community about the role of their ethnicity in their lives. The model is comprised of three stages: *diffusion-foreclosure*, in which attitudes and feelings about ethnicity are unexplored, and there is little or no interest in ethnicity; *moratorium*, in which minority adolescents become painfully aware of the significance of their ethnicity and how it is undervalued in the dominant culture, leading to a search for more information about their ethnic group; and *identity achievement*, which is characterized by resolution of identity conflicts and achievement of a healthy bicultural identity.

Helms' (1993) White Identity Model describes the movement toward a nonracist white identity through two phases and six "statuses," three within each phase:

Phase I: Abandonment of racism

Status 1: Contact, in which white individuals first encounter black people and develop various thoughts and feelings based on limited exposure and depending on the individuals' upbringing.

Status 2: Disintegration, "involves the conscious, though conflicted, acknowledgment of one's whiteness while recognizing the moral dilemmas associated with being white" (Evans et al., 1998, p. 7 8).

Status 3: Reintegration, in which the individual consciously accepts the idea of having a white identity while accepting social stereotypes and concluding that blacks are inferior and whites are superior.

Phase II: Defining a nonracist white identity

Status 4: Pseudo-independence, or white liberalism, is a time of intellectualism as the individual questions the assumption of black inferiority and begins to acknowledge the ways whites perpetuate racism; white standards still prevail and racism is more subtle.

Status 5: Immersion-Emersion, includes the replacement of stereotypic images with more accurate information about blacks, the conscious questioning of the individual's racial identity, and emotional and cognitive restructuring in search of a new identity.

Status 6: Autonomy, is characterized by the internalization, nuturance, and application of the new white identity; race is no longer threatening and the individual actively seeks new knowledge about other cultures and works to eliminate all forms of oppression.

Josselson's (1987) theory on identity formation in women describes women in the four groups originally proposed by Marcia (1966): *foreclosures, identity achievements, moratoriums,* and *identity diffusions.* Foreclosures "graduate from college with identity commitment but without experiencing identity crisis" (Evans et al., 1998, p. 57). They choose their life course at an early age and do not deviate from their chosen path. Their choices mirror those of their parents, they experience little or identity change, and they find security in their relationship, not in their work. Identity achievement women severe their familial ties and reorganize their sense of self to form distinct identities. They are more concerned with valuing themselves, as opposed to seeking affirmation. They tend to be both relationship and career oriented, flexible, resilient, and confident in themselves and their choices. Moratoriums are young women who are in "an unstable time of experimenting and searching for new identities" (Evans et al., 1998, p. 60). They are conflicted about adopting new values other than their parents', they may become paralyzed by this identity conflict, and guilt-ridden by their choices that do not reflect earlier family values. Some regress to those earlier values, while others move on to become Identity Achievers. The last group, identity diffusions, are characterized by a lack of crisis and commitment, they are the least healthy psychologically of all the groups, and they tend to withdraw from situations and relationships. Josselson (1987) described them as falling into one of four subgroups: *severe psychopathology, previous developmental deficits, moratorium diffusion,* and *foreclosed diffusion.*

The two most contemporary theories of gay, lesbian, and bisexual (GLB) identity development are those of Cass (1979) and D'Augelli (1994). Cass's theory is psychosocial in nature, describing how homosexual identity develops through a sequence of six stages of increasing awareness, acceptance, and integration. Stage 1, identity confusion, is marked by the person's earliest awareness of homosexual thoughts and feelings. Confusion and anxiety may accompany this awareness, and if the individual resolves these feelings in a positive way, he or she moves on to the next stage. Negative resolution leads to foreclosure. In Stage 2, identity comparison, the individual admits the possibility of being homosexual; he or she may then seek out others who are gay or lesbian in an effort to learn what it means to be homosexual. The person may feel alienated about being different, may try to change, may maintain a straight public persona, and may seek professional help. Stage 3, identity tolerance, is characterized by increasing commitment to the possibility of being gay or lesbian. The individual typically seeks experiences with other gay or lesbian persons, and if those experiences are positive, moves on to the next stage. Negative experiences may result in identity foreclosure. At Stage 4, identity acceptance, the person has continued and increasing contact with other homosexuals, leading to positive acceptance, as opposed to mere tolerance. He or she may choose to "come out" or may remain closeted in some or most environments. Stage 5, identity pride, is characterized by even more positive valuing of others' homosexuality, by increased pride in the person's sexual identity, and possibly in active participation in gay issues and advocacy. Anger at the oppressive dominant society may be felt and expressed. Finally, in Stage 6, identity synthesis, the individual integrates his or her sexual identity with the other aspects of self, and good and bad can be seen in both homosexuals and heterosexuals, and comfort and security are found within his or her sexual identity.

In contrast to Cass's approach, which is typical of psychosocial theories in that it is essentially an age-stage and ontogenetic model, D'Augelli (1994) stressed the plasticity of the identity and the complex interplay of three sets of variables that influence the ongoing development of sexual identity: (1) personal subjectivities and actions (personal meanings and behavior patterns), (2) interactive intimacies (parents, family, peers, and partnerships), and (3) sociohistorical connections (social customs, policy, law, and cultural concepts). Framing the interaction of these sets of variables within the life-span human development view, D'Augelli saw it as influencing six "identity processes" (p. 319):

1 Exiting heterosexual identity
2 Developing a personal lesbian-gay-bisexual identity status
3 Developing a lesbian-gay-bisexual social identity
4 Becoming a lesbian-gay-bisexual offspring
5 Developing a lesbian-gay-bisexual intimacy status
6 Entering a lesbian-gay-bisexual community

D'Augelli's model reminds us that lesbian-gay-bisexual identity develops within a complex interplay of social, interpersonal, and intrapersonal processes that "are mediated by the cultural and sociopolitical contexts in which they occur" (p. 324).

Cognitive Structural Theories

Cognitive structural theories, which draw heavily from the work of Piaget (1952), attempt to explain the intellectual development students attain as a result of the college experience. They are similar to psychosocial theories in that they view development as sequential and necessitating an optimal amount of dissonance for progression. However, because they are concerned with intellect rather than personality and social skill, they differ from psychosocial theories in that they do not view progression as age-related.

Perry's (1970) theory of intellectual and ethical development and Kohlberg's (1981) theory of moral reasoning are two highly respected cognitive structural theories. Unfortunately, in developing their theories they did not consider a diverse student population. Hence, scholars have critically examined them and developed theories which attempt to give voice to populations not included in their research. We briefly summarize both Perry's and Kohlberg's theories below and then describe follow-up scholarship that built on this research.

Perry (1970) theorized that cognitive and ethical development occurred through nine stages, or "positions," as he preferred to call them. The theory is best summarized by describing four of the most significant positions—*dualism, multiplicity, relativism,* and *commitment.* Dualism is characterized by a view of the world in terms of right and wrong, good and bad. Dualistic students expect to be given answers from authorities and are uncomfortable with ambiguity. Students begin the move from dualism to multiplicity when cognitive dissonance occurs—for instance, when two experts disagree on an issue (Evans et al., 1998). Multiplicity, meaning the acceptance of the existence of multiple perspectives on any given issue, is distinguished from relativism by its disinterest in defending a perspective. Relativism views the world as contextual but nevertheless recognizes the need to support an opinion.

Commitment is perhaps the most interesting, and controversial, of all positions in Perry's scheme. It is in this stage that Perry moves his theory from one of intellectual development to one concerned with ethical development. Students now begin to make commitments to people, ideas, and values and have developed an ability to make mature judgments. Kitchener and King (1994) have critiqued this stage because of its shift in emphasis from cognitive development to ethical development, or as they view it to an identity development or psychosocial theory. Nevertheless, Perry's theory has been employed extensively by instructors, advisors, counselors, and other professionals who work with college students (Stage, 1988).

Building on the work of Perry, Kitchener, and King's (1981, 1990) reflective judgment theory includes seven stages that can be subdivided into three categories. The theory has been critiqued for its similarity to Perry's scheme (Rodgers, 1989), as the description of each category indicates: *prereflective thinkers* do not recognize the uncertainty of knowledge; *quasireflective thinkers* realize the uncertainty of knowledge but have difficulty drawing their own conclusions; and *reflective thinkers* realize knowledge claims must undergo a rigorous evaluation process and are capable of using a rational process of inquiry.

Belenky, Clinchy, Goldberger, and Tarule (1986) also built on Perry's theory while acknowledging the work of Carol Gilligan (1982, described below), although they attempted to capture the reasoning processes of women, which they propose differ from men's. Women's epistemological development is grouped into five major perspectives: silence—subject to the whims of external authority; *re-*

ceived knowledge—receiving and reproducing knowledge from authorities; *subjective knowledge*—conceiving personal, private, and subjective knowledge; *procedural knowledge*—learning and applying objective procedures for obtaining and communicating knowledge; and *constructed knowledge*—creating knowledge using both subjective and objective procedures.

Baxter Magolda's (1992) model of epistemological reflection offers a four stage model of intellectual development. Because she designed her research with gender as a focus, the dual patterns within the first three stages offer the most interesting research findings. The four stages and corresponding patterns include: *absolute knowing*—receiving knowledge and mastering knowledge; *transitional knowing*—interpersonal and impersonal knowing; *independent knowing*—interindividual and individual knowing; and *contextual knowing*. Women tend to reflect the patterns of received knowledge, interpersonal knowing, and interindividual knowing, although Baxter Magolda (1 992) indicates that she found more similarities than differences between men's and women's ways of knowing.

Kohlberg (1981) presented another cognitive structural theory focused specifically on how people make moral judgments. Kohlberg described a six stage model of moral development that includes three levels, each with two stages:

Level I: Preconventional
    Stage 1: blind obedience and fear of punishment
    Stage 2: individualism and reciprocity
Level II: Convention
    Stage 3: attempts to be viewed as a good person
    Stage 4: respect for authority and social order
Level III: Postconventional
    Stage 5: view of the existence of a social contract and human rights
    Stage 6: universal ethical principles

Although Kohlberg indicated he had no empirical evidence to support the existence of stage six (Kohlberg, Levine, & Hewer, 1983).

As a result of her studies with Kohlberg in which women consistently scored at lower stages of development, Gilligan's (1982) research led her to an alternative view of moral development based predominantly on women's experiences. Whereas Kohlberg's theory of moral development reflected a bias toward autonomy and justice, Gilligan demonstrated that women view morality from a perspective of care and relationships with others. She proposed a theory composed of three levels: *Level I: orientation to individual survival*—a focus on one's own survival and individual desires; *Level II: goodness as self-sacrifice*—the individual will sacrifice self-interest in order to be accepted by others; *Level III: morality of nonviolence*—essentially a belief in doing no harm to others coupled with the idea of actively caring for both others and self.

Cognitive structural theories are applicable in a variety of settings, including judicial councils, honor councils, and any student groups concerned with ethical dilemmas. In addition, because of their focus on cognitive development, cognitive structural theories have relevance for faculty interested in how students learn and reason through moral dilemmas.

Typology Theories

Typology theories are descriptive and explanatory in that they attempt to describe personality types and explain why one person might respond differently than another to the same situation. One does not grow out of one personality type and progress to another one. It is true, however, that a person can change personality types over the course of a lifetime. But one does not follow any developmental sequence through the life cycle, as is the case with developmental theories.

One of the most widely used typologies is the Myers-Briggs (Myers, 1980) personality type inventory. This theory draws on Jung's (1960) work on personality and proposes that personality has eight preferences within four dimensions: *introversion* and *extroversion, sensing* and *intuition, thinking* and *feeling,* and *perceiving* and *judging.* These eight preferences allow for 16 different personality types. A dominant preference usually arises within each dimension, thus defining one's personality type. One of the reasons this theory is used so much is the development of an easily administered inventory. The Myers-Briggs Type Inventory has been used in roommate assignments, mediating conflicts, and assisting student organization members in better understanding one another.

Although Holland's (1985) theory of vocational personalities and environments is used primarily by career services professionals, it is applicable to all student affairs work. Focusing on the relationship between personality and environment, Holland theorized that people seek out the environments that are most similar to their personality type and allow them to express themselves (the so-called "person-environment fit"). He proposed six personality types, of which everyone has one dominant and two subtypes: *realistic, investigative, artistic, social, enterprising,* and *conventional.* This typology can be helpful for working with student organizations and, as mentioned, for work with students considering career options.

With the publication of the *Student Learning Imperative* (American College Personnel Association, 1994) typology theories describing learning styles have become increasingly significant. Any help we can provide faculty members with understanding how students learn will go a long way toward building bridges between academic and student affairs. The most commonly used theory of learning styles was developed by Kolb (1985), who describes preferred learning styles of students both in and out of the classroom. He describes four categories or learning styles: *convergers, divergers, assimilators,* and *accommodators.* Finally, the Clark and Trow (1966) typology describes four types of students: *academic, collegiate, vocational,* and *nonconformist* according to a high or low commitment to ideas and to their institution. This typology can help us understand various student reactions to campus issues and may help faculty members consider the differences students bring to learning situations.

Gardner (1983) developed a theory of multiple intelligences that is of growing importance for college student learning. His theory and subsequent research challenge traditional simplistic notions of bicategorical verbal and mathematical intelligence. This body of work describes and provides evidence of a multitude of intelligences that are typically ignored or undervalued in formal educational settings. To *logical-mathematical* and *linguistic intelligences*, Gardner adds *musical, spatial, bodily-kinesthetic, interpersonal,* and *intrapersonal.* For a summary of theories focusing on learning see Stage, Muller, Kinzie, and Simmons (1998).

COLLEGE ENVIRONMENT THEORIES

College environment and campus culture theories attempt to explain the context—the physical and human aggregate characteristics of a setting—within which student development takes place. Essentially, this area of research is concerned with the interaction between the person and the environment.

Strange (1994) suggested four propositions concerning the influence of campus environments on student development. Proposition 1 suggests that educational environments restrict and enable individuals by the form and function of their natural and synthetic physical characteristics. Thus, the terrain, climate, architectural design, and spacing of the campus all combine to either enable or restrict student behavior. Proposition 2 suggests that educational environments exert a conforming influence through the collective, dominant characteristics of those who inhabit them. This represents the idea of a "person-environment fit," similar to Holland's (1985) theory discussed above, in which students seek those environments that allow self-expression in a positive and reinforcing manner. Proposition 3 suggests that educational environments, as purposeful and goal directed settings, enable or restrict behavior by how they are organized. Campuses can be seen as dynamic or static, centralized or decentralized, and formal or informal. Campuses that are dynamic, decentralized, and informal tend to encourage greater participation and involvement of students, hence promoting student development (Astin, 1985; Strange, 1981, 1983). Proposition 4 suggests the effects of educational environments are a function of how members perceive and evaluate them. This last proposition by Strange (1994) introduces the idea that the meanings attached to campus environments are socially constructed by the people who inhabit them. Thus, the focus now shifts from the physical environment to the perceived environment—what Moos (1979) referred to as the social climate. In their study, Kuh, Schuh, Whitt, & Associates (1991) concluded that certain institutional cultures can promote student involvement in out-of-class experiences and foster student development. However, one cannot understand the culture without viewing it through the eyes of the individuals inhabiting that environment. The meaning that students associate with the campus culture—its history, stories, ceremonies, heroes and heroines—is essential to the understanding of a college environment (Manning, 1994).

College environment and campus culture theories and research can be helpful to student affairs administrators attempting to place a problem or issue in perspective. Understanding the environmental or cultural context of the problem can help an administrator see the bigger picture and perhaps redefine the problem. Also, environmental and cultural theories help an administrator understand that students develop within a cultural, social, and physical context that can either promote or discourage growth.

COLLEGE OUTCOMES AND IMPACT STUDIES

Feldman and Newcomb (1969) summarized a wealth of research data to describe the impact of college on students. Since that time there have been literally thousands of studies to determine how students change and benefit as a result of the college experience. The major difference between this research and student development theory is that it includes outcomes separate from cognitive and psychosocial development, such as income level, job satisfaction, participation in community service, marriage and divorce rates, alcohol consumption, attendance at cultural events, and voting habits to name just a few.

Following up on this seminal work, Pascarella and Terenzini (1991) conducted a meta-analysis of the literature on college students, and drew conclusions quite similar to Feldman and Newcomb (1969) and Bowen (1977). As a result of the college experience: students develop more abstract, critical, complex, and reflective ways of thinking; their values and attitudes become more liberal and tolerant; they have an increased interest in cultural and artistic activities; they develop more positive self-esteem; they develop a wider variety of intellectual interests and have an increase in their psychological maturity; they develop more principled reasoning skills in judging moral issues; and they have higher earnings, greater occupational status, career mobility and attainment (Pascarella & Terenzini, 1991). Not surprisingly, they found that residing on campus maximizes opportunities for involvement in college life which, in turn, maximizes opportunities for student development and has a significant impact on retention.

Astin (1993) compiled some of the most significant research yet on college impact, including both longitudinal and multi-institutional data. He divided student outcomes into a taxonomy that includes three dimensions: type of outcome (cognitive and affective), type of data (psychological and behavioral), and time (during and after college). The results of Astin's research are too numerous to discuss here, but a few general findings are worth mentioning. Student-faculty interaction outside the class results in increased student satisfaction with faculty quality of instruction, and individual support services, and has significant positive correlation with every academic attainment outcome and every self-reported area of intellectual and personal growth. Additionally, Astin's data has confirmed that "the student's peer group is the single most potent source of influence on growth and development during the undergraduate years" (1993, p. 398). Given these findings, student affairs professionals are well advised to promote the interaction of students with faculty members and to use peer groups to work with students.

Given the findings from this extensive body of research, college impact studies can help student affairs practitioners justify expenditures on programs and services. Student learning and growth are clearly demonstrated to occur as a result of the experience a student has on campus, both inside and outside the classroom. These studies also serve to remind us that learning and growth occur over time, are cumulative, and are interrelated with one another. Student development theories explain how the learning and growth occur, while college impact studies prove that it does occur.

ORGANIZATION AND ADMINISTRATIVE THEORIES

As institutions of higher education have grown in complexity so have the theories to explain their organization and administrative structures. The hierarchical nature of many organizational theories simply does not explain the unique structure of higher education. Baldridge, Curtis, Ecker, & Riley (1977) described five distinguishing characteristics of academic organizations: *goal ambiguity*—almost anything can be justified or attacked; *client service*—students demand to be part of the decision-making process; *unclear technology*—not having a simple technology for dealing with the minds, bodies, and spirits of human beings; *professional staffing*—faculty members are professionals who demand autonomy and peer evaluation and have divided loyalties; and *environmental vulnerability*—being vulnerable to opinions of external key constituents.

Given these characteristics one can understand why Cohen and March (1974) referred to decision making in higher education as organized anarchy. They described a situation in which "each individual in the university is seen as making autonomous decisions. Teachers decide if, when, and what to teach. Students decide if, when, and what to learn. Legislators and donors decide if, when, and what to support" (1974, p. 33). Thus, decisions are made through negotiations and a incidental coming together of problems, choices, and decision makers.

Weick (1976) described the relationships among elements of educational organizations as loosely coupled, providing a contrast to the assumption that the elements of organizations are tightly linked together through shared goals, intentional actions, and rational decision-making processes. One can understand this conceptualization by considering how little an academic department may depend on an administrative office to accomplish its objective. This is not to suggest departments are completely autonomous, rather that they are less dependent on one another than, for instance, two groups of workers on an assembly line.

Although no theories describe the increasing significance of the legal environment on student affairs work, there is a growing body of research to help the practitioner respond to these issues. Gehring (1993) suggests that there are four primary relationships between students and their institutions: *constitutional* (particularly First, Fourth, and Fourteenth Amendment issues); *statutory* (civil rights acts, FERPA/Buckley, the drug-free schools, student right-to-know, and campus security acts); *tort* (negligence, defamation, and state laws concerning alcohol and violence); and *contractual* (explicit/implicit, written or oral). Finally, Kaplin and Lee (1997) recently published a legal guide for student affairs professionals that offers essential information on legal issues practitioners address on an almost daily basis.

ISSUES OF DIVERSITY AND MULTICULTURALISM

Currently, no greater challenge faces higher education than the changing demographics in America. Every week the *Chronicle of Higher Education* has at least one article on an issue that can generally be categorized as diversity-related. Affirmative action, hate speech and hate crimes, political correctness, and the so-called "culture wars" of the academic canon can all be categorized as diversity issues (Chang, Witt-Sandis, Jones, & Hakuta, 1999). Student affairs administrators and scholars have often attempted to help their campuses understand the complexity of this issue (Blake, 1985; Manning, 1988; Moore, 1990; Taylor, 1986). The administrator of the 21st century who can help campuses develop programs, services, and policies to maximize the positive effects of diversity and multiculturalism will be essential to the success of the institution.

Stage and Hamrick (1994) developed a model for campus-wide development of multiculturalism. This model, based on Evans's (1987) model for fostering moral development, suggests that administrators utilize a multidimensional approach to fostering diversity on campus. The model suggests that there are two possible targets of intervention, institutional (entire campus or sub-group) or individual (one person or a group of persons). Actions taken by an administrator are seen as implicit or explicit, and planned or responsive. Hence, a policy on harassment is viewed as targeting the entire campus in an explicit and planned manner. An administrator responding to an incident of harassment as an opportunity to discuss free speech and civil rights is viewed as targeting an individual in an implicit and responsive manner. According to the model, the most effective manner for developing a multicultural campus is to have every possible combination of intervention targets and responses utilized by campus administrators.

Jacoby (1993) described a model referred to as SPAR (services, programs, advocacy, and resources) that can help administrators develop a comprehensive approach to enhancing the experience of a diverse student body. Administrators are encouraged to consider: *services*—should be both general for student body and specific for particular student groups; *programs*—again, should be provided generally for student body and specifically for particular student groups; *advocacy*—student affairs staff must be informed of the needs of students and advocate on their behalf; *research*—all services, programs, and advocacy must be based on research data. At the core of this model is the assumption that an institution is willing to do a critical self-assessment on the appropriateness of its services to diverse student groups.

CONCLUSION

These five bodies of literature form the intellectual foundation of the student affairs profession. The purpose of the summaries described above and the annotated bibliography provided below is to assist the reader in responding to the cases in this book. It is our hope that you refer back to this chapter as you begin work on the cases. The practice of using the theories and research described in this chapter will help develop your skills in applying theory in practice as you progress to "real" situations.

ANNOTATED BIBLIOGRAPHY

This annotated bibliography was selected to provide further reading on theories and research described in this chapter.

Anderson, J. (1988). Cognitive styles and multicultural populations. *Journal of Teacher Education, 39*(1), 2–9.

This article describes differences in cognitive styles between multicultural populations. Suggestions for new pedagogical perspectives and practices are offered. Comparisons of western and nonwestern cultural groupings are offered in such areas as worldviews, writing styles, cognitive style, and use of symbolic imagery. This article should prove important for educators interested in learning more about multicultural learning perspectives.

Astin, A. (1985). *Achieving academic excellence: A critical assessment of priorities and practices in higher education.* San Francisco: Jossey-Bass.

In this book Astin compiles the results of his years of work using the Cooperative Institutional Research Program (CIRP) data set, encompassing more than 1,000 institutions of higher education and over 500,000 students. He describes the results of some of the most significant research yet on college impact, including both longitudinal and multi-institutional data. He uses a taxonomy of student outcomes that includes three dimensions: type of outcome (cognitive and affective), type of data (psychological and behavioral), and time (during and after college). His work extends and expands the findings of many others who study college students as well as provides background for areas of research that have been little studied.

Baldridge, J. V., Curtis, D. V., Ecker, G. P., & Riley, G. L. (1977). Alternative models of governance in higher education. In I. V. Baldridge & T. E. Deal (Eds.), *Governing academic organizations* (pp. 2–25). Berkeley, CA: McCutchan Publishing.

Discusses the distinguishing characteristics of academic organizations, including such things as goal ambiguity, client service, problematic technology, professionalism, and environmental vulnerability. According to the authors, these characteristics distinguish academic organizations from other types of organizations (i.e., government, industry). Three models of academic governance are described: academic bureaucracy, university collegium, and the university as a political system. Additionally, issues of leadership under each model are discussed. This chapter should prove useful for anyone interested in combining organizational theory and academic governance research.

Barr, M. A., & Associates (1993). *The handbook of student affairs administration.* San Francisco: Jossey-Bass.

Perhaps the most useful book on organization and administrative practices for student affairs professionals, this book offers the reader the most comprehensive research on the organizational aspects of student affairs administration. The book is divided into five parts: the administrative environment of student affairs, organizational and management issues, essential skills and competencies for student affairs managers, acquiring and developing administrative skills, and administrative challenges for the future.

Baxter Magolda, M., & Porterfield, W. D. (1985). A new approach to assess intellectual development on the Perry scheme. *Journal of College Student Personnel, 26,* 343–351.

This article describes the initial validation of a new and comprehensive rating manual designed to enhance the accuracy of measurement of the Perry scheme. A brief review of the Perry scheme and the limitations of available instrumentation to measure the scheme are discussed. Additionally, a description of the initial test of the measure of epistemological reflection (MER) and follow-up studies addressing its reliability and validity are offered.

Belenky, M., Clinchy, B., Goldberger, N., & Tarule, J. (1986). *Women's ways of knowing: The development of self, voice and mind.* New York: Basic Books.

Using William Perry's theory of intellectual and ethical development as a point of reference, this book describes five major epistemological categories that ultimately describe women's ways of knowing or making sense of the world. These five categories includes: Silence, in which women view themselves as mindless and voiceless, depending on the voices of external authorities; Received Knowledge, in which women see themselves as capable of receiving and possibly reproducing the knowledge of the external authorities; Subjective Knowledge, a position in which women begin to view knowledge as subjective and personal; Procedural Knowledge, in which women are invested in learning, obtaining, and communicating knowledge in an objective fashion; and finally Constructed Knowledge, a perspective in which women view all knowledge as contextual, and themselves as capable creators of new knowledge. This study includes much of the text from interviews with 135 women, 90 of whom were students.

Caple, R. B., & Newton, F. B. (1991). Leadership in student affairs. In T. K. Miller & R. B. Winston, Jr. (Eds.), *Administration and leadership in student affairs: Actualizing student development in higher education,* 2nd ed. (pp. 111–133). Muncie, IN: Accelerated Development.

This chapter discusses leadership in student affairs, providing perspective, current trends, and future expectations and focuses particularly on the changing nature of administration. It describes the usefulness of theories to the administrator and offers suggestions to the administrator on today's quickly evolving campus.

Chickering, A. W., & Reisser, L. (1993). *Education and identity,* 2nd ed. San Francisco: Jossey-Bass.

The book updates and revises Chickering's first edition by the same title, making his theory more contemporary and more applicable to diverse populations. His theory was developed focusing on the traditional-aged college students. The theory describes student development along seven major dimensions, referred to as "vectors," including competence, emotions, autonomy, identity, interpersonal relationships, purpose, and integrity. Conditions and arrangements on campus that foster or stifle development as well as analysis of six major sources of influence on campus are described.

Clark, D. L. (1985). Emerging paradigms in organizational theory and research. In Y. Lincoln (Ed.), *Organizational theory and inquiry: The paradigm revolution* (pp. 43–78). Beverly Hills, CA: Sage.

The author offers a description and analysis of the emerging paradigms in organizational theory and research originally described by Schwartz and Ogilvy (1979). Characterizations of the classical organizational paradigm, such as simple systems, hierarchical order, and linear causality, are contrasted with the emergent organizational paradigm, which is characterized by complex systems, hierarchical order, and mutual causality. This article offers a comprehensive summary and analysis of a paradigm shift that appears to be taking place in organizational theory. It should prove stimulating for anyone wishing to challenge their assumptions about how organizations work.

Conyne, R. K. (1991). Organization development: A broad new intervention for student affairs. In T. K. Miller & R. B. Winston, Jr. (Eds.), *Administration and leadership in student affairs: Actualizing student development in higher education,* 2nd ed. (pp. 73–109). Muncie, IN: Accelerated Development.

This chapter focuses on the usefulness of organizational development for student affairs administrators. Theories of organizations as well as environmental theory provide a backdrop for guidelines that should prove useful to campus administrators. Potential uses of organizational development for higher education administration is explored.

Conyne, R. K., & Clack, R. J. (1981). *Environmental assessment and design.* New York: Praeger.

This book offers administrators a model for conceptualizing, classifying, measuring, and implementing environmental design. A historical context for environmental design and suggestions for critical training and competent and ethical practice are suggested by the authors. An exhaustive bibliography is included for students or administrators wishing to further explore environmental design. This book should help those interested in answers to questions such as: What is an environment? How does a practitioner assess an environment? How can an environment be altered or changed? And what are the implications of environmental design?

Creamer, D. G., & Frederick, P. M. (1991). Administrative and management theories: Tools for change. In T. K. Miller & R. B. Winston, Jr. (Eds.), *Administration and leadership in student affairs: Actualizing student development in higher education,* 2nd. ed. (pp. 135–157). Muncie, IN: Accelerated Development.

This chapter offers a brief and easily understood summary of the major theories of administration and management including a helpful chart that classifies major theorists. From these theorists, 15 basic concepts about management are presented, and the implications of these for management are discussed. The chapter then turns to providing helpful interpretation on the application of such theories to student affairs practice.

Dannells, M. (1997). *From discipline to development: Rethinking student conduct in higher education.* ASHE-ERIC Higher Equation Report, vol. 25, no. 2. Washington, DC: George Washington University, Graduate School of Education and Human Development.

This monograph examines the many issues related to student conduct, institutional standards of behavior, and using developmental approaches to student discipline. Dannells recommends student affairs collaboration with faculty in creating curricular and cocurricular strategies for making the code of conduct a part of community building on the campus.

Evans, N. J., Forney, D. S., & Guido-DiBrito, F. (1998). *Student development in college: Theory, research, and practice.* San Francisco: Jossey-Bass.

This book could easily serve as the main text for a graduate course on student development theory. In fact, because of its emphasis on the application of student development theory, it would make a great companion text for students struggling with the cases in this book. The authors have divided the book into five parts: understanding and using student development theory, psychosocial and identity development theories, cognitive-structural theories, typology theories, and reflecting on theory in practice.

Gehring, D. (1991). Legal issues in the administration of student affairs. In T. K. Miller & R. B. Winston, Jr. (Eds.), *Administration and leadership in student affairs: Actualizing student development in higher education,* 2nd ed. (pp. 379–413). Muncie, IN: Accelerated Development.

This chapter reminds us of the increasing relevance of legal issues in the administration of student affairs. It provides a particularly useful summary of the most relevant legal responsibilities of student affairs administrators and cites cases that set precedent for specific issues. Finally, a list of further readings is provided.

Gilligan, C. (1982). *In a different voice: Psychological theory and women's development.* Cambridge, MA: Harvard University Press.

This book offers the scholar and practitioner some insights into how women's development and thinking differ from men's. Using three separate studies—the college student study, the abortion decision study, and the rights and responsibilities study—Gilligan documents the different "voices" she hears in how women reason through a variety of moral dilemmas. She validates and offers insight into how women use a morality of care and responsibility while connecting and attaching themselves to the issue or dilemma. A three stage theory of morality is offered as an alternative to Kohlberg's six stage theory.

Hollander, P. A., & Young, D. P. (1991). Legal issues and employment practices in student affairs. In T. K. Miller & R. B. Winston, Jr. (Eds.), *Administration and leadership in student affairs: Actualizing student development in higher education,* 2nd ed. (pp. 415–445). Muncie, IN: Accelerated Development.

This chapter provides the student affairs administrator with useful guidelines for employment and personnel practices. Cautions about the mistakes of uninformed but well-meaning employers are particularly useful. General guidelines for student affairs administrators are provided.

Huebner, L. A. (1979). *New directions for student services: Redesigning campus environments.* San Francisco: Jossey-Bass.

This sourcebook focuses attention on the interaction between the student and the institution, and the implications of this interaction for the student services professional. This so-called "ecosystem perspective" is defined in an historical context, and descriptions are offered of ways the perspective is used in a variety of settings, including residence halls, counseling sessions, and a dean of students office. A critical examination of the ecosystem perspective is also presented.

Kaplin, W. A., & Lee, B.A. (1997). *A legal guide for student affairs professionals.* San Francisco: Jossey-Bass.

This book is a much-appreciated adaptation of Kaplan and Lee's larger project, *The Law of Higher Education.* Offering a summary of the legal issues that student affairs administrators face, this book is divided into 12 chapters. The superb organization of the book makes it a true guide for student affairs administrators, meaning that a professional person could utilize it as an easy-to-use reference when a legal issue arises. The 12 chapter titles reflect the comprehensiveness of this book: Overview of postsecondary law; The college and trustees, administrators, and staff; The legal status of students; Admissions and financial aid; The campus community; Academic policies and concerns; The disciplinary process; Students' freedom of expression; Student organizations; Intramural, club, and intercollegiate athletics; The college and local and state governments; The college and the federal government. The book also offers a selected annotated bibliography for further reading.

Knefelkamp, L., Widick, C., & Parker, C. A. (1978). *Applying new developmental findings: New directions for student services,* No. 4. San Francisco: Jossey-Bass.

This monograph offers descriptions and analysis of several student development theories and human development models. Included are the following: Erik Erikson's theory of psychosocial development; Arthur Chickering's theory of student development; William Perry's theory of intellectual and ethical development; Lawrence Kohlberg's cognitive stage theory of the development of moral judgment; Jane Loevinger's model of ego development; Douglas Heath's model of maturing; and Roy Heath's model of personality typologies. In addition to the theories and models of student development, the authors have included an introduction discussing the uses and value of theories, a chapter on challenges that new students present to the student affairs profession, and a brief annotated reference list.

Kohlberg, L. (1981). *Essays on moral development: The philosophy of moral development: Moral stages and the idea of justice.* New York: Harper and Row.

This book, volume one of a three volume set, focuses on the philosophy of moral development and justice. (Volume two focuses on the psychology of moral development and volume three on education and moral development.) This volume consists of a number of essays, including a description and a defense of Kohlberg's theory of moral development. The book is organized in four parts dealing with the aims of education, the idea of justice, legal and political issues, and problems beyond justice. Naturally, a detailed description of Kohlberg's theory of moral development is presented. In brief, Kohlberg introduces a six stage theory in which individuals move from a punishment and obedience orientation (preconventional level) to interpersonal conformity (conventional level) and ultimately to an orientation based on universal ethical principles (postconventional level).

Kuh, G. D., Schuh, J. H., Whitt, E. J., Andreas, R. E., Lyons, J. W., Strange, C. C., Krehbiel, L. E., and Mackey, K. A. (1991). *Involving colleges: Successful approaches to fostering student learning and development outside the classroom.* San Francisco: Jossey-Bass.

This book offers a glimpse into the culture of several institutions deemed "involving colleges," colleges which successfully involve students in out-of-class experiences, while providing insights into how every institution can promote student involvement. The book is divided into three parts. Part one offers a justification for the study and describes the characteristics of an involving college. Part two, the most comprehensive of the three, describes how involving colleges promote student learning and development. For those readers interested in the distinguishing characteristics of large, small, and urban institutions the authors have described each one in some detail. Part three describes how institutional agents can develop opportunities for student involvement. This book is required reading for anyone interested in promoting out-of-class experiences for students.

Masland, A. T. (1985). Organizational culture in the study of higher education. *Review of Higher Education, 8,* 157–168.

This article describes the recent influence of organizational culture in the study of organizations. The author offers a definition of organizational culture, examines how it has been applied to higher education, describes how the influence of organizational culture can be uncovered, and discusses the relevance of the study of organizational culture for researchers and practitioners. A brief analysis of the importance of organizational sagas, heroes, symbols, and rituals to uncovering manifestations of organizational culture is presented. This article should prove useful for those wishing to find out about the practical and theoretical uses of the concept of organizational culture.

Miller, T. K., & Winston, R. B. (1991). Human development and higher education. In T. K. Miller & R. B. Winston Jr. (Eds.), *Administration and leadership in student affairs: Actualizing student development in higher education,* 2nd ed. (pp. 3–35). Muncie, IN: Accelerated Development.

This chapter briefly discusses the evolution of higher education and the increasing relevance of theories of human development for the field. The usefulness of several of the theories is discussed with regard to the student affairs profession.

Moos, R. H. (1979). *Evaluating educational environments.* San Francisco: Jossey Bass.

This book offers a framework for evaluating environments. It focuses primarily on two distinct environments: university student living groups and the classroom settings of junior and secondary high schools. Suggestions for practical applications for changing educational environments and implications of these changes are offered. It attempts to describe and measure the environment and how people create and are influenced by this environment. Two measures of the college environment, the University Residence Environment Scale (URES) and Classroom Environment Scale (CES) are reintroduced and discussed by the author. This book should prove important reading for educators working to improve the environment of a residence hall, fraternity, sorority, or classroom.

Morgan, G. (1986). *Images of organization.* Beverly Hills, CA: Sage.

This book offers insight into the art of organizational analysis through the use of a variety of metaphors. These metaphors include organizations as machines, organisms, brains, cultures, political systems, psychic prisons, flux and transformation, and instruments of domination. One full chapter is devoted specifically to developing the art of organizational analysis and includes suggestions for using metaphors to read, understand, manage, and design organizations. A set of bibliographic notes is included for those wishing to further explore any specific metaphor. This book should prove useful for educators wishing to learn more about organizational analysis and the use of metaphors in conjunction with organizations.

Pascarella, E. T., & Terenzini, P. T. (1991). *How college affects students.* San Francisco: Jossey-Bass.

This book reviews and summarizes over 2,600 studies on the impact of college on students across a 20-year period. The book is organized into chapters according to specific outcome studies and within chapters organized into a discussion of between-college and within-college effects. The book includes a useful methodological appendix for those interested in conducting their own research on college students.

Perry, W. G. (1970). *Forms of intellectual and ethical development in the college years.* New York: Holt, Rinehart, & Winston.

This landmark book describes the Perry theory of intellectual and ethical development. Perry's theory describes the college student as progressing through nine stages, or positions, from basic duality, in which the world is seen as black and white and authorities are always right, to multiplicity, where multiple perspectives and diverse opinions are seen as legitimate, to relativism, which is seen as a kind of sophisticated multiplicity where opinions and judgments are based on evidence and logic, and finally commitment, where students make choices and decisions in the awareness of relativism. In addition to a first-hand description of Perry's theory, this book offers the reader an analysis and description of the study as well as Perry's own critique of the study.

Rodgers, R. F. (1991). Using theory in practice in student affairs. In T. K. Miller & R. B. Winston, Jr. (Eds.), *Administration and leadership in student affairs: Actualizing student development in higher education,* 2nd ed. (pp. 203–251). Muncie, IN: Accelerated Development.

This chapter focuses on some of the major theories of college student development. The author offers a brief history of paradigm development in student affairs, with student development being the most recent, although not the dominant, model (Rodgers asserts the student services model is dominant). Three of the four kinds of developmental theory are reviewed: psychosocial theories, including Erikson and Chickering; cognitive-structural theories, including Kohlberg, Gilligan, Perry, King, and Kitchener; and typological theories and models, including Carl Jung and Myers-Briggs (person-environment interaction theories are covered in a separate chapter). This chapter offers a brief, yet coherent, overview for readers interested in obtaining a broad understanding of some of the most prevalent theories of student development.

Schuh, J. H. (Ed.). (1990). *Financial management for student affairs administrators.* Alexandria, VA: American College Personnel Association.

This book offers a perspective on current financial conditions, presents detailed views by several authors of expensive services, and aims to help young professionals "understand and appreciate the linkage between financial support and student affairs services and programs" (p. x), and improve their skills in money management. Since the real-life situations presented in case studies often have fiscal implications, this book is included here.

Stage, F. K., Anaya, G. L., Bean, R. P., Hossler, D., & Kuh, G. D. (Eds.). (1966). *College students: The evolving nature of research.* ASHE Reader Series. Needham Heights, MS: Simon & Schuster Custom Publishing.

This compilation of previously published articles and book chapters addresses what we know about today's college students and how we know it. It highlights the latest in college student research and takes a critical look at the research methods used. It uses a transformational perspective on research, characterized by three features: "1) all students' experiences are viewed as source and subject of pertinent facts, priorities, and research problems, 2) the resulting research is to provide useful and helpful explanations of these problems, and 3) the researcher is neither objective nor distanced from those who are the focus of the research, but is 'in the same critical plane.'" (p. xiv).

Stage, F. K., & Manning, K. (1992). *Enhancing the multicultural campus environment: A cultural brokering approach.* New Directions for Student Services, No. 60. San Francisco: Jossey-Bass.

This monograph reviews current literature focusing on diverse students and racial tensions on college campuses. A model is presented for incorporating a "cultural broker" perspective in student affairs practice. Applications of the model to various aspects of student affairs administration are described.

Stage, F. K., Muller, P., Kinzie, J. & Simmons, A. (1998). *Creating learning centered classrooms: What does learning theory have to say?* ASHE-ERIC Highs Education Report Volume 26, No. 4. Washington, DC: The George Washington University.

This monograph reviews learning theories that are relevant to academic learning on the college campus. The book focuses on research conducted at the college level and, using case studies, exemplifies the theory being discussed. The book ends with a chapter that reviews the needs for research by specific theory and a chapter that juxtaposes current popular methods for teaching with the relevant theoretical perspectives.

Straub, C., & Rodgers, R. (1986). An exploration of Chickering's theory and women's development. *Journal of College Student Personnel, 27,* 216–224.

This article describes a study conducted by these authors to test Arthur Chickering's (1969) psychological theory that men and women from the ages of 17–25 share common developmental tasks. Two hundred forty-one college students and adults were used in a cross-sectional study to determine their psychological development. The hypothesis that for some women Chickering's "developing autonomy" vector may come later in their psychological development and the "developing mature interpersonal relationships" vector may come earlier was tested. These authors found evidence that supported a sequence of developmental tasks for women that differed from Chickering's theory.

Walsh, W. B. (1973). *Theories of person-environment interaction: Implications for the college student.* Iowa City, IA: The American College Testing Program.

This monograph, consisting of seven chapters, offers five different theoretical viewpoints on person-environment interaction. These include: Barker's behavior setting theory, the sub-cultural approach, Holland's theory of personality types and model environments, Stern's need × press = culture theory, and Pervin's transactional approach. Each of the chapters devoted to the five theoretical viewpoints is divided into six basic parts: an introduction, background and development, the theory, research, evaluation, and implications. In addition, an introductory chapter discusses the relevant issues, the individual-environment relationship, and the nature of theory. Finally, the author offers a comparison of theories.

Weick, K. (1976). Educational organizations as loosely coupled systems. *Administrative Science Quarterly, 21,* 1–19.

This article provides a contrast to the assumption that the elements of organizations are tightly linked together through shared goals, intentional actions, and rational decision-making processes. The author offers an argument that organizations are actually loosely coupled systems in which elements of organizations are loosely tied together and often times act independent of one another. Educational organizations are used as the example and should offer researchers and practitioners an alternative perspective to how educational organizations are organized. Research priorities are suggested for those wishing to probe further into this alternative perspective.

REFERENCES

American College Personnel Association. (1994). *The student learning imperative: Implications for student affairs.* Washington, DC: Author.

Astin, A. (1985). *Achieving academic excellence: A critical assessment of priorities and practices in higher education.* San Francisco: Jossey-Bass.

Astin, A. (1993). *What matters in college? Four critical years revisited.* San Francisco: Jossey-Bass.

Baldridge, J. V., Curtis, D. V., Ecker, G. P., & Riley, G. L. (1977). Alternative models of governance in higher education. In J. U. Baldridge & T. E. Deal (Eds.), *Governing academic organizations* (pp. 2–25). Berkeley: McCutchan.

Baxter Magolda, M. (1992). *Knowing and reasoning in college: Gender-related patterns in students' intellectual development.* San Francisco: Jossey-Bass.

Belenky, M., Clinchy, B., Goldberger, N., & Tarule, J. (1986). *Women's ways of knowing: The development of self, voice, and mind.* New York: Basic Books.

Blake, J. H. (1985) Approaching minority students as assets. *Academe, 71*(6), 19–21.

Bowen, H. (1977). *Investment in learning: The individual and social value of American higher education.* San Francisco: Jossey-Bass.

Caple, R. B. (1987a). The change process in developmental theory: A self-organization paradigm, Part 1. *Journal of College Student Personnel, 28,* 4–11.

Caple, R. B. (1987b). The change process in developmental theory: A self-organization paradigm, Part 2. *Journal of College Student Personnel, 28,* 100–104.

Cass, V. C. (1979). Homosexual identity formation: A theoretical model. *Journal of Homosexuality, 4,* 219–235.

Chang, M., Witt-Sandis, D., Jones, J., & Hakuta, K. (1999). *The dynamics of race in higher education: An examination of the evidence.* Washington, DC: The American Educational Research Association.

Chickering, A. W. (1969). *Education and identity.* San Francisco: Jossey-Bass.

Chickering, A. W., & Reisser, L. (1993). *Education and identity,* 2nd ed. San Francisco: Jossey-Bass.

Clark, B. R., & Trow, M. A. (1966). The organizational context. In T. Newcomb & E. Wilson (Eds.), *College peer groups: Problems and prospects for research* (pp. 17–70). Chicago: Aldine.

Cohen, M., & March, J. G. (1974). *Leadership and ambiguity: The American college presidency.* New York: McGraw-Hill.

Conyne, R. K. (1991). Organization development: A broad new intervention for student affairs. In T. K. Miller & R. B. Winston, Jr. (Eds.), *Administration and leadership in student affairs: Actualizing student development in higher education,* 2nd. ed. (pp. 73–109). Muncie, IN: Accelerated Development.

Conyne, R. K., & Clark, R. J. (1981). *Environmental assessment and design.* New York: Praeger.

Creamer, D. G., & Frederick, P. M. (1991). Administrative and management theories: Tools for change. In T. K. Miller & R. B. Winston, Jr. (Eds.), *Administration and leadership in student affairs: Actualizing student development in higher education,* 2nd. ed. (pp. 135–157). Muncie, IN: Accelerated Development.

Cross, W. E., Jr. (1995). The psychology of Nigrescense: Revising the Cross model. In J. G. Ponterotto, J. M. Casas, L. A. Suzuki, & C. M. Alexander (Eds.), *Handbook of multicultural counseling* (pp. 93–122). Thousand Oaks, CA: Sage.

D'Augelli, A. R. (1994). Identity development and sexual orientation: Toward a model of lesbian, gay, and bisexual development. In E. J. Trickett, R. J. Watts, & D. Birman (Eds.), *Human diversity: Perspectives on people in context* (pp. 312–333). San Francisco: Jossey-Bass.

El-Khawas, E. (1966). Student diversity on today's campuses. In S. R. Komives, D. B. Woodard, Jr., and Associates (Eds.), *Student services: A handbook for the profession,* 3rd ed. (pp. 64–80). San Francisco: Jossey-Bass.

Erikson, E. H. (1963). *Childhood and society,* 2nd ed. New York: Norton.

Evans, N. J. (1987). A framework for assisting student affairs staff in fostering moral development. *Journal of Counseling and Development, 66,* 191–194.

Evans, N. J., Forney, D. S., & Guido-DiBrito, F. (1998). *Student development in college: Theory, research, and practice.* San Francisco: Jossey-Bass.

Feldman, K., & Newcomb, T. (1969). *The impact of college on students.* San Francisco: Jossey-Bass.

Gardner, H. (1983). *Frames of mind.* New York: Basic Books.

Gehring, D. D. (1993). Understanding legal constraints on practice. In M. J. Barr & Associates, *The handbook of student affairs administration* (pp. 274–299). San Francisco: Jossey-Bass.

Gilligan, C. (1982). *In a different voice: Psychological theory and women's development.* Cambridge, MA: Harvard University Press.

Helms, J. E. (1993). Toward a model of white racial identity development. In J. E. Helms (Ed.), *Black and white racial identity: Theory, research and practice* (49–66). Westport, CT: Praeger.

Holland, J. L. (1985). *Vocational preference inventory (VPI): Professional manual.* Odessa, FL: Psychological Assessment Resources.

Jacoby, B. (1993). Service delivery for a changing student constituency. In M. J. Barr (Eds.), *The handbook of student affairs administration* (pp. 468–480). San Francisco: Jossey-Bass.

Josselson, R. (1987). *Finding herself: Pathways to identity development in women.* San Francisco: Jossey-Bass.

Jung, C. G. (1960). *The structure and dynamics of the psyche.* New York: Bollingen Foundation.

Kaplin, W. A., & Lee, B. A. (1997). *A legal guide for student affairs professionals.* San Francisco: Jossey-Bass.

Kitchener, K. S., & King, P. M. (1981). Reflective judgment: Concepts of justification and their relationship to age and education. *Journal of Applied Developmental Psychology, 2,* 89–116.

Kitchener, K. S., & King, P. M. (1990). The reflective judgment model: Ten years of research. In M. L. Commons, F. A. Sinnett, F. A., Richards, & C. Armon (Eds.), *Adult development: Vol. II. Models and methods in the study of adolescent and adult thought* (pp. 63–78). New York: Praeger.

Kitchener, K. S., & King, P. M. (1994). *Developing reflective judgment: Understanding and promoting intellectual growth and critical thinking in adolescents and adults.* San Francisco: Jossey-Bass.

Kohlberg, L. (1981). *Essays on moral development. Vol. 1: The philosophy of moral development: Moral stages and the idea of justice.* New York: Harper & Row.

Kohlberg, L., Levine, C., & Hewer, A. (1983). *Moral stages: A current formulation and a response to critics.* (Contributions to Human Development Series, Vol. 10). New York: Praeger.

Kolb, D. A. (1985). *Learning style inventory: Self-scoring inventory and interpretation booklet.* Boston: McBer.

Kuh, G. D. (1996). Organizational theory. In S. R. Komives, D. B. Woodard, Jr., and Associates, *Student services: A handbook for the profession,* 3rd ed. (pp. 269–294). San Francisco: Jossey-Bass.

Kuh, G. D., Schuh, J. H., Whitt, E. J., Andreas, R. E., Lyons, J. W., Strange, C. C., Krehbiel, L. E., & Mackey, K. A. (1991). *Involving colleges: Successful approaches to fostering student learning and development outside the classroom.* San Francisco: Jossey-Bass.

Manning, K. (1994). Metaphorical analysis in a constructivist study of college rituals. *Review of Higher Education, 18*(1), 45–60.

Manning, K. (1988, September). The multi-cultural challenge of the 1990s. *Campus Activities Programming,* 52–56.

Marcia, J. E. (1966). Development and validation of ego-identity status. *Journal of Personality and Social Psychology, 3,* 551–558.

Moos, R. H. (1979). *Evaluating educational environments.* San Francisco: Jossey-Bass.

Moore, L. M. (1990). *Evolving theoretical perspectives on students.* New Directions for Student Services, No. 51. San Francisco: Jossey-Bass.

Myers, I. B. (1980). *Gifts differing*. Palo Alto, CA: Consulting Psychologists Press.

Parker, C. A. (1977). On modeling reality. *Journal of College Student Personnel, 18,* 419–425.

Pascarella, E. T., & Terenzini, P. T. (1991). *How college affects students.* San Francisco: Jossey-Bass.

Perry, W. G. (1970). *Forms of intellectual and ethical development in the college years.* New York: Holt, Rinehart, & Winston.

Phinney, J. S. (1990). Ethnic identity in adolescents and adults: Review of research. *Psychological Bulletin, 108,* 499–514.

Piaget, J. (1952). *The origins of intelligence in children.* New York: International Universities Press.

Rodgers, R. F. (1989). Student development. In U. Delworth, G. Hanson, & Associates (Eds.), *Student services: A handbook for the profession,* 2nd ed. (pp. 117–164). San Francisco: Jossey-Bass.

Rodgers, R. F. (1991). Using theory in practice in student affairs. In T. K. Miller & R. B. Winston, Jr. (Eds.), *Administration and leadership in student affairs: Actualizing student development in higher education,* 2nd ed. (pp. 203–251). Muncie, IN: Accelerated Development.

Sanford, N. (1962). Developmental status of the entering freshman. In N. Sanford (Ed.), *The American college: A psychological and social interpetation of the higher learning* (pp. 415–434). New York: John Wiley & Sons.

Stage, F. K. (1988). Student typologies and the study of college outcomes. *Review of Higher Education, 1,* 247–257.

Stage, F. K., Anaya, G. L., Bean, R. P., Hossler, D., & Kuh, G. D. (Eds.). (1996). *College students: The evolving nature of research.* ASHE Reader Series. Needham Heights, MS: Simon & Schuster Custom Publishing.

Stage, F. K., & Hamrick, F. A. (1994). Diversity issues: Fostering campuswide development of multiculturalism. *Journal of College Student Development, 35,* 331–336.

Stage, F. K, & Manning, K. (1992). *Enhancing the multicultural campus environment: A cultural brokering approach.* New Directions for Student Services, No. 60. San Francisco: Jossey-Bass

Stage, F. K., Muller, P., Kinzie, J., & Simmons, A. (1998). *Creating learning centered classrooms: What does learning theory have to say?* ASHE-ERIC Higher Education Report Volume 26, No. 4, Washington, DC: The George Washington University.

Strange, C. C. (1981). Organizational barriers to student development. *National Association of Student Personnel Administrators Journal, 19*(1), 12–20.

Strange, C. C. (1983). Human development theory and administrative practice in student affairs: Ships passing in the daylight? *National Association of Student Personnel Administrators Journal, 21*(1), 2–8.

Strange, C. C. (1994). Student development: The evolution and status of an essential idea. *Journal of College Student Development, 35,* 394–412.

Straub, C. (1987). Women's development of autonomy and Chickering's theory. *Journal of College Student Personnel, 28,* 198–205.

Straub, C., & Rodgers, R. F. (1986). An exploration of Chickering's theory and women's development. *Journal of College Student Personnel, 27,* 216–224

Taylor, C. A. (1986). Black students on predominantly white college campuses in the 1980s. *Journal of College Student Personnel, 27,* 196–201.

Weick, K. (1976). Educational organizations as loosely coupled systems. *Administrative Science Quarterly, 21,* 1–19.

Chapter 3

Case Analysis in Action

Michael Dannells and Frances K. Stage

While many day-to-day decisions made by administrators have quantitative elements (dollars spent, students served, staff hired), solutions evaluated in case-study analysis tend to be qualitative. The broad campus issues presented in a case usually entail emotional involvement of the actors and conflicts in values that must be taken into account in the resolution. From a range of solutions that can be generated for a case, some will be more feasible than others. This feasibility can be ascertained through consideration of numerous factors including costs involved, ease of implementation, availability of resources, personalities of key characters, and fit with the mission of the college. While many of the elements for weighing the feasibility of a solution have no fixed numerical value, they can be evaluated against the similar elements of an alternative solution for the same case.

To gain the most as a case-study analyst, one needs to have direction in sifting through these multiple qualitative and quantitative elements. The purpose of this chapter is to provide an algorithm of sorts, a general guide to aid in the analysis process. The analysis presented here is by no means perfect, and the questions generated are not necessarily exhaustive nor definitive. However, it represents an organized approach to case-study analysis that is used in sorting multiple considerations. Later in the chapter, a case study and sample analysis are presented to provide guidance to the novice analyst.

STEPS IN ANALYSIS

Every case study, like every major campus issue, has many possible solutions. A set of very general questions must be answered every time a case is analyzed:

1 What are the decision issues presented in the case?
2 What facts are essential for understanding and dealing with the issues?
3 What additional information must be collected?
4 Who are the principal decision makers and what roles do they play?
5 Are there any theories that might be relevant to the decision issues?
6 What alternatives are available to the principal decision makers?
7 What are the advantages and disadvantages associated with each alternative?
8 What course of action (long-term and short-term) will be taken?

These eight questions form the basis for an approach to case study that can be used to analyze the cases in this book.

Analysis of the Problem

The first question applies in any analysis of a campus problem or issue. What are the decision issues faced by the actors in the case study? Usually, the major issues seem obvious. Frequently, short-term issues might mask long-term issues, such as absence of campus policies and procedures. Practice identifying decision issues helps keep the case-study analyst from being too shortsighted or narrow in resolving campus dilemmas.

Essential Facts

In the second step you are looking for information that is essential in dealing with the issues discovered above. You must separate the chaff from the wheat. This step involves practice recognizing important facts and separating them from those that are merely colorful and that help to make a good story.

Additional Information

This step follows directly from the above step; is any additional information needed? As you envision yourself in the role of the case professional, the protagonist, if you will, is there anything else you need to know? Are there any documents or facts usually available on a college campus that are relevant and were not provided here? What are current legal precedents for action that may be taken? To whom might you need to talk to gather further information? Remember that decisions makers seldom have all of the information they might want or need, and often they must make reasonable guesses or assumptions about certain key facts. This step reminds the analyst to be explicit about her or his assumptions.

Key Actors in the Case

The next step requires the identification of key actors in the case. Of course the administrator or professional who is caught in the dilemma is included. Additionally, usually one or more of her or his supervisors are involved, if only from the standpoint of judging the outcome. In some case presentations, the principal decision makers must be ferreted out from within the body of the case. They include those who will likely take some sort of action or react to the action you take in resolving the case. Other key players, sometimes called stakeholders, may include powerful persons who may not be directly involved but seem to have strong opinions on ways to resolve issues. Identifying the decision makers and stakeholders and verbalizing the roles they play gives the analyst practice considering a variety of perspectives for decision making.

Relevant Theory or Theories

The fifth step, identifying relevant theory, is the most individual of those in case-study analysis. Anyone who is familiar with some of the myriad theories discussed in Chapter 2 will have their favorites. At this stage, the case study analyst attempts to link a theory (or theories) to the case. Sometimes more than one theory may be appropriate. At any rate, no one theory is necessarily the theory to be used; application of a theory is very personal. A theory that works for one person may not be helpful to others. In the resolution of the case presented later in this chapter, several theories are discussed relative to the case. In any class or workshop, differences of opinion will occur as to which is the most helpful and relevant.

Alternative Solutions

The greatest creativity in case-study analysis comes in the sixth step. Here the analyst, informed by the intervening steps, generates alternative solutions for each of the issues described in step 1. At this stage the analyst is free to let his or her imagination roam. In the next step, the seventh, the constraints on the solutions are addressed.

Advantages and Disadvantages of Alternatives

In answering the seventh question—what are the advantages and disadvantages of each alternative?—the analyst must be mindful of several considerations. Possible reactions to the alternatives by each of the major characters must be assessed. Support by external as well as internal campus constituents must be considered. Legal responsibilities of the institution cannot be forgotten. The mission statement of the institution or future visions of the campus could be factors. And, of course, the availability of resources must be realistically weighed.

Course of Action

Finally, a reasonable course of action, one that includes resolution of both short-term and long-term issues, must be selected in light of the work from the previous steps.

ANALYZING A CASE

The presentation of the following case provides information that allows you to enter a new campus setting. The case is described as realistically as possible and in as detailed a manner as is practical. First you, the analyst, are provided with context, characters, and facts about the case. Through this information you enter the scene of the problem or issue. Next, you are provided a chronological unfolding of events that are presented as a problem to be resolved or a goal to be achieved. As you read the following case, you are encouraged to suspend reality for a while and to lose yourself in the reading of the events. Try to feel, as the administrator would, the urgency and the emotions of the situation.

In the remainder of this chapter, the case will be presented and then analyzed according to the steps presented here. This analysis should provide a useful guide to those using this book.

Pizza Bashing at Highland University
Marilyn J. Amey
Michigan State University
David W. Hardy
Attorney

Setting

Highland University is a comprehensive university located in a quiet town in the rural midwest. The university was founded in the 1800s and has always been a favorite for state residents because of its quality academic programs and picturesque campus. Over the years, the student population has grown to about 20,000 and recruitment has extended beyond state borders, although most students are still in-state residents. There has always been a strong student culture here in part due to a winning athletic tradition and in part because of the overall homogeneity of the population—most students are from fairly small cities and towns, often farming communities. In the last decade, the admissions office has made strides in the recruitment of minority students to campus, which has been one of President Jackson's priorities. Although still not statistically integrated, minority students represent almost 8% (approximately 3% African American, 3% Asian American, and almost 2% Latin American) of the current student population and for many long-time Highland U faculty and staff, the university can now be considered a diverse community. Yet, with diversity has come increased tensions between student groups on several fronts: inequitable funding of student programs, lack of minority representation among faculty and staff, limited academic course offerings that depart from western traditions, and a poor track record of awarding scholarship monies to qualified minority students.

Also of note is that one year prior to the incident of this case, the Black Student Union brought to campus an African American activist of some renown as part of Black History Month. The head of the Conservative Student Association countered by bringing a member of the Ku Klux Klan to campus for a lecture, claiming freedom of speech as a central tenant in the university's handbook. As a result, although the speech thankfully passed with minimal confrontation, the atmosphere around campus suffered as a result. Members of the Student Affairs staff have still not fully recovered from the incident and, in many ways, have become somewhat skeptical of their ability to foster acceptance of diversity under the current policies and practices of the institution. Alice Mayor, the dean of Student Life, has spoken several times about trying to revise the student handbook and about engaging with key members of the Academic Affairs unit about diversity issues but she has been told by many of the president's staff that "now is not a good time."

Characters

Carol Reed, University student, employed by local pizza franchise, who was the target of the "pizza bashing."

Rich Kennedy, Assistant dean of Student life, in charge of Greek Life and Discipline, he reports directly to the dean of Student Life and has been with the University for two years. Rich has come from another predominantly white university in a nearby midwestern state.

Brian Stewart, University student and member of the Rho Delta Epsilon fraternity. He also was also involved in the "pizza bashing."

Les Winter, president of Rho Delta Epsilon fraternity and past-president of the Conservative Student Association who brought a Ku Klux Klan member to campus last year.

Ray Marshall, University student and member of the Black Student Union, who, at times, tends to prefer a more radical approach to problem solving.

Vanessa Durbin, Advisor to minority student groups and a member of the Student Affairs staff. She graduated from Highland U two years ago, and many were surprised when she applied for her job. Often she had expressed dislike of the university and its policies regarding African American students.

Alice Mayor, Dean of Student Life, has been with the university and in her present position for almost 15 years. Promoted through the ranks, Dean Mayor has often been touted as evidence of Highland's progressive stand on hiring women

into senior positions. She is one of only two women staff at her level and reports to the vice president for Student and Alumni Affairs.

Dwight Jackson, President, is in his 11th year as president of Highland. Many
positive changes have occurred during his tenure including increased student
enrollment, improved academic programs, the inception of several doctoral
programs, and increased alumni giving. He envisions his legacy to the university as one of enriched cultural awareness and consistently includes in each
baccalaureate speech a reminder that Highland is "on the cutting edge."

You are Rich Kennedy, assistant dean of Student Life, in charge of Greek
Life and Discipline. It has been a long, sometimes turbulent year on campus and
you will be glad to see the end of spring semester in your second year. There are
only six weeks left of the semester and most students are beginning to heavily
focus on course work and preparation for final exams.

Case

Friday 11:30 p.m. Carol Reed is a Highland U sophomore who works part-time
delivering for a local pizza franchise. She arrives at the Rho Delta Epsilon house
to deliver a pizza which was ordered by one of the brothers. As Carol enters the
house, she is aware that a party has been going on during the evening; empty beer
cans and bottles are scattered around the foyer and stereos can be heard from
around the house. Brian Stewart, a member of the fraternity and the person who
ordered the pizza, comes down the main house stairs to meet Carol and receive his
pizza. He grumbles something about the pizza being late and that he should not
have to pay. Carol notices that Brian has been drinking and seems quite annoyed,
so she quickly tries to explain that, even if the pizza was delivered a few minutes
late, she still must collect payment for the pizza. Brian is not deterred and repeats
his complaints more loudly. At first Carol stands firm in her resolve but when
Brian proceeds to call her a "black bitch," she decides to forego the pizza money
and leave the house quickly. Placing the pizza on a nearby table, Carol heads for
the door. With an angry remark, Brian picks up the pizza and throws it at Carol as
she is exiting the fraternity, striking her in the back of the head. A little stunned,
but more upset than hurt by the incident, Carol quickly leaves the fraternity.

Once back at her place of employment, Carol repeats her story to coworkers
and is encouraged to report the incident to the police. Somewhat hesitantly, Carol
decides to call the local police as well as the University police. Before the night is
through, Carol files formal assault charges with both police departments against
Brian Stewart.

Saturday. First thing Saturday morning, you are awakened by the University
Police with news of the pizza incident and the official report filed against Brian

Stewart. Responsible for student discipline, you follow your normal routine and separately call both students into your office. Carol Reed is still upset about the incident but you assure her that she has done the right thing and that proper steps will be taken to admonish Brian Stewart. Before meeting with Brian, you rummage through your files because his name sounds familiar. Sure enough, the year before, Brian was on disciplinary probation for "serious hazing" during fraternity rush. You get a sick feeling in your stomach that your well prepared "student affairs" approach may not register with this guy, but you proceed anyway. Brian seems quite undisturbed by the event, other than admitting to a serious hang-over. He claims that "Ms. Reed" has blown the incident out of proportion and that hitting her had been an accident if it had happened at all; he had decided he no longer wanted the pizza and meant to throw it to the ground and was fairly sure the pie had not actually struck Carol Reed. Although you're not buying the tale, you record his comments and let Brian know that proper procedures will be followed according to the university disciplinary code. For now, you feel things are under control and drop a summary memo off for Dean Mayor so she'll see it when she comes into the office on Monday.

About 10:00 Saturday night, you get a call from one of the university police officers on duty. The officer tells you that Les Winter, president of Rho Delta, is concerned about a crowd that is gathering on the lawn of the fraternity house. The officer adds, "Wasn't Winter the guy who orchestrated that Ku Klux Klan member coming to campus last year that caused such a mess?" The officer's memory serves him well. Without waiting to hear more, you get over to the house, after asking to make sure several officers will join you there, "just to be on the safe side." When you arrive, about 20–25 people have gathered on the lawn. You recognize several students from the Black Student Union on campus as well as several members of the African American Network from town. The crowd is agitated; they want racial reforms, starting with Brian Stewart's dismissal from school. Fortunately, the fraternity brothers are staying inside the house and, for the most part, are not encouraging antagonistic behavior. You go into the house and briefly speak with Les, telling him not to provoke the crowd and to make sure that Brian stays clear of any more trouble until Monday. You then go outside to disband the group, suggesting an alternative forum for this discussion on neutral ground. You ask the student leaders to meet with you, the dean of Student Life, and members of the fraternity on Monday. They agree to the meeting but assure you that if the matter is not resolved satisfactorily, they will take matters into their own hands.

Upon arriving home, you decide to telephone Dean Mayor even though it is now close to 11:30 p.m. You explain the events of the last 24 hours, including the pending meeting with members of the fraternity and leaders of the Black Student Union scheduled for Monday. The dean supports your actions and suggests that you have done all that presently can be accomplished. Although you are uneasy about the recent events, you drop off to sleep only to be awakened around 3:00

a.m. by the university police saying they have gotten a second call from Les Winter who claims some of the earlier protesters have returned and are trying to enter the fraternity house.

You quickly go back to the fraternity. This time, the fraternity members and protesters are more vocal, engaging in cat calling. The group is much smaller this time but you recognize Ray Marshall as the leader. Ray was in the earlier group of protesters but kept a low profile. Now, he and several other male Black Student Union members are leading the fray. They are visibly angry and want immediate action to rectify what is now being referred to as the "pizza bashing." You reiterate the earlier agreements that a meeting would take place between appropriate representatives of all parties on Monday, but Ray is not deterred. He starts a chant, calling for the disbanding of the Rho Delta house, dismissal of Brian Stewart, Les Winter, and others involved with African American oppression, and your resignation as a protector of such racial bigots. Recognizing that Ray is unlikely to easily be dissuaded you do your best to remind others in the protest group of the efforts being made to appropriately deal with Brian Stewart and that other infractions will be dealt with accordingly but that the entire fraternity should not be punished for the actions of one. With perseverance and patience, you and the police officers eventually disband the protest group but Ray assures you as he leaves that "this is not over yet! "

Sunday. Things are relatively quiet on campus, although the local paper has gotten hold of the story. Statements by Carol Reed and Les Winter appear in one story, recounting the events of Friday night. But the story that most catches your attention is an article addressing local reaction to the events in which a number of prominent citizens express their concern about the incident, its handling by the "university staff," and what they deem a "lack of institutional support for the African American student community." Later that day you notice some picketers on the sidewalk outside the fraternity house and recognize several of them as citizens cited in the article. Fortunately, the rest of the day proceeds without incident.

Monday. Dean Mayor calls a 7:00 a.m. strategy planning meeting for the student life staff. She received several phone calls on Sunday and is expecting a surge today as well. The dean reinforces with the staff that the university has disciplinary procedures to address student complaints such as that which was filed by Carol Reed. However, apparently there is some concern "higher up" about whether the university should have gotten involved given that, at the time of the incident, Carol was employed by a local business and on private property (the fraternity house). Given the steps you have already taken, and have promised to take, you are feeling somewhat uncomfortable with what sounds like an "about face" in policy, if not in practice. Dean Mayor assures you that she stands behind your decisions to date but warns the group that new ground is being broken in university/fraternity relations and that everyone needs to be aware of the future ramifications of actions taken. She decides to meet with the student groups separately but asks you to be at the meetings. She has also invited Vanessa Durbin, the advisor to minority student groups, to attend. The dean dismisses the staff meeting, reminding the group that President Jackson is very concerned about the "alleged incident" and the amount of press coverage it is receiving. Dean Mayor says the president's advisory board wants things to be handled quickly and quietly. "After all," the advisory board has told Dean Mayor, "there are now only six weeks left of classes and then students will be gone for the summer anyway."

As you leave the strategy session, Vanessa Durbin stops you in the hall to comment on your handling of the situation. "I'd have kicked that white supremacist frat off campus so fast, they wouldn't know what hit them. They're just a bunch of racists. Somebody at this university has to take a stand," she says and heads to her office. Picking up your mail, you note "emergency" phone messages from the Minority Academic Affairs Office, the head of the African American network in town, the Civil Rights Office, the local ACLU, and the presidents of the Student Hispanic Association and the Gay and Lesbian Student Group. You suddenly feel like it will be a very long day.

Events of the Following Week. The atmosphere around campus is tense, but the week proceeds without significant incident. Stories about the "pizza bashing" are basically removed from the campus and local papers with the exception of the editorial page, where rather narrow-minded "Letters to the Editor" continue to appear. You clip them from the paper diligently, noting how many have been written by Ray Marshall and by members of the Conservative Student Association (CSA); you are somewhat relieved that Les Winter's name has not appeared on any editorials, given his current role as president of Rho Delta and past role as president of CSA. Two particular letters from the campus paper catch your attention. One is written by Ray, setting out a list of demands to which "any university truly interested in diversity" would agree, including the hiring of a vice president for African American Affairs, building an African American Cultural Center, providing scholarships for African American students, and hiring a Minority Affairs officer to oversee retention efforts on campus. A second letter, appearing a day later, offers a brusk retort to Ray's demands, suggesting that "to give in to such archaic pressure tactics would mean that soon the Chinese students are going to want their own center, and the Mexicans will want special scholarships . . . " The racist overtones of the letter disturb you and you wonder who in the university community might have written such an editorial but the writer had requested anonymity. The dean's meetings with the student groups on Monday and Tuesday do little to resolve the conflict. Les Winter feels it is inappropriate to disband the fraternity for the actions of one member but agrees that Brian should be reprimanded for his behavior and suggests racial awareness sessions with a counselor on campus. Carol Reed is still upset about the incident; she has not enjoyed the instant celebrity status minority groups have afforded her. The whole affair has disrupted her academic and home life. She wants Brian punished but also wants the whole thing to "go away."

The incident seems to have caused even greater dissent among the African American student population. Black Student Union, which has never been overly radical, continues to take an active role in trying to address the issue of racism on campus and has suggested launching a series of programs throughout the end of the semester and into next year. The Black Panhellenic Organization wrote a stern rebuke of the fraternity actions for public dissemination but you hear from several greek student leaders that most Black Panhel members are very disgusted with the institution's response and question your objectivity as well. Finally, several members of BSU, including Ray Marshall, make it known that they are "through with cooperative action" and break away to form their own activist group. This group organizes several small rallies each day at different points around campus. Although the numbers of participants is relatively small (no more than 75–100 students) and no institutional activities are really disturbed, news coverage of the rallies is incredible and certainly keeps the issue of discrimination on campus alive.

Friday, one week from the original incident. Vanessa Durbin comes in to your office to tell you that "justice will finally be done." She is referring to another rally which has been taking place in front of the library for the last half-hour. By her report, most of the minority student groups are represented as well as several other groups with "axes to grind." Vanessa estimates that there must be at least 500 students involved. You look out the office window to see the group is starting to walk away from the library and Vanessa tells you "they're heading for the administration building to see the president and they're going to stay until he talks with them! They have a list of demands and Jackson is going to have to do something about them or . . . well . . . I wouldn't want to see what happens if he turns them down today. It's about time Jackson and his cronies realize they can't just ignore us any longer!" Looking down at your watch, you realize that it is 11:00 a.m. and both the president and Dean Mayor are off campus today until almost 5:00 p.m.

As the assistant dean of Student Life, what alternatives do you have?

Analysis of the Case

In order for you to analyze the case, you must provide answers to the eight questions put forth at the beginning of this chapter: 1) What are the decision issues presented by the case? 2) What facts are essential for understanding and dealing with the issues? 3) What additional information must be collected? 4) Who are the principal decision makers and what roles do they play? 5) Are there any theories that might be relevant to the decision issues? 6) What alternatives are available to the principal decision makers? 7) What are the advantages and disadvantages associated with each alternative? and 8) What course of action (short-term and long-term) will be taken? Moving through this series of questions, you sort out the elements that allow you to arrive at a solution for the case.

Decision Issues

This case presents a complex set of decision issues, with various degrees of immediacy. Most immediate, of course, is the situation you, as assistant director of Students Rich Kennedy, are faced with: a large and apparently agitated crowd moving toward the president's office. What will you do *now*?

You and Highland University face myriad other, seemingly less pressing, but in the long-run, even more important issues: How can the recent racial tensions be addressed in a way that will lead to a community with greater appreciation of diversity and with less divisiveness? To what extent is the apparent attitude of the members of Rho Delta Epsilon systemic in the predominantly white fraternity-sorority system? What is the appropriate range and focus of jurisdiction for the university's judicial system? (Should it extend to behavior off-campus? Should it be limited to individuals or can it address living groups as a whole—e.g., an entire fraternity—etc.) How should the disciplinary case of Brian Stewart be handled so that he is treated fairly and educationally, and the confidentiality of his university record is maintained in the face of pressure to make the outcome public? What support should be offered to Carol Reed? Should the campus newspaper publish anonymous letters to the editor? How can Vanessa Durbin's supervisor(s) address her behavior in this situation? What might be done in crafting university policy and in staff development to improve the competence, confidence, and morale of the student affairs staff in relation to the climate surrounding diversity issues at Highland?

This set of questions frames the decision issues and forms a template for an analysis of the case. (Do you see other issues in the case that should be addressed?) By answering the remainder of the eight questions with which this section began, you develop solutions to the decision issues.

Essential Facts

Given the foregoing framing of the issues, what facts are essential for understanding and dealing with the case? Answers to this question typically can be found within the body of the case study. In this particular case, the facts are presented in chronological order. The Setting provides important history and background, including such salient facts as: this is a public (presumably) university with a high profile in the state and with a central administration that is highly sensitive to external public relations; Highland is becoming more diverse, and that has caused tensions, particularly apparent between the Black Student Union (BSU) and the Conservative Student Association (CSA); the president of the fraternity where the "pizza bashing" occurred is the past-president of CSA; the BSU has a vocal and "radical element" in Ray Marshall; the precipitating incident included a racist epithet in a predominantly white fraternity house off campus where alcohol was present; both Brian Stewart, the "basher," and Carol Reed, the "bashee," are students; Brian is already on disciplinary probation; Carol was physically unhurt, but upset by the incident, and she filed assault charges with both the local and the campus police; the student affairs staff, presumably including you Rich Kennedy, do not feel they have the full support of the administration in fostering diversity and lacks confidence in its ability to function effectively in this environment; the advisor to minority student groups, Vanessa Durbin, is openly hostile toward Highland because she believes it has been unjust toward African Americans; racial tensions have increased greatly over the past week and the university has been in the public eye more than usual; the president is worried about bad press, and the president's advisory council has told Dean Mayor it wants a quick and quiet resolution by the semester's end in five weeks; an agitated crowd of about 500 (Vanessa's estimate) is headed for the administration building and the president's office; and President Jackson and Dean Mayor are away from campus today.

Additional Information
Examination of these facts leads directly to question number three: what other important information must be collected? Given the urgency of the immediate situation, you (Rich Kennedy) would certainly want to know first hand the size and mood of the crowd. Other immediate questions come to mind: To what extent are the campus police and possibly other agencies involved with the crowd? Who are the leaders of the crowd and what are their demands? What is the nature of your relationship with the leaders of the crowd and with the African American community on campus? Where are the president and Dean Mayor and are they are reachable by phone? Is the vice president for Student and Alumni Affairs available? In the absence of immediate supervision, are you empowered to make decisions in this situation? If you do act, to what extent will the dean support you? Does this situation fall under the university's emergency procedures, and if so, who is charged with the responsibility in such a circumstance? (What other immediate questions run through your mind as you put yourself in Rich Kennedy's place?)

Regardless of the outcome of the immediate situation with the crowd, some other information would be useful to inform more long-term decisions. What is the true nature of the gap between the rhetoric and the reality of Highland's commitment to diversity and multiculturalism? What are student affairs staff hiring and training like? What is the university's policy about off-campus student behavior? . . . about student group behavior? What is the university's policy regarding racial and sexual harassment, and might Brian Stewart's behavior fall under it? Assuming the crowd situation did fall under Highland's emergency policy and procedures, how well did they work? What kind of alumni support can Rho Delta Epsilon muster, and to what extent will the president be influenced by it? What campus-wide and living group alcohol education programs and diversity training are in place? Who works with fraternities and how effective is she or he? Are there "cultural brokers" (Stage & Manning, 1992) on the campus and who are they?

Key Actors in the Case

The fourth question asks who the principal decision makers are and what roles they play? In this case study, most of them are listed under the heading Characters. You are cast in the role of Rich Kennedy, and you have become something of a lightening rod for the mounting racial tensions at Highland. You have a very pressing decision: What, if anything, do you do about the crowd headed toward the president's office? The pressure of this decision is exacerbated by the immediate absence from campus of two other important decision makers: the president and the dean of students. Other critical decision makers include Vanessa Durbin, Ray Marshall, and possibly the vice president for Student and Alumni Affairs, about whom information in this case is strangely absent. Other important decision makers in the crowd situation are the chief of campus police or the senior officer on the scene, and the individual officers themselves.

In addition to the characters listed in the case, other long-term decision makers would likely include the BSU, the CSA, Rho Delta Epsilon (the leadership of the chapter, the national office, and the alumni), the Greek affairs advisor, the student government, the news media and those who attempt to influence it on behalf of Highland, the editor of and the advisor to the campus newspaper, the leadership of the other minority student organizations, the president's advisory council and, of course, the board that governs the university. Given the systemic and deep-seated nature of campus culture and the issues that surround diversity and multiculturalism, one might argue that virtually every member of the campus community is touched by, has a stake in, and will make individual decisions that will influence the long-term outcome of this case.

Relevant Theory or Theories

The fifth question asks whether any theories might be relevant to the decision issues. Several theories could be considered germane to the issues and might inform the decision made by the principal actors. Your handling of the crowd situation could be informed by the literature and theory of constructive crisis management, most of which comes from the field of organizational development (Creamer, 1993). Hopefully, you are familiar with a practical model of managing campus crisis like Duncan's (1993), that provides a convenient checklist of actions to be taken. Various environmental assessment theories (e.g., Moos, 1979) could help you and others better understand what is happening at Highland in terms of the social climate of the campus. You and the other white university administrators could learn much from the literature on racial identity development (e.g., Helms, 1990).

Constructive management of the campus environment as it moves from a monocultural to a multicultural one could be guided by the cultural brokering model of Stage and Manning (1992). Highland might consider "the development of a comprehensive approach to meeting the needs of the diverse groups of students" (p. 21) like that of the SPAR (services, programs, advocacy, and research) model (Jacoby, 1991). To better understand and work with some of the key actors in the case (Stewart, Winter, Marshall, & Durbin) theories of cognitive-structure and theories of human development (e.g., Kohlberg, Perry) might prove useful. The legal and disciplinary issues in the case could be considered in light of the most recent law (Kaplin & Lee, 1997) and contemporary developmental approaches to student discipline (Dannells, 1997). Carol Reed should probably be referred to counseling, where the counselor might well employ any one of a number of counseling theories, possibly including a cross-cultural perspective like that of Atkinson, Morten, and Sue (1993). The issues related to staff morale and supervision might be best addressed with some understanding of the theories and concepts of human motivation, staff development, and organizational development.

Many theories, not just those suggested here might be helpful to you as you contemplate the issues. However, it is best for you to settle on four or five theories with which you are most familiar rather than confusing the issues with an elaborate evaluation incorporating a dozen theories.

Alternative Solutions and Advantages and Disadvantages of Each

Answers to the sixth question—what alternatives are available to the principal decision makers?—and the seventh question—what are the advantages and disadvantages associated with each alternative, will be considered together.

As the crowd approaches the president's office, you are faced with several alternatives. You could do nothing and let events run their course. This has the advantage of not making mistakes of commission, but also the disadvantage of appearing ineffectual and possibly even irresponsible to your superiors. You could call the campus police, which has the advantage of protecting university property and individuals from harm should the crowd's behavior become violent, but may have the disadvantage of aggravating the situation if the police do not assume a low profile. You could make some quick phone calls to the president's office and the vice president's office, informing them of the situation, and trying to assess if the president and Dean Mayor are reachable by phone. These calls have the advantage of giving your superiors a "heads-up," can provide advice, and may bring the president and the dean back to campus, but they may delay you in taking more direct action related to the crowd. You could confront Durbin's unprofessional behavior and try to enlist her cooperation in dealing with the crowd. The viability of this option would depend greatly on your relationship with her and on your correct reading of her ability to respond to an appeal to her professionalism. You could gain an ally, or you could provoke a nasty exchange. You could approach the crowd and make a first-hand assessment of the volatility of the situation. If the crowd is approachable, you could assume a nonconfrontational demeanor, address its leaders, ask their intentions, inform them of the absence of the president, and possibly offer to arrange a future (perhaps the next day) meeting of select leaders of the group and the administration. The advantages and disadvantages of this course of action swing on your ability to correctly read the situation and to deal effectively with the crowd as a negotiator and mediator. You would be taking direct action and could demonstrate genuine concern for the needs of minorities at Highland. You also might put yourself at risk or inflame the situation.

After the resolution of the immediate situation, Highland and its principal decisions makers will have many alternatives, depending largely on how truly it values diversity and the extent to which it wants a multicultural campus. It could stonewall the demands of the leaders of the minority group(s) and it could white-wash the situation with rhetoric but no genuine action. This may be attractive to an administration highly sensitive to bad press, but it may only delay and exacer-bate the serious problems underlying the current crisis. Alternatively, Highland's leadership could begin serious negotiations with its minority constituency and develop an action plan designed to move it to a truly inclusive community. This situation would have the disadvantage of leadership publicly "owning" the diver-sity-driven issues, while it would have the advantage of allowing Highland to be true to its mission and creating an environment where all could enjoy to their fullest extent the fruits of its educational and developmental offerings.

Several mid-range alternative courses of action might be taken at Highland, especially in relation to the fraternity and to Brian Stewart. A more formal hear-ing and resolution of the disciplinary issue for both the group and the individual could be held, or Highland could await the outcome of the criminal process. The advantage of proceeding with its own process is that Highland would be taking responsibility, which would send an important message to Ray Marshall and oth-ers who believe the university does not care about justice. The disadvantage is that by taking action before the outcome of the criminal charges against Stewart, Stewart's lawyer may seek an injunction to stop the university process, perhaps costing the university considerable legal staff time and possibly fraternity and sorority, or at least Rho Delta Epsilon, alumni support.

The fraternity might be dealt with in several ways. Because of its history of hazing, and in light of the alcohol-related behavior of Stewart, its national organi-zation could be called in, it could be required to face peer review in Highland's Inter-Fraternity Council (IFC), and it could be required to undergo alcohol educa-tion or multicultural education training or both. The advantages of dealing with RDE as a unit could send a powerful message to the community of predominantly white Greek-letter social organizations and to the minority community. The dis-advantage of lost alumni support could arise here, also.

Other decision issues require an analysis of alternative courses of action in-cluding: follow-up support for Carol Reed; the student newspaper's publishing anonymous letters; Vanessa Durbin's seeming loss of professional objectivity, her continued identification with the students despite her university role, and her hos-tility toward the administration; and the morale and confidence of the student affairs staff in handling diversity-related issues. What alternative solutions do you see for these decision issues, and what advantages and disadvantages would you assign to each?

Course of Action to be Taken
Finally, the last question asks, what course of action (short-term and long-term) will be taken? To answer this, you must decide on the relative merits of the alter-natives, weighing their advantages and disadvantages.

In the short term, you must alert campus police (assuming they are unaware) and the president's office of the crowd; you should try to reach the president and the dean (at least leaving messages); you must decide if you have an ally in Vanessa Durbin; and you should personally assess the volatility of the situation. If you feel you can approach the crowd, you should at least inform its leaders of the current unavailability of the president, communicate genuine concern, and try to negotiate a later meeting with a representative group. Upon the return of the president and dean, you should meet with them, updating them on the situation, including your efforts and the behavior of Vanessa. You must convey the demands of the crowd's leaders and communicate the depth of their feelings. At this point you might seek to engage Vanessa in the conversation as a "window" into the seriousness of the demands of the group and of the broader climate at Highland. You should also seek guidance about the next steps to take regarding the disciplining of Brian Stewart and the fraternity.

President Jackson, Dean Mayor, and perhaps the president's advisory council must listen carefully to the demands of Ray Marshall and others, and develop both a short- and long-term strategy for addressing them. At issue is the genuineness of Jackson's visions of enriched cultural awareness and putting Highland on the cutting edge of inclusiveness and multiculturalism. To the extent that he and his administrative team have a true commitment to those ends, they would be well-served to employ the "cultural broker" model noted in the theory section of this analysis. The situation has developed to the point where handling it quickly and quietly, and stalling until the school year is ended, is not a prudent strategy; nor is it the right thing to do given the expressed values of the institution. In fact, the spin doctors should be brought in to make public Highland's plan for addressing the demands of its minority constituency by taking a bold and progressive action to move the campus from a monocultural to a multicultural one.

Dean Mayor and Rich Kennedy should meet to review the most recent events and, with advice from the university's legal counsel, come to some clear understanding of how the cases of Brian Stewart and his fraternity should be handled with fairness, firmness, and without further delay. Subsequent contacts and discussions must include the fraternity's national headquarters, the IFC leadership, and the person responsible for alcohol education.

As Rich Kennedy, you must follow up in support of Carol Reed. You should try to determine how upset she is, to what extent the situation is interfering with her school work, and if necessary, refer her to a counselor or perhaps an advocate from the women's center. You must meet with the editor and advisor of the campus newspaper and ask them to review their policy of publishing anonymous letters.

Dean Mayor and the vice president for Student and Alumni Affairs must come to grips with the issue of staff morale in student affairs at Highland. If the president is to employ a progressive model like cultural brokering, he will have to turn to his student affairs professionals, and they will have to function effectively and with the confidence that their efforts will have the support of the central administration.

CONCLUSION

An important point for users of this book to understand is that no single correct analysis of a case exists. Indeed, case analysis may be thought of as an art, as unique to the individual performing the analysis as decision making is to the campus administrator. The interplay among the various elements of the case will be weighed differently by each analyst. Hence, one of the values of analyzing cases in a group situation; many alternative, equally valid and viable solutions are presented.

Unlike many case studies, those in this book do not end with a set of neatly described questions to be answered in the solution of the case. Instead, as in real life, cases end with the professional in the throes of a dilemma or attempting to follow a supervisor's instructions. Hopefully, again as in real life, the case study analyst will refer to the questions provided in this chapter to develop her or his own solutions.

Additionally, an important point to remember is that no attempt should be made to generalize from one case to another. The purpose of using the case-study approach to learning is that what works in one situation may not work in another. Finally, case-study analysis in class or another group setting reinforces the give and take of collegiality and team decision making in higher education. Much of our professional education helps us learn what one *should* do as a student affairs administrator, Let us now turn to the following cases and begin to develop our own unique style for *how* to do it.

REFERENCES

Atkinson, D. R., Morten, G., & Sue, D. W. (1993). *Counseling American minorities: A cross-cultural perspective*, 4th ed. Dubuque, IA: Brown & Benchmark.

Creamer, D. G. (1993). Conflict management skills. In. M. J. Barr & Associates (Eds.), *The handbook of student affairs administration* (pp. 313–326). San Francisco: Jossey-Bass.

Dannells, M. (1997). *From discipline to development: Rethinking student conduct in higher education.* ASHE-ERIC Higher Education Report, vol. 25, no. 2. Washington, DC: George Washington University, Graduate School of Education and Human Development.

Duncan, M. A. (1993). Dealing with campus crises. In M. J. Barr & Associates (Eds.), *The handbook of student affairs administration* (pp. 340–348). San Francisco: Jossey-Bass.

Helms, J. E. (1990). *Black and White racial identity; Theory, research, and practice.* New York: Greenwood Press.

Jacoby, B. (1991). Today's students: Diverse needs require comprehensive responses. In T. K. Miller & R. B. Winston, Jr. (Eds.), *Administration and leadership in student affairs: Actualizing student development in higher education,* 2nd. ed. (pp. 281–307). Muncie, IN: Accelerated Development.

Kaplin, W. A., & Lee, B. A. (1997). *A legal guide for student affairs professionals.* San Francisco: Jossey-Bass.

Moos, R. H. (1979). *Evaluating campus environments.* San Francisco: Jossey-Bass.

Stage, F. K., & Manning, K. (1992). *Enhancing the multicultural campus environment: A cultural brokering approach.* New Directions for Student Services, No. 60. San Francisco: Jossey-Bass.

Part Two

Case Studies

Chapter 4

Cases in Organization and Administration

Few crises on campus escape the attention of those responsible for the administration of the college. Additionally, a satisfactory solution of any problem within a subunit of the campus requires consideration of the total organization. The cases presented in this chapter focus on broad campus issues affecting institutions as a whole and student affairs divisions in particular.

In "Student Dissent at Warren Community College," Flo Hamrick describes a campus conflict over the naming of a building for a woman scientist who followed a questionable (by today's standards) line of research. In "Doing More with Less: Creatively Downsizing or 'Rightsizing'" by Susan R. Komives, one of the issues focuses on a young professional who struggles over loyalty to his institution in a crisis and his own professional growth and development. In Katie Douglas's "Less Drinking or Professional Sinking?" a young student affairs professional struggles for recognition and stature in campus meetings. In "The Freshman Applicant Everyone Seems To Know (and Hate)" by Bill Tobin, an influential politician attempts to influence the admission decision for a questionable applicant. Janice Dawson-Threat's "The New Dean" struggles with conflicting priorities on a small college campus. In "Honesty and Integrity" by Vicki Rosser, officials grapple with the reality of budget reductions on a large public university campus. Finally, Scott Brown's "Birth of a Learning College" focuses on efforts to move one campus toward a learning centered environment.

As you work on this first set of cases you will get a view of the student affairs division as a whole along with some current prevalent issues.

Student Dissent at Warren Community College
Florence A. Hamrick
Iowa State University

Setting

Warren Community College, now part of a state community college system in the northwest, has served the metropolitan area of Warren as well as the 12-county regional area since its founding 74 years ago as Jackson Technical Institute, a private college founded to provide specialized technical training for workers employed by regional industries. The majority of WCC's 9,000 students are enrolled in four programs: environmental sciences, engineering technology, computer science, and a general education curriculum leading to transfer to 4-year colleges. Students completing these programs have enjoyed successful careers or continued their studies at various universities.

Due in part to its longstanding focus on sciences and technology, male students continue to predominate at WCC. Achieving greater gender diversity has been a priority for the last ten years. Thanks to aggressive recruitment—particularly at the local high schools—women student enrollment has almost doubled in the last ten years, growing from 15% to 28%. Minority enrollment has remained generally steady at 18–20% over the past ten years. The average age of female students is 22, and for male students, 27.

Characters

Angela Reeves has been WCC's dean of Student Services for the past six years. She reports to the vice president for Instruction and Educational Services.

Adele Willis is WCC's president and the first woman to hold that position. She became president two years ago.

Henry Larson is a 29-year-old student majoring in environmental sciences.

Phil Connors is a 19-year-old student who plans to transfer to the state university and pursue a History degree. He is an officer in WCC's Humanities Club.

Brenda Fountain is a 20-year-old student and president of the Women in Science Club. She is an engineering technology student.

Jaime Ramirez is the 31-year-old president of the Student Government He is enrolled in the computer science program.

Jim Russell is WCC's placement director.

Dennis Austin is the vice president of Instruction and Educational Services.

Case

As Angela Reeves, you are responsible for counseling and advising students, overseeing the developmental education and tutoring offices, registering student organizations, coordinating student-family events, and advising student government and proposing students for membership on WCC committees. You also work closely with the Placement Office to organize career-related events for alumni and current students.

During your first years at WCC, you were surprised by the pride students and alumni expressed in the quality of their WCC education. You had not attended a community college yourself and did not anticipate seeing much school spirit or active alumni involvement at a community college. The fit between you and WCC has been good, and you suspect that your undergraduate degree in chemistry has lent credibility to your dealings with students and faculty at this type of institution. You have received two Outstanding Staff Member awards and one Outstanding College Service award, selected by a college-wide committee. You have earned a reputation as a level-headed and respected student advocate.

Because of plateaus and cutbacks over the past 15 years in the state funding for higher education, WCC had to defer a great deal of building maintenance. In recent years, some buildings have fallen into serious disrepair. President Willis was hired specifically to address this problem by the nine-member locally-elected Board of Trustees. Current board members have business, civic, or educational backgrounds, and all are from WCC's 12-county region. With full support of the Board, President Willis has worked aggressively to raise funds for building renovation and new construction. Just this week, following the Board of Trustees' monthly meeting, President Willis made a speech unveiling plans for next year's celebration of the 75th anniversary of WCC's funding. The first building renovation at WCC in five years will coincide with the anniversary.

Thanks to the generous support of many prominent WCC alumni and business donors, Grand Hall, a classroom and office building dating back to the founding of WCC, will be renovated and renamed to honor Anna James, a nationally prominent biologist during the mid-to-late 1800s who was born in a rural area near Warren. One of her nephews was a member of the founding WCC faculty. President Willis noted that James Hall will be the first WCC building named in honor of a woman and will serve as a symbol of WCC's commitments to excellence and diversity. During the 12 months before Grand Hall's rededication as James Hall, a full schedule of WCC anniversary events will be held—including several seminars on the lives and legacies of Anna James and other scientists with WCC connections.

The week after President Willis' announcement, Henry Larson sent an e-mail posting to a number of WCC students, asking them to distribute it widely among students. Henry's brother Charlie, a recent graduate of the state's flagship university, had conducted research on Anna James as part of his senior honors thesis and had discovered correspondence from the last 15 years of her life in which she articulated her beliefs in phrenology. Phrenology, a science that has since been widely debunked, emphasized correlations between an individual's character and the topography of the skull and facial features. Charlie had discovered writings that appeared to substantiate Dr. James's support of phrenology's ability to explain intellectual and dispositional shortcomings of racial groups other than northern Europeans. With Charlie's permission, Henry distributed excerpts from Charlie's honors thesis in the e-mail message along with Henry's conclusion that James's beliefs were racist and undermined her public legacy as a serious scientist. Henry's e-mail concluded: "If we are serious about our status as real scientists and WCC's reputation as a credible institution, we can't let this building be named after someone who subscribed to such ridiculous beliefs. As students, we have to get this decision changed. There will be a meeting at 7 p.m. this Thursday in the Biology Building Conference room to talk strategy."

Soon Charlie's findings and Thursday's meeting—only one day away—have become the talk across campus. In your informal conversations with students, you hear a variety of reactions. During a meeting about an upcoming Humanities Club trip, Phil Conners complained: "Don't people understand historical context? Lots of scientists in those days were intrigued with phrenology. If you let science run its course, flawed theories will be rejected and good science will be continued. You know, geologists who tried to predict earthquakes used to be crackpots not so long ago. Now monitoring geologic conditions and statistically modeling earthquake probabilities are routine. Things change."

Later that day Brenda Fountain stopped by your office and remarked: "I'm really not sure what I think about this. It was so exciting to think that a building here would be named for a woman who was so prominent, but what I hear about her personal beliefs is reprehensible. Still, what about her contributions to the field? I know that she was responsible for so many advances that would have been lost after her death if not for her key research assistant. I read a biography that gave him credit for the fights he regularly undertook to make sure she received credit for her work. She really didn't get fair consideration of her accomplishments while she was living or even after her death, and I think she deserves to be honored."

Jaime Ramirez also stopped by: "You know, I'm really disappointed. I just got back from a meeting with Willis and asked her if she would come to the meeting Thursday to talk about the naming decision and the information we've since received. She said that she would be out of town on a fundraising trip but that she'd send a development officer to answer any questions we had about the decision. She said the decision was firm, though, and she was not considering re-opening the process. There are so many students who have very strong opinions about this. What do students need to do to be taken seriously here? You'll be at the meeting, won't you?" You assure Jaime that you will attend.

One meeting on your Thursday afternoon calendar is with Jim Russell. You and Jim update each other on progress toward a Career Fair to be held next month, and then your conversation turns to James Hall. Jim says, "I'm worried about this. On my calls to employers, they're starting to hear about the phrenology stuff, and they're asking a lot of questions. The established companies—no problem. They know us, and I'm prepared to take the joking. But the newer high-tech companies that are thinking about relocating to this area—well, this is influencing how they see us and it makes it more difficult to get past that and emphasize the quality of our programs. With these new people, perceptions are so much more important and this is shaping up to be a real threat to our reputation."

As you're wrapping up your work Thursday afternoon, you get a call from a faculty member in Engineering. You chat briefly about his son, with whom you worked when he was a WCC student two years ago. Then the professor tells you, "My neighbor is good friends with two of the major sponsors of the James Hall renovation. Both of them received faxes yesterday from Henry Larson along with a copy of the e-mail he had sent around campus. One of the supporters is a local NAACP chapter leader and has also been an adjunct instructor here. Apparently, he was really furious that he hadn't known about this and planned to call the president today. Wow, the students sure are taking this and running with it. I've never seen anything like this in my 20 years at WCC."

As you are gathering your papers for the meeting, Dennis Austin calls and asks you to stop by his office. He says, "Have you seen the afternoon newspaper?" He hands you the opinion page featuring a guest editorial by two male WCC students, described in the byline as a 26-year-old white student in computer sci-ence and a 19-year-old African American student in the general education pro-gram. Their column contains passages attributed to Dr. James's correspondence and the students' concluding recommendation that WCC scrap the naming plans and search for a person worthy of this honor. "What's going to happen with this meeting tonight?" Dennis asked. "Willis has made it clear to all of us on her team that she's not going to change her mind on this. We have to back her up and smooth things out with the students. How can you get the students to back off? WCC had gotten so much positive publicity from the anniversary announcement, but now it's all turning sour. We've got a lot riding on this and I'm counting on your help, Angela. Call me at home after the meeting is over."

What do you do?

Doing More With Less:
Creatively Downsizing or "Rightsizing"
Susan R. Komives
University of Maryland

Setting

Two hundred year old Waverly College is nestled in a wooded ravine on the outskirts of Centerville, a town of 100,000 people in the northeast United States. The
north side of Waverly College touches the south side of local Centerville State
University, a regional state university of 19,500 students. Centerville has a large
population of highly educated professionals and is the home for the state headquarters of several insurance, banking, and regional medical facilities. Centerville
is rapidly becoming a bedroom community of Urbanopolis, just 30 minutes away
by interstate.

Founded as a liberal arts college, Waverly is now known for its business
management and computer technology programs and for a fine Humanities focus
with specialties in Art History, Creative Writing, and Performing Arts. Indeed,
Centerville residents have historically looked to Waverly as the cultural center of
the community.

Waverly enrolls 1,500 students from across the country; 500 of these students are local, part-time adult students taking evening and special weekend courses.
Ten years earlier, Waverly enrolled 2,300 traditional age residential students.

Characters

Dr. Anne Lanham, dean of Students, has been at Waverly for eight years. She has
a Master's in College Student Personnel, a Ph.D. in Higher Education Administration, and has built a highly regarded student affairs division. She is creative
and appreciated on campus particularly by the student affairs staff. She serves
as the discipline officer and advises the student judicial council. She is accessible to students but more and more of her time in the last three years has been
spent in college-wide budget and planning sessions. She has full autonomy and
the support of President Jamison to lead her division as she deems appropriate.

Josh Gibson, director of Student Affairs, runs a popular one man show and is
truly a one person multi-function office. He coordinates orientation, commencement, the Class Councils, leadership programs, serves as advisor to student
government, IFC, and Panhellenic and works with all clubs and organizations.

Janet Minor, director of Financial Aid, is withdrawn and seems reticent. Janet earned a BA in Economics at Waverly ten years ago and is still acquiescent around her former faculty. She has responsibility for new and continuing student awards, student employment programs including college work study and, with a part-time office clerk, manages a large aid program.

Maria Fernandez, director of Placement, is new to Waverly, having joined the staff this year from her position as assistant director of Career Planning and Placement at Centerville State. She is lively and outgoing and has already established several new programs including a mentor program for seniors, an externship program in Urbanopolis, a "Senior Survival Week" helping seniors plan their transition, and, with Dean Lanham's blessing, has established an Internship Council to examine more co-op programs and internships for Business majors. Maria just gave Anne a draft of a proposal to link older students as mentors with traditional age freshmen to aid retention.

Dr. Bob Johnson, director of the Counseling Service, has been at Waverly for 25 years following his APA internship at Centerville. In addition to personal counseling and short term therapy, the Service houses the career planning function. Bob feels strongly that career counseling must remain in the Counseling Service to be the legitimate presenting problem many students claim when they really come for personal counseling. Bob is close friends with many teaching faculty and has served as chair of Campus Senate for two terms. He does no direct service with students, but administers the Counseling Service. Bob supervises three full-time counselors, one of whom has a specialty in career issues.

Mary Gamble, director of Resident Life, also serves as acting dean in Anne's absence. Mary has reorganized residence life in recent years and has lost half of her ten person staff as housing enrollments have shrunk. Her most recent innovation is to attempt to attract top notch staff by combining their residence life role with a .25 time commitment outside residence life in some function like student activities, career placement, or admissions.

Michael Rhodes, continuing as hall director, told Mary that he prefers a .25 time assignment in the career services function. He has a Master's in higher education administration with no formal counseling course work, but is interested in exploring that dimension of his professional development.

Karen Williams is the president of the Student Government Association. Karen was just elected to her role and is very dependant on Josh for guidance. She seems manipulated by a group of rising seniors and is often encouraged by them to take a stronger, abrasive position although she is collaborative in one-to-one situations with administrators.

Facts:

1. While retention rates have held steady at 65% persistence to graduation, new student enrollment is on a downward plunge. For the fifth year in a row, the admissions office has not met their projected enrollments.

2. Commitment to Waverly is high among long time staff and faculty. Morale is fragile because faculty and staff are faced with no raises for the second consecutive year. Nearly 85% of the faculty are tenured and few new faculty are hired annually. Open positions in academic departments are not filled and courses that must be covered are handled by part-time faculty if at all. Faculty teach eight courses per year and are reviewing a proposal to add a ninth course to their load. The Religion and Philosophy department and Early Childhood Education program have recently been eliminated with only service courses retained. Part-time faculty on overload from Centerville and from the local professional community have increasingly provided needed specialties at low cost.

3. Operating budgets are thin and it is not uncommon for staff to bring their own pads of paper and pens after mid-March each year when spending freezes are announced.

4. Student affairs has lost five of its ten residence directors through normal attrition over the last three years as buildings have been closed and assignments shifted. Morale in Student Affairs is surprisingly good due to a strong commitment to a shared vision of student development in a residential college and close relationship with others in student affairs, as well as with students and faculty.

5. To attract bright staff and spread the student affairs staff talent to campus needs, the continuing five residence life positions have been combined with .25 time assigned outside residence life for next year. The specific .25 outside assignments have not been set. Four new hall directors have signed contracts to come to Waverly. They all hold Master's degrees from counseling and student development programs and understand they will be contacted shortly to match their preferences with the campus needs for their .25 time supplemental assignment prior to starting their positions.

6. Tuition and fee increases have topped 10% annually, but due to declining enrollment numbers, the budget is often in the red. Further budget reductions loom on the horizon.

7. The Student Affairs division is comprised of 19.5 full time equivalent (FTE) staff: the dean, directors of Residence Life, Financial Aid, Placement, Student Activities, Counseling Service, three counselors, five hall directors, five full-time secretaries, and a part-time clerk. Paraprofessionals work in residence life and the career resource room.

Case

You are Josh Gibson, the director of Student Activities. You have had four great years of experience at Waverly after having graduated from a Master's program at Centerville State. You enjoy your work and orientation and have been talking with Dean Lanham about your plan to seek a full-time position at a larger university, which could well branch into any of the specialties you have had a chance to develop. You tell Dean Lanham and the other directors at your usual Monday morning staff meeting that you will *not* be back next year—you got the job at the University of the Midwest!

After joyous clapping and hugging congratulations for your success from your colleagues, Dean Lanham asks for your comments and advice for next year. Your assessment of the area is that more attention is needed for a growing international student population, adult students and their needs, commuters, and leadership. The new Black Student Union is growing, but structurally floundering and needs more staff support. You are pleased that nearly 200 students are involved in some leadership positions and highly involved on campus. You'd love to see another full-time staff member although you know that's not likely.

Your resignation announcement is well timed. The Division is planning a "whole world" retreat [their humorous term for all professional staff in student affairs] for Friday this week to look at organizational models for next year and you can participate without feeling like you need to defend your turf. The agenda for this annual retreat is usually to assess the year, set goals for next year, identify teams and form ad hoc groups to join together for new interventions, and develop the five outside assignment functions for the hall directors. While Dean Lanham chairs the group, there is a great deal of shared leadership and mutual responsibility. Units have been tightly coupled and know each other's functions well. You always enjoy these off-campus retreats; it's good to spend time with student affairs colleagues from across campus and everyone leaves feeling very valuable to the overall student experience.

Monday 3 p.m. Dean Lanham calls. She has just come from the president's cabinet meeting with a new goal to raise retention rates dramatically next year. The president wants to see 10% increase in freshmen retention and 15% increase in sophomore to junior retention. He is also considering a hiring freeze. She says these items will be added to the Friday retreat agenda and is calling all department heads to let them know. She asks if you could give some thought about how the division might handle your functions differently if the position cannot be filled.

Monday 7 p.m. You finally get home from a dinner meeting. You start an outline of topics to include in your Friday presentation: What are the legitimate student concerns about possible budget reductions? What should student government's role be in the decisions Waverly has to make? Which of your functions are essential for Waverly's mission and student body needs? Which functions should be shifted to other units (on or off campus)? What functions could be handled by teams and ad hoc groups or other flexible structures? Which could be handled by student paraprofessionals or new human resource models? Which functions should be dropped? How should the new .25 time assignments of the hall directors be handled? You plan to draw a new organizational chart and think that intersecting circles may help you more than lines and boxes. Somehow this feels like Master's comps all over again and wearily you put aside your notes and just go to bed.

Tuesday 10 a.m. Karen is distressed about your plans to leave. Not only will she miss you personally, she is desperately worried that your position will be cut and that all your functions will be dispersed or not handled. She says she was talking to some student senators last night, and they commented that, "we pay a fortune to go here and should get more for our money not less!"

Wednesday Morning. *The Weekly Waverly,* the school paper, carries an interview with the VP for Business Affairs. He announces budgets will be cut again for next year and he is quoted as saying "No area can go untouched." You call Dean Lanham but she is in an emergency meeting in the president's office.

Thursday Noon. Karen appears in your doorway looking distressed. She says the senators are talking about a student protest over reduction in services and cuts in faculty if the budget story is truthful. She would like to head this off but doesn't know what to do. Fortunately, the next SGA meeting is not until next Monday night, so she thinks there is some time for planning. You call Dean Lanham to alert her and agree to bring this up at the retreat on Friday; she confides in you that the news is true and student affairs will have to take the "hit" of one more full-time position somewhere.

Thursday 12:30 p.m. You finally get to the campus deli for a late lunch and run into Bob Johnson. He sits down to tell you how sorry he is you are leaving and wishes you well. He asks your opinion of Michael Rhodes and shares that he likes Michael but has some concerns about someone without any counseling background working as a staff member in career counseling. Bob thinks it will violate their standards. You feel a bit awkward hearing this and encourage him to talk with Mary.

You decide you better get back to a draft of a possible organizational model that would shift your functions to other existing units to be ready with creative solutions for Friday's retreat.
What will you propose?

Less Drinking or Professional Sinking?
Katie B. Douglas
University of Rhode Island

Setting

Pride University (PU) is known as the flagship institution in a southern state postsecondary education system. The total student enrollment at Pride is approximately 14,000 students (11,000 undergraduates and 3,000 graduate students). Nearly 45% of the student population lives in on-campus residential housing facilities. These facilities consist of 14 residence halls clustered in three residential areas, with each area having its own dining commons. Most of the remaining student population commutes to campus from within a 50-mile radius. PU is located in a small village, but the state's fourth largest urban area is approximately 15 miles from campus.

Characters

James Porter, director of Residence Life, has been working with the residential student population at Pride University for 15 years. He came to Pride immediately after earning a Master's degree in College Student Personnel. Initially, James served as residence hall director. He was promoted to an area coordinator position after two years. In this position, which he held for five years, James supervised several residence hall directors and worked closely with the area's Facilities and Operations as well as Dining Services managers. While an area coordinator, James enrolled as a part-time student in Pride's Higher Education Administration doctoral program. When the associate director of Residence Life job opened up, James applied for and was selected for that position. After three years as the associate director, James not only had earned his Ed.D. but also had been promoted to director of Residence Life upon the retirement of the incumbent. He has been in the director position for five years. James' leadership style is highly collaborative, and he is known for commitment to multicultural issues and dedication to the students at Pride U. James reports to the vice president for Student Affairs.

William Stanford, dean of Students, has been at Pride University for 28 years. During his senior year as an undergraduate at a small, private, liberal arts college in the state, he served as the Student Body President. He began his career at Pride as the director of Student Activities, while also pursuing a Master's in public administration at PU. Eventually, William's title at Pride also included "and assistant dean of Students." Eighteen years ago, when the previous dean of Students retired, William was promoted to this position. He has a no-nonsense management style coupled with a warm, friendly interpersonal style. He is well-known and liked by many students, staff, faculty, and alumni. William, or Dean Stanford as he is known to most people, reports to the vice president for Student Affairs.

Paul Timmons, M.D., director of the Student Health and Wellness Center, has been at Pride U. for three years. He came to Pride after five years in a private group practice, although prior to that he worked for 12 years in University Health Services at a public, postsecondary institution that was located in a different geographic region of the United States. When his wife had a career opportunity in the urban area close to Pride U., they decided to move and he joined a private practice. Eventually, the director of the Student Health and Wellness Center position at PU became available and Dr. Timmons was recruited to fill the position. Although fairly new to his position, Dr. Timmons has established himself as a collegial leader who operates with a community health perspective. He reports directly to the vice president for Student Affairs.

Michael Adams, Alcohol-Drug Education Services coordinator, has been in this position at Pride for two years. He came to Pride after completing his doctoral program in counseling psychology, with a speciality in substance abuse issues. In order to do outreach activities as well as hire additional staff (which includes graduate student interns with PU's Counseling and Consultation Services), Dr. Adams relies on soft money or grant revenue. He is well-respected among his colleagues for his grant-writing abilities. Michael reports to Dr. Timmons.

Olivia Felds, Residence Life Area coordinator, came to Pride University two years ago. Prior to this, she had served for three years as a complex director at a large, public, flagship institution located in an urban area in a different geographic region of the United States. This director position was the first professional position that Olivia held after earning her Master's degree in Student Affairs in Higher Education. During her two years at Pride, Olivia has earned the respect of students and colleagues with her collaborative leadership style and commitment to multicultural issues. She reports to James Porter.

Case

Within a month after the residence halls opened for yet another academic year at Pride, a number of the Residence Life hall staff members are showing signs of severe stress. This stress is primarily a result of dealing with several alcohol-related incidents that required the transporting of students with life-threatening blood alcohol concentrations to the nearest hospital. This hospital is about 14 miles from campus via mostly rural roads. It takes over 15 minutes by ambulance to get to the hospital, and the ambulance service is staffed by part-time Emergency Medical Technicians who receive training through PU's Student Health and Wellness Center. Statistics kept by the Office of Student Residence Life show there has been a steady rise in the number of such alcohol-related incidents at Pride over the previous three years.

The student newspaper has begun printing stories on the number of drinking-related incidents that take place on campus, and an editorial ran with the tone, "What do you expect when there's nothing else to do on this campus?" The stories in the student newspaper are starting to attract the attention of the print and broadcast media from the nearby urban area as well as local and state politicians, many of whom graduated from PU.

On a bi-weekly basis, the two directors and the dean who report to the vice president of Student Affairs (i.e., director of Residence Life, dean of Students, and the director of the student Health and Wellness Center) meet to discuss campus issues. Typically these meetings are held on a casual basis, such as over lunch. The men have decided that in their next meeting they will discuss strategies for addressing the increase in the number of alcohol-related incidents occurring on campus. They have asked Michael Adams to join them. Also, they decide to meet in a room located in the student union so that they can have use of a chalkboard as well as an overhead projector, if needed. Dr. Timmons and Dean Stafford especially are interested in learning more from Michael about a workshop he recently attended on using fines as a way of addressing this issue.

Two days before this scheduled meeting, James Porter learns he must attend another meeting instead. James asks Olivia Felds if she will attend the alcohol-related incidents meeting on his behalf. He specifically asks Olivia because he knows that she did field work with a community-based alcohol intervention program while earning her Master's and has expertise related to judicial sanctioning. Olivia does indeed know the research and practices related to these areas, and she is pleased that she has been asked to represent the director of Residence Life in this meeting. Olivia prepares for the meeting by developing a list of possible intervention strategies for implementation at Pride.

When Olivia arrives at the meeting, Dr. Timmons and Dean Stanford already are present. They great her warmly, and Dean Stanford asks how her transition to Pride U. is going. She responds by saying that this year feels especially good to her since her first two years at Pride had been professionally rewarding and enjoyable. Michael arrives and the group begins to talk about the rise in the number of alcohol-related incidents on campus. Dean Stanford asks Michael to explain what he learned in the workshop about fines. Michael gives a brief presentation about the workshop and advocates using fines in the residence halls at Pride. He proposes that fines be given as an "immediate sanction" when a residence life staff member encounters a blatant violation of alcohol policies. Basically, this means that Resident Assistants would write "tickets," and predetermined fines would need to be paid by those ticketed. There would be due process procedures established for appealing such tickets, and other sanctions might also be given to Pride students during typical judicial proceedings,

Olivia raises questions about placing paraprofessional students in such a role. Also, she talks about how the research and practices that she is familiar with do not show the effectiveness of using fines to decrease the number of alcohol-related incidents, especially on a long-term basis. Dean Stanford says he has been in this line of work for a number of years and regardless of what the literature says, he thinks this is a worthwhile approach to try at Pride U. Olivia brings up some studies that have shown other approaches to preventing and addressing alcohol-related incidents in college residence halls. Dean Stanford says to Olivia, "Just write down the information about fines and make sure Porter receives it." Neither Dr. Timmons nor Michael seem to take any particular notice of this comment and the men continue to discuss the fining idea. Olivia sits there stunned, and feels as though Dean Stanford is trying to relegate her to the role of a note taker. Although she occasionally comments during the remaining 20 minutes of the meeting, Olivia does not see an opportunity to present any more of her ideas.

Upon returning to her office, Olivia types up a summary of the "facts" presented at the meeting for the director of Residence Life. As she types the memo, she becomes increasingly angry about the interpersonal dynamics in the meeting. She wonders why she seemed to be disregarded: Was it because the men seemed to know each other so well both professionally and personally? Was is it because of her age or perceived lack of experience compared with others in the group? Was it related to her gender? The more she pondered the situation, the more upset she becomes; she thought that after five years of successful post-Master's experience, she had established her credibility as a professional in Residence Life.

She attaches a note to the summary memo that lets James know she would like to talk with him about the dynamics of the meeting. When she drops off the materials the following morning, James is in his office. He asks, "So, how did the meeting go?" Olivia explains that she summarized the content of the meeting in a memo, but said she did not feel as though her input was very welcome in the group. James says that the group knows each other quite well and that is probably what she was sensing. He also says that he would like her to continue to be his representative in that group until this issue is resolved, especially since he has just been assigned another major project that requires immediate attention. Olivia tells him that she would prefer to not be a part of future meetings of this group because the men seem to want his direct input. She does not mention the questions that she pondered the day before, especially since she is very concerned that something be done as quickly as possible to reverse the escalating number of alcohol-related incidents among residential students. She fears that if something is not put in place soon a student will die from alcohol poisoning. She asks James if she can have some time to think about whether she will continue to be the representative from Residence Life to this group. James suggests that they discuss it tomorrow morning during their prescheduled weekly meeting. Also, he wants to discuss her ideas for addressing the number and severity of the alcohol-related incidents on campus.

Olivia thanks James for listening and proceeds to her area staff meeting. As usual, she has a very full day ahead of her; a day that will leave little time for personal reflection. She knows, though, that she must make the time to decide what to tell James in the morning.
What does Olivia tell James in the next morning's meeting?

The Freshman Applicant Everyone Seems to Know (and Hate)
William Tobin
Indiana University

Setting

One of the key issues facing many senior admissions officers, perhaps more often than they care to admit, is the political and economic influences in the admissions process. This issue can impact the morale of the staff and the credibility of the office. A recent example is not only illustrative, but no doubt a familiar occurrence. Nearly every school with even moderately selective admission standards is faced with that borderline student whose success or failure at the institution is difficult to foresee, and often predicated on individual maturity and motivation rather than preparation and past performance.

As in the following example, the decisions made not just by an admissions director, but also the president and provost have various impacts on the institution and the people who work there. Some of these results can be positive, others negative; some intended, others unanticipated.

Janine is the director of Admissions at a medium sized regional public university located in the Midwest. As an indicator of the importance the institution attaches to the role of admissions director, the provost and vice president for Academic Affairs also awarded Janine the concurrent title of assistant vice president for Academic Affairs. Her staff consists of an associate director, five assistant directors, and several admissions counselors, along with support personnel who fulfill vital functions in the office. Shortly after her arrival six years ago, Janine convinced the administration to move toward more selective admissions criteria after a history of virtually open admission for state residents. This caused some controversy among citizens of the state, but was warmly applauded by the faculty, who for years chafed under the popular notion that the university was the state's dumping ground for ill-prepared under-achieving students.

After enjoying a period of relatively robust growth in new student enrollments, the university suffered three straight years of declines ranging from 4–5% per year. In addition, income from state appropriations remained stagnant during the period (or even declined slightly when adjusted for inflation). Since the university is not a significant player in the research dollars market, any growth in the budget is tied to growth in enrollments, whether by recruitment or retention.

During the course of her tenure at the university, Janine was asked a number of times to give "special consideration" to applicants whose parents were people of substance in the community because of their wealth or political influence. There were a number of occasions when the athletic department brought pressure on her office to admit students whose records did not meet the published criteria. Janine approached each of these on a case by case basis, taking care not to establish a precedent for these kinds of special exceptions that would give the appearance of favoring the privileged. Nevertheless, she is experienced and shrewd enough to understand that admitting these students can have a positive impact that goes far beyond any problems created. One example was a scholarship awarded to talented but economically disadvantaged students. The scholarship was endowed by the parents of a borderline student. Another instance was the new parking garage on campus which may or may not have resulted from the admission of the son of a friend of the lieutenant governor's. Although no one would want to imply causation, the support of the lieutenant governor during the debate in the legislature on approving the bond issue for the garage came at a critical time.

The president has made it clear to Janine that he does not sell spaces in the freshman class, but neither of them is naive enough to believe that an exception to the admission requirements does not have some kind of quid pro quo attached to it, however unspoken that attachment might be. On the other hand, the most recent case of bending with the winds of political opportunity proved to be particularly explosive.

The Case

During the past academic year the admissions office received an application from the son of a state legislator whose academic record was close to, but did not meet in several respects, the minimum standards for conditional freshman admission to the university. The student's father is a prominent member of the powerful House Ways and Means committee, and thus in a position to exert influence on the manner in which taxpayer dollars are appropriated, so the president was especially eager to see that the student received what he called "full consideration."

In most instances this student's record was close enough to the cutoff point that an exception could have been made, but in addition to poor academic performance in high school, the student was expelled during his junior year for bringing a gun to school, and had a juvenile record for assaulting a teenage girl. Although as a juvenile offender the record should have been sealed, news of the assault was common knowledge in the student's high school, and it came to the attention of the admissions counselor who visits that school on behalf of the university. Further complicating the issue, the parents of the victim in the assault case wrote letters to the president and vice president for Student Affairs, professing their strong opposition to the student's admission. Although it is not clear how news of this student's application became an open secret among several staff members, the point is moot since the bell has already been rung. Concerns were then raised by senior members of the Student Affairs Division that this student could pose a threat to other students and disrupt the orderly conduct of university business. Of special concern to just about everyone with knowledge of the situation is the student's conduct.

Clearly the university could benefit from the political good will generated by admitting this student, but members of the dean of Students' staff expressed concerns about the admission of the student. The dean of Residential Life also expressed strong opinions on the subject since the student would be living on campus during his freshman year. The faculty-dominated admissions committee, which ordinarily serves as an advisory body, asked that they be allowed to review the case. The student's guidance counselor even took the extraordinary step of recommending against admission on the section of the application reserved for such comments.

The president could have easily issued an edict to admit the student if he so chose, but did not want to give the appearance of such a high-handed manipulation of policy for the benefit of such a controversial student. Consequently, this item of business was handed to the admissions director for "appropriate action."

While this situation is somewhat extraordinary in the context, it also presents decision makers with a rather typical dilemma. Namely that in many cases we are seldom presented with a choice between a really good solution and a really bad solution. More likely we are faced with choices in which we are attempting to minimize damage, reduce hurt feelings, or reduce the number of constituents who find the action taken intolerable. This is just such a situation. Regardless of what action the director of Admissions takes, there will be some negative fallout with one campus constituency or another, perhaps more than one. Of no less concern to her personally is the effect that any decision would have on her relationship with her superiors, the president and provost, who through the artful but feint political language of the university administration have, to her ears, made their positions clear. And she fully understands the pressures that they are under. Many influential legislators view the university as just another state agency that can and should be manipulated by the legislative body that funds it.

On the other hand, the president and provost are fully cognizant that the university community, especially the faculty, prizes its independence above all other attributes, and often resents the meddling of outsiders in the traditional functions of the academy (i.e., teaching, research, and service), which includes deciding who is taught. The director believes that this is a significant factor in the president's attempting to be above manipulating the process for political capital because there are those on the faculty who believe that he is not one of their own, but an administrator bent on eroding their steadily dwindling perquisites.

The provost asks the admissions director to meet with him next to week to discuss the matter. Assume the role of the director of Admissions. What will you present to him and what will your recommendations be?

The New Dean

Janice Dawson-Threat

University of Missouri-Columbia

Two months ago you became the new dean of Students at Livingwell, a private liberal arts college. As a recent graduate of a professional education program with a focus in student affairs and with three years experience as a Hall Director, you felt equipped to assume professional responsibility for this position.

Livingwell College has 3,000 students and is located two and a half hours from any major airport. Approximately one third of the students are commuters and graduates of small rural community high schools that surround the college. Another third of the students are specially recruited from three major urban area high schools that have targeted bright and hard working students who did not blossom until late in their junior year. Those accepted showed visible improvement in their grades by their senior year, and had national test scores slightly above the sixtieth percentile. The final third of the students are those who sought out Livingwell College as the children of alumni, as students affiliated with the International Student Enrollment program, or for the particular commitment of the college to a Liberal Arts curriculum and to providing a seamless learning experience.

At least half of the students were attracted to the college because of the work-for-tuition program. Race, gender, and ethnicity ratios vary with each annual class enrollment. African American students comprise between 6–10% of any class. Hispanic students range from 2–4% and international students range from 5–12%. The male-female class ratio ranges from 3:1 at the senior level to 1:1 at the first year level.

At the beginning of the year, in your initial meeting with the president, he told you he expects you to develop a plan to restructure the student affairs division to meet several goals:

1. Enhance the commitment made by the trustees to provide an excellent undergraduate curriculum in the liberal arts so that students learn to appreciate the finer things in life.
2. Increase the involvement of students in campus activities.
3. Increase the interaction between commuter students and resident students through out of class activities.
4. Improve the professional development of staff employed in the Student Affairs division, particularly those under your direct supervision.
5. Create a means for students to communicate with the dean of Students and other administrators about issues and concerns on campus.

After holding a series of meetings with key staff members to learn the history and perspective of the campus, you now examine your notes. In two weeks you will present your action plan to the president for your first year as dean. Below are notes from your meetings.

Financial Aid Director. Mary provides spreadsheets that show numbers of students, amounts of grants and loans awarded, total cash paid per student, and total tuition waived as part of the work program. She also took the liberty of getting a copy of the residence hall budget and reported that those operations were at a break even point. She felt the previous dean did an excellent job of balancing the budget while maintaining the correct balance between the hall operations and her ability to provide financial aid packages to students.

Mary says she heard the president say that he wanted to double the involvement of students in campus activities, but she advises against doing anything that would place the budget in the red. Since the president frowns upon department budgets going over allocations, she recommends you avoid taking any action on his request. She believes it would benefit both the financial aid office and the residence hall to attract the recommended number of students from wealthier families. This cash paying group would be less troublesome and have more time to actually devote themselves to a greater appreciation for college life than those who participate in the work-for-tuition program.

Meeting with both Hall Directors. Roger is director for the junior/senior hall. His building is also one third first-year students. Joan is director for the first- and second-year hall with about one fourth of the building housing juniors and seniors. The directors spoke of the planned renovation of both residence halls. Roger and Joan think the idea of installing computers in every room is great, especially if the work is completed over the summer. Since only one building can be renovated at a time, Joan was hoping to have this summer off and not participate in the freshmen orientation program. Roger wondered if he would have temporary help if Joan left for the summer and if his building is completed next summer can he plan a leave?

Both directors reported they were having problems with the resident advisors who were part of the work-for-tuition program. They were not available during required hours and often complained that they couldn't complete their studies because of the numerous interruptions. Roger says that he has to repeatedly explain that they have the opportunity to study because their tuition has been waived in exchange for the work. He feels the work is the first priority. Joan tells her resident advisors that although school is the first priority, she cannot allow them to retain the position if they can't handle their classes and the job. Both directors ask you to reduce the financial obligations of these students by allowing them to reduce the number of required hours they must be on duty. They feel that reduced hours could permit them to hire more students and therefore provide more free time for students to become involved in campus activities, something they know the president wants to see happen.

Additionally, Joan reminds you that she is having a problem between the students from the urban areas and the rural areas. It doesn't matter what the floor project or activity—the outcome is always the same—students becoming angry with one another.

Roger's hall projects are not going well; his students are absolutely apathetic. He had agreed to fund a 100 foot banana split for Springfest last year but the money was not used. He also believes there are racial problems brewing in the hall but whenever he asks about it, everyone says there is nothing going on. It's his observation, however, that all the intramural teams, event committees, and dining hall seating arrangements are always racially divided. That says problem to him. Finally, Roger hands you a list of questions that was compiled by members of his staff.

Notes from Concerned Resident Advisors:
1. They are asked to be on duty for too many hours. Can't get to the library at a decent hour in the evening.
2. Why can't students pick their own work hours? What do you do when you want to be in a club, but can't participate because the hall director has assigned specific work hours that interfere?
3. How can they qualify to be a resident advisor on a quieter floor? How many years do they have to be a resident advisor for the underclassmen?
4. Why do they have to spend so much time planning goofy events like building 100 foot banana splits?
5. Can you suggest what to say when the urban students don't want to room with the rural students? Black students with the white students? A senior with a sophomore?
6. How does one become a hall director?
7. There are rumors that tuition is going up to help hire more resident advisors. Is it true?
8. Is it true that commuter students will be able to take meals in the residence hall? Where will all the students sit?
9. Why are these meetings always at 7:00 a.m.?
10. Do we have the freedom to talk with you directly any time?

Meeting with Commuter and Resident Association. Jackie and Sam are the presidents of the two hall associations. Their first concern is that commuter students receive more club funding than resident students. Their examples for this were the radio station, newspaper, and union board, which are dominated by commuter students, and receive more money than any other organization. As resident hall students, they feel they should receive an additional portion of funds to create a Hall newspaper and be allowed to sponsor one concert a year during the "Steak Out Barbeque" each year. They also feel the idea of installing computers in every room is great, but they would like the option of both IBM and Mac to be contained in one computer. They have a concern that students will express a preference for a given room or hall if the machines do not have both platforms.

Eileen, who is the president of the Commuter Association, thinks the charge that commuters receive more money is preposterous. Participation in the radio station, newspaper, and union board only changed last year. Resident students still control the intramural sports program and student government. Eileen doesn't like the idea of installing computers in every resident hall room unless commuters will have equal access to use them. Since they won't be available during the night hours, she feels a lease or check out arrangement would be fair so commuters can take computers home and use them.

Eileen expressed concern that resident hall students receive student leadership training. They have resident advisors and hall directors to work and advise them. Commuter students are treated like outside clubs. The leaders rarely come into contact with any one from the dean's office. She wonders how student leaders who are commuters can receive more one-on-one leadership development and service.

Leaders from the Radio Station, Newspaper, and Union Board. Although their concerns were presented in various contexts, the issues were basically all about diversity. Each thought the other groups were getting more than their share of resources. No one seemed to recognize their own problems but they were clear about the problems of the other organizations. Concerns expressed for the radio station included: not enough hours of the right kind of music, and prime time hours filled with heavy metal and rap music. The Union Board was criticized for only booking country music bands and classical artists, and the campus newspaper was accused of only carrying negative stories about black students.

Meeting with both Assistant Deans. Jim is responsible for the residence halls, the radio station and the Union Board. He is an alumnus of Livingwell College who majored in music. Jim grew up in the Livingwell Community and graduated from a high school with a senior class of 80 students. The only time Jim has been away from Livingwell was to serve in the Armed Services for two years right after high school. While in the service he worked with the music division and toured the country with the Armed Services band. He developed an expertise in entertainment booking and that's how he qualified for his current position.

Malika is responsible for the commuter students, the newspaper, and all other clubs and activities, as well as special needs services such as women affairs, minority affairs, and so forth. Malika has a Master's degree in history and was active as an undergraduate in student activities. The previous dean met her at a conference and offered her the opportunity of becoming an assistant dean with the possibility of securing the dean's position. The terms of her advancement were based on his retirement and her receiving more advanced education. She is presently disappointed that she was not selected for the dean position but she is committed to helping until her resignation takes effect next August. She plans to return to graduate school and pursue a Ph.D. in history.

Jim expresses concern that the hall directors and the Resident Hall Association presidents don't listen to him. He attends their meetings and tries to advise them on program planning and budget concerns. It is his assessment that both halls seem to pull in opposite directions.

Malika is pleased with the development of the commuter students association. She has managed to negotiate the option of commuter students' being able to purchase a meal ticket which can be used in the resident hall dining area. She believes if the commuters could eat with the resident students, some of the barriers that divide them would come down. Both assistant deans are concerned that they have not attended any professional development conferences for two years and wonder if that is something you will provide for them in the future.

Open Meeting with Students. No one stops in for the first 45 minutes.

3:25 p.m. Sally, a white female, senior resident student, in her last semester stopped in to say she is very excited that Livingwell finally hired a professional to be the dean. She is the outgoing president of the Student Government and has attended all the regional, state, and national student government conferences. She also worked in the summer as an intern for the state representative in the capital city. She feels she has met numerous types of deans of students so she voted in the affirmative for your selection as dean.

She wanted you to know that it was a milestone when she was elected president of the Student Government. All previous leaders have been male students and the only reason she thought she won was because of her past experience working as an intern in the state capital. Knowing that most of the women students don't have that type of experience, she wondered what you would do as the new dean to eliminate sexism within campus organizations.

Preparing the Report

Looking over your notes, you begin to formulate a plan of action that includes staff development as well as redeployment of budget funds. People seem to have very different assumptions and beliefs about student affairs and its role in higher education. You begin by spelling out for the president a small number of achievable goals for the student affairs area. You also decide to develop a new organizational structure with careful attention to coordination of communication and responsibility. Finally, you explain some of the theories utilized by student development professionals to help the president understand and decide where to place developmental emphasis on a phase by phase basis.

You begin writing your report.

Honesty and Integrity
Vicki J. Rosser
University of Hawaii at Manoa

Setting

Dilemma University is a public research university located in the west. Approximately 17, 000 students attend the university. Since 1992 the university has sustained consistent budget cuts. A once flourishing allocated budget of more than $331 million (FY 1992–93) has now been reduced to $267 million (FY 1997–98). The decrease in funding represents more than 64 million dollars in the university's operating budget in four years. In 1992 there were more than 4,841 faculty and administrators. Today those numbers have been reduced substantially, reflecting decreases of 10% in each category.

Characters

Vice President Thomas is the senior vice president of Planning and Policy for the university. He is meticulous, hard working, and well-respected by his peers and those who report directly to him. Vice President Thomas's staff prepares many presentations for the Board of Regents (BOR), and he is often called upon by the president for special projects.

Vice President Johnson is the senior vice president for Student Affairs. She is well known throughout the system for her ability to run a tight ship. She grooms her staff, frequently promotes individuals within her areas of responsibility, and demands a high level of work and loyalty from her staff.

Jack is the director of Institutional Research for Student Affairs. He has been the director for five years, and he is the only director to hold this position in a newly created department. Jack reports directly to Vice President Johnson in Student Affairs.

Doreen is Jack's secretary in the Institutional Research Office in Student Affairs. She has worked for Jack since the office was created five years ago. Doreen is very loyal to Jack. She is pleased that he has confidence in her to run his office.

Wanda is a full-time researcher in the institutional research office for student affairs. She is considered the senior institutional researcher in the office and has been working under Jack for more than three years. Wanda is a doctoral student in the department of Political Science.

Zena is also a full-time institutional researcher working in the research office for student affairs. She has worked with Wanda and Jack for three years. Zena's major

is Human Resources and she just finished her Master's degree. After graduation, Zena will leave the office to pursue her doctorate at another institution.

Tina is a part-time graduate research assistant in the Office of Planning and Policy.
She reports to Vice President Thomas and for several years she has prepared
special projects for him to present to the Board of Regents. Tina is pursuing a
second career in higher education and is a full-time doctoral student in the
department of Educational Administration. Tina has a strong interest in statisti-
cal methods, data analysis, and institutional research.

The Case

One afternoon Tina was working with her mentor on her research presentation for
the National Association of Student Personnel Administrators (NASPA) when
she received a call from Vice President Thomas. Tina was asked to come to his
office immediately. Tina was thrilled with the sense of urgency and the idea that
the president may need some sort of a data response to a BOR request. She loved
the thought of having another project and working closely with Vice President
Thomas.

As the conversation with Vice President Thomas began, Tina knew this was
not to be the type of project she hoped to have. Instead, Tina was told that due to
budget and staff reductions, her position working with Vice President Thomas
was to be eliminated. The news, however, was not all bad. Vice President Thomas
negotiated with Vice President Johnson that Tina could become an applicant and
interview for a part-time student research position with Jack, the director of Institutional Research for Student Affairs. Although no promises or guarantees were
made to Tina regarding the position, she was pleased with the opportunity to apply for another part-time research position with full benefits. Most of all, this
position would allow her to continue her doctoral studies and research on a full-
time basis. Tina did not want to jeopardize the quality of her doctoral experience.

The following day Tina called Jack to set up an interview. He said that he was too
busy preparing for NASPA that week and asked if they could meet some time
after the trip. In the meantime, Jack suggested that she submit an application with
her vita to his secretary Doreen. Tina agreed to submit all the paperwork and she
was willing to set up an interview appointment after the NASPA annual meeting.

A week later at the annual meeting in Chicago, Tina ran into Jack after a
research paper session. Jack asked Tina if she would like to go and get a cup of
coffee. Tina agreed. While at the coffee shop, Jack offered Tina the graduate student research position in his office. Jack said, "you were the best qualified, besides, anyone that can work with Vice President Thomas with all his scruples can
work for me and Vice President Johnson." Tina was pleased, but also very uncom-

fortable with the fact that she didn't officially interview for the position. Jack shook her hand and then ran off to another session. Tina was a bit taken back and began to question whether she had earned the position on merit and qualifications or from her political ties with Vice President Thomas.

On Tina's first day in her new position Jack and Wanda were not in the office. Tina cheerfully introduced herself to Doreen and Zena and asked if there was anything she could do to help. Doreen gave her a book on institutional research and told her to start reading. Zena acknowledged Tina then walked away to her carrel. As Tina sat at her desk, she noticed that there were no supplies at her desk and asked Doreen where she could get a pencil and some other supplies. Doreen pointed and said, "there are supplies in that cabinet, go ahead and get your own, but don't be greedy."

Three days later, Jack and Wanda returned to the office; as they entered the office area, both were giggling and smirking. After they settled into their offices, Tina approached Jack and asked him if there were any projects assigned to her. Jack gave Tina the raw data from a student exit survey from the university for the past three years and asked her to clean up the data entry errors, run some descriptives, make some pie charts, and forward the results to Doreen. Realizing he was late for a meeting, Jack jumped up and dashed out of the office. Moments later, Wanda approached Tina and informed her that she was in fact the senior researcher in the office and that Tina should go through her first before going to Jack. Tina nodded her head slowly and apologized if she had inadvertently gone over her head. Wanda walked away and said there was no problem "this time around." Wanda then looked at Doreen and said she was leaving and would be tied up in meetings for the rest of the day.

A few weeks passed and Tina turned in the results of the student exit survey to Doreen. Although Doreen seemed pleased with the quality of Tina's work, she showed little, if any, emotion or appreciation toward Tina. Again, Jack and Wanda were not in the office so Tina decided to run further analyses on the data. Beyond the descriptive statistics, Tina discovered many powerful trends in student perceptions over time regarding their choices to exit the university. Tina was so surprised with these obvious results, she continued to investigate the data and took the initiative to write up an extensive report from the student exit survey. She placed the report and data analyses on Wanda's desk for her review. Throughout the month Tina worked hard and kept to herself, trying not to intrude into anyone's territory. She did, however, collect enough nerve to ask Wanda the status of her student exit survey report. Wanda told Tina that she was still editing the report and reverifying the analyses.

One afternoon Jack and Wanda stopped by the office to announce that in addition to Wanda, Zena and Tina were going to be funded to attend a research training session on the east coast. Everyone was pleased with the opportunity to receive advanced institutional research training. Although Tina didn't say anything, she was shocked that the funding was approved while the administration was cutting people and positions. Moreover, Tina just heard that Zena was leaving the institution at the end of the summer to pursue her doctorate at another institution, and further, Tina was only a part-time student researcher in the organization.

The following month Wanda, Zena, and Tina flew to the research training together. Midway through the first day of training, a trainer approached Tina and asked her if Wanda and Zena, who were absent, were going to attend the rest of the research sessions. Tina shook her head in astonishment and said she didn't know. At lunch time, Tina ran over to the hotel and rang both of their rooms; there was no answer. She assumed she had missed them and returned to the training sessions. Later that afternoon, both were still nowhere to be found and the trainers again asked Tina about them. Feeling very uneasy, Tina again called their rooms, but there was no answer. This time she left a message and asked them to call her immediately and that everyone was worried about them. The next morning there was still no sign of Wanda and Zena. Tina went to the training coordinator and expressed her concern that something may have happened to them. The coordinator agreed and said he would contact hotel security and the police. He suggested that Tina should go back to the training sessions and that he would call her if necessary.

As the morning training session ended, both Wanda and Zena walked into the room laughing and giggling. Tina walked up to them and asked if they were ok. Both smiled and said, "Oh yes, we had a blast!" "We went to the city yesterday and did lots of shopping and sight seeing."

Tina asked, "Didn't you get my message, we were worried."

"Yes," they replied, "but we got back to the hotel early this morning and we were too tired to call."

Tina gasped, "We were so worried, we even called hotel security and the police!"

Wanda then yelled at Tina and said, "You're the one that had us awakened early this morning?" Tina reiterated that she and the trainer were very worried about them. Wanda put her nose in Tina's face and said, "Mind your own business." Shocked by what she had heard and not wanting to make a scene, Tina just walked away.

After the research training was completed, all the participants gathered to catch their shuttle vans to the airport. Tina noticed that Wanda was not with the group. The trainer had also noticed Wanda's absence and asked Zena if she knew if Wanda was going to the airport with the rest of the group. Zena, holding back her laughter, said that she had left last night to meet her boss at another research meeting. For some reason, Tina was not surprised and speculated that Jack and Wanda's relationship could be more than platonic.

Upon Tina's return to the office, the mood was quiet and uncomfortable. Tina felt that it was very important that Jack, as the director, should be informed of Wanda and Zena's behavior at the research training sessions. When Jack arrived at the office, Tina asked to speak with him. In Tina's mind, the issues of honesty and integrity strike at the core of Wanda and Zena's behavior. Both had squandered scarce institutional resources. Tina told Jack the entire story, and added that she was truly embarrassed as an employee of the institution. Without any reply, Jack nodded at Tina and thanked her for coming to talk to him.

That afternoon, Vice President Johnson requested that all the student affairs units attend a special meeting. Vice President Johnson announced that Wanda had written an exemplary report on the results of the student exit survey and she wanted to personally recognize Wanda for her excellent work. Vice President Johnson went on to say that because of Wanda's report, the administration is better able to make informed decisions affecting student retention policies. Therefore, the administration is sending Wanda to a national meeting to present the results of her study. Everyone was pleased with Wanda's fine accomplishment and congratulated her for her contribution. Tina was stunned and dismayed by Wanda's incredible breach of honesty and integrity.

The following morning, Vice President Johnson called Tina and asked her how she was adjusting to her new work environment. Tina replied that everything is fine. Vice President Johnson seemed pleased and said, "Great, then you wouldn't mind providing me with an honest perspective of the research office's performance. I would like to meet with you this afternoon at 2:00 p.m. in my office." Tina paused for a moment then confirmed the time and the place for the meeting. After hanging up the phone Tina sat back and began to contemplate the dilemma of Vice President Johnson's request to honestly discuss the unit's overall work performance.

Birth of a Learning College
Scott C. Brown
University of Maryland

Setting

Brubaker College is a moderately selective, tuition-driven institution founded 148 years ago by the Anglican church, with whom it has had only nominal ties since 1933. The school was an all-men one until 1972, when it reluctantly admitted women. Today, the ratio between men and women is almost at parity with 52% men and 48% women. The student body is comprised of predominately white, middle class students. Brubaker's location in a rural setting in the upper midwest has made it difficult to attract historically underrepresented groups, but a special scholarship fund and aggressive recruiting has kept the African American population at 3%. Hispanic, Native American, and Asian American students together compromise 2.3% of the overall population of the college's 2,800 undergraduate students. Brubaker College typically draws heavily from the surrounding four states, and east to the Great Lakes region. About 20 years ago, there was an influx of students coming from the New England area. Admissions from that area plateaued nine years ago, and have been declining since.

The college was originally founded to teach men to be "right of mind and character" and has had a fair to middling reputation in the modern languages and literature, and in several disciplines in the sciences. The school typically prepares liberally educated students who pursue careers in teaching or business. Although it is not on par with more highly selective institutions, students are quick to defend their bucolic surroundings as an ideal backdrop for college. Campus traditions are strong: All first-year students run around the college chapel tower three times as the bell tolls twelve times at midnight during the first full moon of the term. There are also stories about the wanderings of "Old Man Brubaker," a ghost who allegedly haunts Allen Hall, the benefactor's original residence and currently the main administration building. The somewhat insulated environment compels students to draw on the institution as their main source of social activities. Eleven local fraternities and several national sororities form the centerpiece of the social life. Although 53% of the campus is affiliated with a Greek organization, the parties are open to the whole campus. There are two historically black Greek organizations, one fraternity and one sorority. In the frozen monotony of February, students will often road trip to Chicago, which is seven hours away.

Current Context

Despite its colorful campus traditions and history, Brubaker College has been steadily losing the competition for desired students to other institutions with a similar profile. Brubaker College has traditionally survived off the tuition dollars of its relatively affluent students, with scholarships available to a select number of students in need. In recent years, the market for the type of student historically desired by Brubaker has been saturated. Brubaker College has been slow to note this trend, identify its origins, and create a strategy in response to the shifting conditions. With only a modest endowment, there have been no plans to counteract the diminishing annual income. As a result, in the last fiscal year, Brubaker's precarious financial situation has become grave. In response to these fiscal emergencies, the Board of Trustees called an emergency summit.

Immediately after spring commencement, the Board of Trustees hunkered down for a long weekend. The Board is comprised of 13 of the college's more illustrious and industrious alumni, and has not always worked well together. Many of the trustees have nothing more in common than the college: Their ages range from 34–78; some have had different collegiate experiences depending on if they graduated pre- or post 1972; there is a vegetarian on one end, and a hog producer who slaughters 9,000 animals a day on the other. But at this weekend session, just having the college in common was enough, and the usual quibbling over minor issues has been mercifully put aside for the task at hand.

After a grueling session, the Board of Trustees finally agreed to reposition Brubaker as a "Comprehensive Learning College for the New Millennium." To clarify their thinking, one of the trustees suggested using a model from a provocative article entitiled, *The Learning Pyramid: Daily Recommended Servings for a Balanced Diet* which she read in an educational magazine earlier that month. The article proposed the creation of a chart with all the desired learning outcomes associated with college attendance, both in and out of class, so a common language of learning could be created for the whole campus. This chart, the article proposed, would serve as a "Rosetta stone" for other campus-wide educational efforts which would then enable more seamless student learning.

Additionally, the article proposed determining what activities will yield these desired learning outcomes, what constitutes a "serving," how many servings a day are necessary, and what "foods" are particularly rich in one or more of the educational "food groups" (e.g. cognitive complexity, practical application of knowledge, etc.). The Learning Pyramid provides a heuristic to incorporate all aspects of a student's experience to make each student a part of his or her education. Inspired, the trustees decided that the Learning Pyramid will be the centerpiece of the new college, and make Brubaker the first institution to attempt to make this proposal a reality. They have decided to use the occasion of the sesquicentennial of their founding to unveil their plans.

Placing an enormous amount of their future on this plan, the trustees sent a special envoy to recruit the author, Faye Attard, to head up the project in the newly created position as dean of Learning. They promised her an unprecedented professional opportunity, and a steering committee of Brubaker's most influential constituents.

Members of the Learning Pyramid Steering Committee

Faye Attard, dean of Learning. Formerly the director of a well-known residential college located in large, public institution on the West Coast. Of her 13 years of work in student affairs, she has spent the last five working with enhancing the residential academic environments and cultivating faculty-student relationships. Although she has had a number of successes in dealing with issues related to holistic learning on her previous campuses, she has never attempted anything on this scale, with this much at stake.

Thomas Buxton, assistant professor of English. Popular with undergraduates for his candor and with-it attitude, he is an outspoken critic of the old guard mindset that seems to prevade Brubaker College. He believes the Learning Pyramid will address many things that are wrong with this institution, and is anxious to implement it.

Corinne Danielson, director of Student Life. She has worked at the institution for 23 years, holding various positions until becoming director eight years ago. She is known as a straight shooter who is deeply committed to the institution. She did not graduate from any type of student affairs program, but does belong to one professional association. She is known for her creative, albeit traditional, activities for students. With the help of a young professor, she has spent a considerable amount of energy trying to spearhead Brubaker College's nascent service-learning effort. Two of her sons graduated from the college about 15 years ago.

Reginald Harriman, president of Faculty Senate, professor of Botany. One of the few faculty in this teaching-focused institution to bring in research money, based on his seminal work on organic pesticides. He thinks the Learning Pyramid is intriguing, but due to the extra amount of work it will invariably entail, its very questionable viability, and somewhat novel analogy, he is doubtful many professors would ever support it.

Anne Lemal, provost. Serving on the committee at the president's behest, she was appointed provost two years ago after a 12-year tenure as the chair of the History department. She was promoted to evaluate and retool the core general education program, but not of the magnitude that is now being suggested. She found much support while she served as chair, but has encountered some surprising resistance in her role as provost.

David Solomon, vice president for Finance. He has tried to articulate the growing severity of Brubaker College's financial situation for seven years, but the Board of Trustees would not accept any significant alterations of their financial plans until the shortfall last year. He knows something drastic needs to be done, but is skeptical that this Learning Pyramid is it.

Leslie Truman, associate professor of Mathematics. She was selected as one of the "10 Scholars to Watch" in a national poll that identifies up and coming mathematics faculty, and is one of the most valued professors on this campus. Known for her interest in her students, her year-end socials at her home for her classes are much anticipated. She is also faculty advisor to the African American student group. Frequently frustrated by the often expressed viewpoint that "only Brubaker graduates could ever understand Brubaker," she was pleased that the college finally hired an administrator who didn't graduate from the institution.

Derek Westerberg, president of the SGA, sole student representative on the Learning Pyramid Steering Committee, and graduating senior, he doesn't quite understand how anything out of class is the same as "real learning," but feels he has always gotten a lot out of his extracurricular activities. Inherently distrusts anything that will alter the "essential Brubaker experience," that he, his father and grandfather enjoyed as undergraduates.

Situation

After one harried week of settling into her new home and office, Dean Attard is scheduled to chair the first steering committee. She enters Brubaker Hall and nods a silent greeting to the president's executive assistant, who directs her to the end of the hall, where the rest of the committee is waiting. Before she enters the meeting room, she pauses to consider her simple but daunting charge: Fully conceive, implement, and assess the Learning Pyramid. She takes a deep breath, puts her hand on the doorknob of Brubaker College's Founders conference room, and steps in.

Chapter 5

Cases in Advising and Counseling

Advisors and counselors on a college campus can be thought of as the "parents" of the university. In their professional roles they must deal with matters as mundane as helping a student decide which general electives to take or as profound as whether or not life is worth living. Everyone who works in student affairs will at some point serve as advisor or counselor to a student no matter how their official job description is worded.

In "When Trauma Comes Marching In" Anne Butler and Michael Dannells describe complications surrounding the campus newspaper's publication of a student's personal problem. Glenda Droogsma Musoba and Frances Stage in "First Generation College Students: Tension Between Faculty and Staff" describe an academic advisor's efforts to work with a student who could be lost in the bureaucracy. "Culture Clash: International Student Incident at Middle Valley University" by Julie Nelson and Florence Hamrick describes students' aggressive behavior toward their teaching assistant as symptomatic of greater campus issues and a young professional gets caught in a web of miscommunication. Harriet Wilkins' "Aiding International Students: Whose Responsibility?" requires college officials to create procedures for a group of students that has fallen through the gaps in the student support net. In "Little Secrets and Chain Reactions: The Case of Ana Maria Lopez at Traditional University," Jeanett Castellanos describes a campus health issue linked to an indiscriminant and possibly malicious student's behavior.

In these cases consider contrasts of our textbook ideals. Campuses that could be cooperative, developmental, and other-serving sometimes are not so.

When Trauma Comes Marching In
Anne Butler and Michael Dannells
Kansas State University

Setting

The University of Peace (UOP) is a state-supported institution in the northwest, with an enrollment of 16,000 undergraduate and 3,500 graduate students. It is located in the state capital, a city of 100,000 people. Approximately 5,000 of UOP's students live on campus in ten residence halls, and another 3,000 live in fraternity or sorority houses, most of which are contiguous to the campus. Eighty percent of its undergraduates are in-state students.

UOP is a land-grant institution, with especially strong academic programs in the applied sciences. In the Carnegie classification system it is a Research II university. Its athletic programs are all NCAA Division I, and it is a member and one of the powers in a major athletic conference. People within the state exhibit a sense of ownership toward, and a great deal of pride in, the university.

UOP administrators and faculty have long been concerned about the role of the Board of Regents. Although the Regents were given the power to determine funding, and to enact policies for the governance of the university, a common criticism of the Regents is that they over-engage in matters pertaining to internal operations. In short, tension is created between the Regents and the administration and faculty as a result of the Regents' proclivity towards micromanagement.

Characters

The President of UOP was hired four years ago by the Regents for his management and promotional skills. He was given the charge to dramatically increase UOP's enrollment, which had steadily declined for the ten years prior to his hiring. Not known for his scholarship, he tends to stay out of the academic arena, allowing his provost to deal with the faculty and with curricular and programmatic issues. Because his strengths lie in working with external relations, he has devoted most of his energies to commercial and economic development, alumni relations, new student recruitment, athletics, and fund raising. Not surprisingly, he tends to become quickly and deeply involved in issues which affect the public image of the institution.

The vice president for Student Affairs has been in her position for 17 years and is three years from retirement. She has spent her entire professional career of 30+ years at UOP. She is well liked by students for her warm, student-oriented philosophy, but many of the student affairs professionals on campus—especially the younger staff—do not respect her as a professional because she has been too compliant in her dealings with the president and his four predecessors. Her management style is best characterized as "big picture," high in delegation, and low in involvement in the details of the areas that report to her. She is proud to be a survivor of several major shake-ups in the central administration at UOP.

You are in your third year as the associate vice president for Student Affairs and dean of Students. Your areas of responsibility include the Counseling Center, Career Services, Disciplinary/Judicial Affairs, the Health Center, Minority Student Center, Student Organizations and Activities, the Women's Center, and the Student Union. You report to the vice president for Student Affairs, who has been generally supportive of you and the initiatives you have fostered in your areas.

Case

On May 15, 1992, Cynthia Bluestem was awarded an Ed.D. from UOP in Counseling and Student Development, after which she stayed on at the University as a member of the Counseling Center staff. In joining the Counseling Center, Dr. Bluestem was excited about continuing her research on eating problems experienced by women college students. She used Post Traumatic Stress Disorder (PTSD) as a theoretical and clinical construct in her research. PTSD is based on a model that seeks to find a relationship between current problems present in treatment and a prior trauma the individual might have experienced. Using the model with women, Dr. Bluestem was able to link eating problems in women with prior traumas such as incest, other types of sexual abuse, and violence. Thus, she was working on expanding the clinical diagnosis and treatment of women to include an assessment of social and background experiences, rather than to make a diagnosis solely on the basis of the symptoms that seem most logically connected to the problem (i.e., extreme dieting and other behaviors exhibited by women anxious about their weight).

Dr. Bluestem's research about the eating problems (anorexia, bulimia, binging, purging, and excessive dieting) experienced by college women resulted in her receiving many requests to provide lectures and to facilitate workshops in classrooms, the Student Union, sorority houses, residence halls, and several places in surrounding communities. As part of her data collection she often spent time getting to know women students by attending women's sports activities, lounging around residence hall lobbies, eating in residence halls, and observing women students in the local bars and eating establishments popular among students.

Invariably, she would ask students if they were aware of eating problems and whether or not they knew women students experiencing such problems. She collected much information and many personal stories using this technique. After a short time women students started seeking her out with concerns and suspicions about their friends or other women they observed in living groups. On several occasions, Dr. Bluestem approached the director of the Counseling Center and the vice president of Student Affairs about the prevalence of eating problems on the campus. She recommended that immediate steps be taken by the administrators to address the problem. Action was never forthcoming and she heard, through word of mouth, that the administrators believed her research to be frivolous and her perceptions about the prevalence of the problem to be little more than a reflection of her preoccupation with feminism.

Through lectures, workshops and personal interactions with students, Dr. Bluestem heightened student interest in eating problems. She often included the following facts in her discourse about eating problems:

- Bulimia, anorexia, binging, and extensive dieting among women students are reflections of the pervasiveness of this problem throughout American society and throughout the world.
- Extensive preoccupation with body size and image in American society is similar to the practice of foot-binding in Asian countries for centuries, and body mutilation and disfigurement in some Third World countries.
- Changing ideas regarding gender roles, often associated with the women's movement, have not liberated women from cultural expectations and standards regarding beauty and body image.
- The multi-billion dollar dieting and advertising industries promote the image that thin is beautiful and fatness is a social problem in need of continual attention. Fat women tend to encounter rudeness, pressure to diet, subtle and sometimes overt hostility, and discrimination based on body size, shape, or both.
- Eating problems are rarely just a passing fad. Women tend to develop these tendencies and behaviors as young girls and many continue struggling for many years, sometimes with extensive therapy in an effort to overcome chronic depression.
- Eating problems are treated, in scholarship, in at least two different clinical models. The medical model relates the problem to physiological factors. The standard psychological model includes biological, physiological, and cultural factors in the study and treatment of eating problems.
- Emerging research challenges the perception of eating problems being confined to largely white, middle-class girls and women, a view quite pervasive in discussions about "the problem." In reality, the problem cuts across race, class levels, and sexual orientation.

Bluestem's assumptions about the causes of eating disorders were endorsed enthusiastically by many women students who attended her lectures and workshops. Consciousness about eating problems was heightened, and more students started stepping forward to discuss their knowledge of the problem, usually starting their descriptions with "I know someone who . . . "

One group of women students decided to organize an open forum that would allow and encourage "victims" to begin speaking out about their experiences. Among the organizers of the forum were: the student government president and several women senators who wanted to pass a resolution requiring the administration to develop an educational program about eating problems as part of the new student orientation program; several graduate students in counseling and student development (male and female); representatives from sororities; women athletes; representatives from residence hall staffs; and two women reporters for the campus newspaper.

The organizing committee was adamant about wanting to assume leadership and to facilitate the forum, stressing that faculty and staff too often take control of this type of forum to promote their own research or publishing agendas. Further, they believed victims would be less willing to express their experiences if faculty or administrators were prominently involved in the forum. Because of this, the director of Student Organizations and Activities, who helped with some of the planning, and the director of the Student Union, in whose building the forum was held, did not attend. Dr. Bluestem was present, but she maintained a low profile by sitting in the audience and not speaking.

The forum had been promoted heavily through campus media and it was well attended that Friday afternoon; about 200 jammed the small auditorium in the Union. The student facilitators asked that all information shared exclude the names of people, yet they asked that each speaker state his or her first name.

Five women addressed the group from the podium. The reporters were especially struck with a particular story. A senior described her ordeal with eating problems that first started during her freshman year when she was selected for the cheerleading squad. The male sponsor of the squad was very strict regarding weight requirements. Because this student had a tendency to gain weight fairly easily, she was constantly nervous and upset regarding the possibility of being kicked off the squad due to weighing over the required weight level. The sponsor required each cheerleader to weigh in, during practices and throughout the season, each Monday, Wednesday, and Friday morning. He allowed no flexibility with this policy. Over the years, many of the cheerleaders complained to each other about the policy, but no one approached the sponsor or the assistant athletic director to whom he reported.

The speaker went on to say that she finally discovered what other girls were doing to keep their weight down. They told her that she was stupid to get depressed worrying about her weight when she could eat as much of anything she wanted and then make herself vomit it back up. Although it seemed gross at first, this student was desperate and caught on fast. At first, it really worked. But recently, she had a problem keeping any food down. It just wouldn't stay down and on several occasions she had vomited blood. She was too scared to tell her family and tried to hide the purging from her roommate and friends. Often she would sneak off to public facilities where she could hide it from people who knew her.

She said sometimes she did not have time to get out of the residence hall and would explain to her friends that she must have contracted some type of virus. She secretly wishes someone would find out about her problem, because now she is depressed about lying to her friends. She feels a strong sense of shame about what she is doing, and while she is concerned about her physical condition, she is afraid if she seeks medical help her family will find out. She described her life as a nightmare and has thought of suicide.

This story so touched and infuriated the two reporters that they decided the cheerleading sponsor needed to be publicly exposed. They convinced their editor of the seriousness of the problems women were experiencing on their campus and felt that a public disclosure would stop the practices described by this woman. The editor consented to run their article on Monday, including a nearly verbatim description of the personal testimony in question. In their zeal and haste to get out the story, neither reporter interviewed the cheerleader or the sponsor.

When she weighed in on Monday, the cheerleader was met with angry and abusive language by the sponsor. Later, she learned that he had tried to reach her by calling her room five times while she was in her morning classes. She was not aware the story was going to be included in the daily newspaper until she was confronted by the sponsor. Feeling angry that she might be kicked off the cheerleading squad because of the article, she felt violated and went to confront the two reporters.

The article generated a lot of interest. By noon the president had received several calls from irate parents and alumni and word about the article had spread to the Regents' office, which had received calls demanding that the sponsor be terminated immediately.

A faculty member who recognized the woman student as the daughter of a powerful state senator decided to tell the senator. Soon after, the executive director of the Regents' office received a call from the senator, demanding that the cheerleading sponsor be fired. Moreover, he felt publication of the article, in a manner that did not protect the identity of his daughter, was just one more example of the student reporters' inability to practice responsible journalism.

The senator, on three previous occasions, had voiced concerns to UOP's president about reporters being out of control and having unbridled power. This was the final straw! He told the executive director that if changes in the governance of the campus paper were not implemented immediately, he would start a campaign among the Regents and state legislators to withdraw funding for the paper. More-over, current allocations for the entire publications unit would be rescinded, and the withdrawal of funds would take place in a matter of weeks. The executive director immediately called the president of UOP.

The president's administrative assistant has just called you to say the senator is on his way to campus to see his daughter and the president, with whom he has an appointment in three hours. The president would like to meet with you and the vice president for Student Affairs in two hours.

You call the vice president's office and learn she is off campus and unavail-able until the time of the meeting with the president, so it seems you will be addressing this situation for the first time with both her and the president.

How do you prepare for the meeting?

First Generation College Students: Tension Between Faculty and Staff
Glenda Droogsma Musoba and Frances Stage
Indiana University

Setting

New River Community College's enrollment is climbing, as they become known as the best price in town for higher education. Their fall FTE enrollment of 11,500 was their highest ever, and their location in the center of a growing northeastern city of 500,000 suggests their future is bright. Their first year student enrollment is 50% traditional age, predominantly White students from the local area with a 3% African American enrollment and 7% Latino enrollment. They are strictly a commuter campus with some students living in urban apartments, and many students living with their families—either their parents or their own families.

New River recently completed articulation agreements with all the major state institutions so transfers to four-year programs are expected to increase. The Advising Center was formed three years ago as part of a retention initiative and is staffed with four academic advisors primarily for first year students. Second year students are usually assigned to a faculty member for advising. While the college is concerned about retention, they do not want to increase the number of advisors because of a strong emphasis in their literature on accessible teaching faculty. Their latest radio advertisement campaign emphasized coming to a college where a professor "knows your name." A faculty advisory board guides the advising center. The faculty appreciates that they no longer need to advise first year students, but they are uncertain that the new arrangement is ideal. Several key players see the Advising Center as part of an administration plan to limit faculty authority. Teaching loads increased by one unit each year when the Center was created.

Characters

Andy Englemeyer earned a Master's in counseling after teaching elementary school for four years. Andy is in his second year as an academic advisor for first year students at New River. Andy loves his job and his students, and his fellow advisors respect him for it.

Raymond Adamez started attending New River as a full-time student in the fall. Raymond is a first generation college student and told Andy that he was the first grandchild in his family to attend college. His family owns a grocery store that his grandfather built after moving to the Midwest as a migrant farm laborer. Raymond is proud of his family and several times has referred to his grandfather as a role model with statements like "if grandpa can build a business out of nothing then I can become what I want to be." Raymond lives with his brother in an apartment near campus and works part-time for the recreation center on campus.

Janice Kerr is the director of the Advising Center under the dean of Students. Janice is an old timer; she was a professor at New River for 24 years before taking on the task of starting the Advising Center three years ago. Janice sees the Advising Center as part of her role as a professor and continues to teach one class.

Bob Roeper is the Physical Education instructor at New River as well as a coach for a local high school swimming team. Andy and Bob have become friends because they frequently see one another at the gym.

Facts

Raymond was put on academic probation after his first semester at New River and now, at midterm of his first year knows that he will likely not fulfill the requirements of his academic contract. Raymond earned a 1.61 semester average for the fall with grades ranging from a 'B' in an American cultures course to an 'F' in Introductory Economics. Raymond is reasonably sure that he will fail the economics course again this semester and be dismissed from college. Raymond is surprised and disappointed because he had good grades in high school and did not spend time studying, especially in his math and science classes.

Case

February 15–16: Andy attends an advising workshop focusing on student self-efficacy. Andy learns that students' performances are impacted by their motivation, which is dependent on their beliefs about their own potential for success. A self-efficacy model suggests that students' conceptions and their locus of control influence their ability to achieve. Therefore institutions and employees, like Andy, can have an impact on students if they implement learning models that enhance students' self-efficacy.

February 19: Andy came back excited and eager to try out some of these new ideas with his advisees. Andy shared his new knowledge at the last staff meeting to mixed reviews. The other advisors were encouraging, but Andy knew they did not quite catch the vision. They have agreed to read Bandura's book on self-efficacy together as part of their on-going staff development.

March 20: Raymond makes an appointment with Andy and shares his concerns regarding his grades for the current semester. Because the hectic period of fall registration has passed, Andy has a little more time than usual and chats with Raymond about his future plans. Raymond was a high school swimmer and had decided that he wanted to be a high school science teacher and swimming coach. Now, with his mediocre grades in science and mathematics, and his trouble with his grade point average, he is at a loss. He feels he's let his family down.

Andy decides to take a different approach with Raymond, who is registered for 16 credits for the fall including Finite Mathematics, Chemistry, Economics 2,

Psychology, and Introduction to Education. Andy wants to apply some of the self-efficacy principles he has learned. Andy offers to appeal Raymond's automatic dismissal and schedules a meeting with Raymond for that Friday to jointly put together a 'success plan.' Raymond leaves with a sense of guarded hopefulness.

After saying goodbye to Raymond, Andy closes his door and takes out his conference materials to refresh his memory. Andy learned that four key kinds of academic experiences are conducive to improving self-efficacy. They are:

1 Mastery experiences in which students experience success or mastery of a skill through actually doing the activity.
2 Vicarious experiences in which students observe their peers or counterparts in mastery experiences.
3 Social persuasion in which other people, peers, educators, or mentors work to convince the student that he or she could be successful.
4 Emotional states in which the student has positive feelings like adequacy and security that enhance performance and beliefs.

March 21: Andy calls Bob to explore some ideas. After exchanging pleasantries, Andy talks to Bob about Raymond's interests. Bob could always use some help with the swim team so he is eager to have Raymond work with him for the fall season.

March 23: Raymond and Andy sit down and formulate a joint plan for the fall semester. Raymond will enroll for a maximum of four courses per semester and meet with Andy every other week. Andy brings up Bob's high school swimming team and the possibility of a co-op experience in coaching four afternoons a week for credit. Raymond loves the idea and is eager to try a different role on the swimming deck. Raymond also enrolls in College Learning Skills and Introduction to Education. Finally he will take the next course in his mathematics sequence, Finite Mathematics. Raymond felt encouraged by the plan and Andy had confidence that Raymond could be successful and believed there was a natural connection between them.

March 26: With the appeal to withhold the automatic dismissal, Andy sends Janice a note that he plans to keep Raymond on his student caseload next year. Janice e-mails back that she has concerns about setting a precedent with this student and is nervous about the reaction of the advisory committee. Janice informs him the advisory committee would be meeting on Wednesday, and she will place Raymond's case on the agenda. Andy is caught off guard by her reaction.

Your task is to take Andy's role and prepare your presentation to the committee on Raymond's behalf. How do you convince the committee to give Raymond another chance and how do you convince them of the value of your plan for Raymond's second year? How will you justify your ongoing involvement?

Culture Clash: International Student Incident at the Middle Valley University

Julie R. Nelson and Florence A. Hamrick
Iowa State University

Setting

Middle Valley University attracts 40,000 students from across the nation and around the world, although residents of this southern state comprise the majority of the student population. Middle Valley is a land-grant, Research I institution, known for its outstanding contributions in the fields of engineering, technology, agriculture, computer science, and natural science. Roughly 8–10% of undergraduate and 20% of graduate students in these fields are international students, many of whom serve as teaching assistants. The percentage of international students on campus has increased 5% overall during the last two years.

The growing number of international undergraduate and graduate students reflects, in part, one of the top priorities of Middle Valley's strategic plan, which is to build its international reputation and reach—primarily through graduate education, international exchanges, and cooperative outreach and research. Strengthening undergraduate education for the predominantly in-state undergraduates represents another top priority of the strategic plan.

As the international presence has increased on campus, so, too, have incidents of verbal harassment, racial slurs, and acts of violence against international students. In recent months, the International Student Office has communicated with the Department of Public Safety to express concern about the growing number of harassment cases. The International Student Office plans to develop an awareness program aimed at enhancing cross-cultural understanding.

Characters

Carolyn Higgins, assistant director in the International Student Office, reports to the director of International Student Affairs. Responsibilities include recruiting international graduate students to Middle Valley and overseeing their academic progress. Carolyn recently implemented an international graduate student exchange program aimed at recruiting and retaining international graduate students. She meets with students once they arrive on campus, often serving as a temporary academic advisor and mentor.

Maggie Johnson, chair of the Zoology and Genetics Department and member of the Faculty Senate, has been a vocal supporter of the international graduate student exchange program.

Juree Wei, international doctoral student in Zoology and Genetics, came to Middle Valley from Thailand. She serves as a teaching assistant for the introductory survey course in Zoology. Juree earned numerous awards for her scholarship since she came to Middle Valley and, through her reputation, drew other Thai students to the Zoology Department.

Jaime White, Carl Bennett, and Steve Ward, undergraduate students enrolled in the introductory survey course in Zoology, struggle to understand Juree Wei's English. Steve Ward, a junior in Business Administration, has been particularly vocal about his frustration.

Burton Ward, Steve Ward's father, feels angry his son cannot understand his teacher when she explains assignments or answers questions in class.

Officer Greg Thomas, Department of Public Safety, has been working with Carolyn Higgins to establish guidelines to ensure the safety and well-being of international students on campus.

Timothy Morton, the dean of Students, has, been instrumental in strengthening undergraduate services in light of the new strategic plan.

Case

As Carolyn Higgins, you oversee programming for International Student Affairs, recruit talented scholars, manage the budget, and serve as advocate for international programs and scholars. Your responsibilities also include managing student visas, welcoming new international students to campus, and serving as a temporary academic advisor for a significant number of international graduate students. You have been working closely with the Provost's Office to develop an international graduate student exchange program. The program has been established, in part, to help meet the needs of Middle Valley's strategic plan.

At times, however, the strategic vision of building Middle Valley's international reputation conflicts with the strategic vision of strengthening undergraduate education for the majority of in-state students. In-state undergraduates, many of whom have never been exposed to students from other countries, have become vocal about their frustrations at not being able to understand their teaching assistants or instructors who come from countries other than the United States, Canada, or England. You hear about tensions among undergraduates and international students from a variety of sources. Sometimes international students relate frustrating situations and racial incidents in passing. Sometimes you hear about incidents indirectly, either from colleagues in other parts of the university or on the editorial pages of the school newspaper, *The Middle Valley Rag.* Sometimes, and increasingly lately, you hear about verbal harassment, racial slurs, and hate-motivated violence from the Department of Public Safety, who send you incident reports involving international students.

This fall semester has been particularly disturbing in terms of the numbers of complaints by in-state undergraduates and international graduate students alike. Five weeks into the semester and already seven formal complaints have been filed by international students with the Department of Public Safety. Two incidents occurred in academic areas on campus, one happened in the cafeteria, and four arose in the residence halls. All of these incidents were relatively minor, involving racial slurs and verbal harassment. In response, you scheduled a meeting next week with Officer Greg Thomas, from the Department of Public Safety, and Timothy Morton, the dean of Students, to discuss the problem and possible long- and short-term policy solutions.

However, this morning Maggie Johnson, chair of the Zoology and Genetics Department, calls you to report that Juree Wei, a teaching assistant from Thailand and an award-winning scholar, felt physically threatened by three male students after her class last Friday afternoon. It is now Monday at 11:00 a.m. After you ask about whether Juree is okay and if the Department of Public Safety has been notified, Maggie tells you what happened.

Jaime White, Carl Bennett, and Steve Ward, all of whom are enrolled in Juree's lab section, stayed after class to ask questions about their assignment. With all other students but Carl and Jaime out of the room, Steve opened his textbook and notebook on top of Juree's desk and asked for an explanation as to why his attempts at solving a problem in the last lab had not matched the answer in the back of the text.

Juree sat at the desk. The three students leaned over the other three sides of the desk, towering over her. As Steve leaned over the front of the desk, his weight shifted the desk backwards bit by bit, slowly pinning the desktop against Juree's body and eventually leaning her chair backwards toward the wall. Steve, wrapped up in expressing his growing frustration with the textbook problem and his inability to determine the appropriate equation, failed to notice the desk's movement backwards and simply kept shifting his feet forward as the desk slowly moved. Growing increasingly frantic at being surrounded by the towering students and the wall, Juree interrupted him with a hurried explanation, hoping that would satisfy him. Instead, Steve pounded his fist on the table and said, "All I asked for was some help, but I can't even understand what you're saying. I've been lost in this class almost all semester and now you're treating me like an idiot! Why don't you learn to speak American?!"

Startled by Steve's anger, Juree jumped out of her seat and fell against the chalkboard as the tilted chair slid from underneath her. Jaime, Carl, and Steve laughed and picked up their books. Jaime said, "Yeah, why don't you go back to China where you belong?" Imitating Jaime and Steve, Carl snorted as they left the room, "What's affirmative action going to hand us next?" Juree panicked and burst into tears. Another Zoology graduate student happened to see her and asked what happened and why she was so upset. Only with the support of the Zoology graduate student did Juree report the incident to Maggie Johnson, chair of Zoology and Genetics.

Maggie tells you that Juree feels devastated by the incident. Maggie called the Department of Public Safety to report the incident when she found out about it last Friday afternoon. Also, Maggie encouraged Juree to make an appointment with you, since you had served as Juree's academic advisor when she first arrived at Middle Valley. In fact, you recruited Juree to attend Middle Valley and followed her progress off and on as she earned recognition for her work. Students such as Juree Wei are just the sort of international graduate students Middle Valley wants to attract. "It's very important that you talk to her," Maggie tells you, "because she sounds terribly upset. She talked about leaving school and returning to Thailand. Apparently these students have been threatening her all semester and she feels afraid and humiliated." You thank Maggie and agree to call Juree as soon as you hang up the phone.

Before you have a chance to call Juree, however, you receive a call from Officer Greg Thomas, a Sergeant for the Department of Public Safety. Officer Thomas wants to give a full report of the incident to you, especially since the two of you will be meeting with the dean of Students next week to develop a strategy for preventing just these kinds of incidents. He has had an opportunity to talk to Steve Ward, Jaime White, and Carl Bennett. All three admit that Juree fell backwards off her chair, but they deny purposely harassing her. Carl Bennett expressed remorse when questioned by Officer Thomas, saying he knew that Steve Ward had wanted to "put her in her place" all semester because Steve could not understand her lectures. But Carl also was surprised at how abrupt and rude Juree had been with Steve when she cut off his question. Carl did not think Steve would go as far as he did in pressuring Juree, but he also did not know what to do other than laugh and get out of there after she fell. Carl played along because the other two were his friends and he had been just as frustrated as they with the class, although he felt sorry about the incident now. Officer Thomas promises to send you a formal incident report.

The following day Juree Wei comes to your office for the appointment you scheduled with her. Juree appears at your door in tears. She is obviously still shaken, upset, and despondent. She is a top scholar in genetics, and you helped the Zoology and Genetics Department recruit her to attend Middle Valley. She has since won numerous awards for her scholarship and is near the point where she will take her preliminary exams. After you calm her down and provide tissues and a warm cup of tea, you listen to her tell the story in greater detail. She tells you that the three students have been making fun of her all semester, particularly focusing on her language ability. For example, they often ask her to repeat a word or a sentence during lecture. When she answers, the three smile and laugh at her amongst themselves during class. She has tried to brush it off, although she admits the comments have been bothering her very much.

You tell her about the Department of Public Safety response and advise her to bring formal charges against the students, but she does not want to do that. In fact, the incident has so shaken Juree's confidence, she is considering leaving Middle Valley altogether. The pressures of American culture (and Ph.D. pressures, too, perhaps) have really been getting to her. Lately, she says, she cries a lot and feels greatly depressed. At times, she fears going into the classroom because of the jeers and mocking behavior of some of her students.

You listen, then strongly encourage her to remain at Middle Valley, pointing out how close she is to completion and reiterating your belief that the three students must be punished for their behavior. This suggestion greatly upsets her; in her country, women do not react that way and draw attention to themselves. She says, "I read the campus paper. I see what happened to some other international students. Just let it go. Maggie offered to have them removed from my section. I don't think they'll do something like this again." There are eight more weeks left in the semester. You explain that unless she presses charges, the students will receive only a slap on the wrist. But she remains firm. She does not wish to draw attention to herself or have her name in the campus paper.

Meanwhile, while Juree is still sitting there, Timothy Morton, the dean of Students, calls to tell you that he just got off the phone with Burton Ward, the father of one of the male students. Apparently, the father is angry that his son has been called in for questioning by the campus police. Timothy tells you Burton Ward said, "Why shouldn't he be frustrated with the instructor? He can hardly understand a word she's saying. We pay good money to send our son to your so-called prestigious institution and how in the world is he supposed to be educated by someone who doesn't speak the English language?" Irate yourself now, but not wanting to upset Juree even further by letting on that the call is related to her case, you tell Timothy you are in the middle of a meeting and will have to get back to him. Before hanging up, he tells you that he gave your number to Mr. Ward in the hope that you might be able to explain the importance of international graduate education at Middle Valley. You thank Timothy and hang up.

You hear a knock on the door. "Come in," you say. Chris Hanson, your new work-study student, enters with a flushed and harried look on his face. "Um," he timidly begins, "would you mind taking this phone call? The guy sounds pretty angry." You ask Juree if she could wait for you in the lobby, and she readily agrees.

"What kind of operation have you got going there?" Mr. Ward begins. You begin to explain the importance of the international graduate program at Middle Valley and how hard the university has worked to attract top international students to campus in an effort to boost the school's international reputation. "What about your local reputation?" he taunts. "How dare you have a uniformed officer waiting to question my son after his history class! How dare you humiliate my son in this way! Do you know how embarrassed he felt to be dragged away like a criminal?" You tell him how upset Juree Wei feels, too, but he cuts you off. "Those people shouldn't come here if they don't speak English. I pay good money to have my son educated there, and how can he learn when the teacher stands up there speaking Chinese?" He slams the phone in your ear.

You ask Juree to come back in your office. She stands by the door and tells you she wants to think things over. You reassure her that none of this is her fault and see her to the door. You make her promise to stop by at the end of the week, and you promise to call tomorrow just to check in with her. She nods and leaves.

A reporter from the school paper calls. Jaime White, one of the undergraduates involved in the incident and a journalism major, alerted his editor about his view of what happened. The reporter on the line wants to interview Juree about her side of the story. You tell the reporter that the police are investigating and that you do not have further comment and doubt the student would either. You recommend that Juree not be contacted. The reporter contacts her anyway, you learn the next day. He got her name from the course syllabus of his friend and knocked on the door of her campus apartment. The reporter told her he was "just following up on the police report." Ashamed and humiliated by the whole incident, Juree becomes alarmingly despondent and seriously considers quitting. She tells you she has already checked airfares back to Thailand.
What do you do?

Aiding International Students: Whose Responsibility?
Harriet Wilkins
Indiana University-Purdue University Indianapolis

Setting

Commuter U. is the urban version of the state's traditional research university. Located in the state capital, Commuter U. has grown rapidly in the past fifteen years, expanding around the university's medical campus. Starting with courses designed as extensions of the main campus, Commuter U. now offers a wide range of undergraduate degrees—from criminal justice to French to nursing to computer technology to biology. Because of the rapid growth of the university, the lack of a central campus, and the large number of part-time instructors, faculty and staff do not know each other well. They feel primary loyalty to their particular school rather than to the university as a whole.

Most undergraduate students come from the counties surrounding the capital and are nontraditional, first generation college students. The average age is 28. Many attend the university part-time and work full-time in offices, factories, and homes in the community. For most students, the university is not the center of their life: their families and work or residential communities receive the focus of their attention.

Unlike the parent research university which has long had a large number of international students, Commuter U. has very few. And many of the students faculty might identify as international are in fact American citizens or refugees or immigrants with permanent resident status who intend to remain in the United States.

Now that the campus enrollment figures have topped 20,000, the central administration has hired several professionals in an effort to improve student services. Frequently, these people don't know each other, nor do they know their way through the decentralized, often ad-hoc paths that have been used in the past for getting things done. Ignored by the central campus and having to cope with a rapidly expanding undergraduate enrollment, local staff and faculty had become quite adept at cobbling together makeshift arrangements to solve immediate problems. As a result, they are not always positive about the more formal procedures some of the new student affairs professionals propose.

Characters

Jim Smith became the vice president for Student Affairs in August, This is a newly created position, with higher profile and status than student affairs had been given in the past. Dr. Smith came with good credentials from a small regional campus in another state, but many local faculty and staff think that one of the local candidates would have been better since they know the particular history of Commuter U.

Connie Webster, director of the Office of Financial Aid, has been at Commuter U. for ten years. She has managed to keep up with the growing demands on the office by hiring and training student assistants and by streamlining office procedures; most of her requests for additional full-time staff positions have been turned down at budget time. Most students at Commuter U. receive some sort of assistance—government aid or employee benefits—so the paperwork load in the office is considerable. Because of the campus's short history as a semi-independent institution, there are no endowed scholarships or private grant funds administered by her office. However, some schools and departments have recently raised money for student scholarships from local industries and organizations; the schools are administering these funds directly.

Ann Baldwin is the director of International Programs. In August, Dr. Baldwin moved from the main campus of the university where she had been an assistant in the Office of International Studies and Programs. She was hired at Commuter U. to help it develop its international image and, in particular, to help schools develop international programs and activities.

Mary Jones, academic counselor, has been a staff member for the university for as long as anyone can remember. She worked in Admissions and for the Registrar's Office before earning her Master's in education. Then she became an academic counselor, first with affirmative action programs whose funding has now run out, then with the special office for returning adult students. For the past three years, she has had the additional responsibility of advising international students, primarily on immigration matters.

Case

At the end of the October meeting of the Advisory Committee to the Office of Financial Aid, a faculty member from the Department of Physics raised an issue. "Did you read in the paper this morning about the African student who died last week? Did you see that the local church he attended is collecting money to send his body home? Didn't the university know about this? Why didn't anybody do anything? I'm embarrassed that something like this could happen."

Vice President Smith, chairing the committee for only the second time and still unsure of names and faces, was taken by surprise. He hadn't seen the article and certainly had not been informed about the student's death. What was the situation with international student advising around here anyway? How could something like this have happened without at least a phone call to his office? Besides, why was the matter being brought up here? What did this have to do with student financial aid?

But before he could offer suggestions about another forum for this discussion, several other members of the faculty and staff entered the conversation. There was more energy in the room than at any point in the previous hour and a half! They talked about the dead student who had apparently been living on very meager funds because he was sending money to his wife and children at home; they talked about donations being collected from faculty in particular departments to get international graduate students set up in apartments before their first teaching assistant stipends came in; they talked about the problems of students who couldn't register because funds from their home countries had been cut off.

Each of the faculty or staff members who participated in the conversation seemed unaware of the other stories; each part of the university seemed to have been dealing with its international students on a crisis by crisis basis. Ms. Webster, however, commented from time to time. Yes, she knew about the registration problem and sometimes had been able to intervene with the registrar in particular cases, but some students told the same story semester after semester. Yes, she occasionally talked with international students about their financial problems, but the university had no funds available for them; after all, this was a campus where most American students did not have enough money to pay for their studies. She thought perhaps Ms. Jones, the person responsible for foreign student advising, had some emergency funds available. Most of the committee members seemed surprised to learn that the university had anyone designated to work with international students.

Vice President Smith looked at his watch. Another meeting, which the president was to chair, was scheduled in this room in five minutes. He had to end the discussion. "Do I have some volunteers who would look into this matter further and bring us a report at the next meeting?" The physics professor, an academic counselor from the School of Dentistry, and a faculty member from the School of Social Work raised their hands. "And, Ms. Webster, would you meet with them and invite Ms. Jones to join you? Perhaps Dr. Baldwin should be invited, too, although she's new to this campus."

You're Connie Webster. It's taken you two weeks since the Advisory Committee meeting to get this sub-committee together. That's a lot of time you could have been spending on other things! And you've learned that international student affairs is a can of worms. Jones thinks her quiet efforts to take care of international students over the years have been unappreciated: after all, she told you, she is responsible only for assisting students on immigration matters and has no emergency funds, but she has often used her own money to help students through personal crises. Now it sounds like the committee is criticizing her for the university's lack of assistance after this student's death. Baldwin was very careful in what she said to you, but she made it clear that she thinks Jones is probably incompetent at worst and unsystematic in her approach to foreign student matters

Little Secrets and Chain Reactions:
The Case of Ana Maria Lopez at Traditional University
Jeanett Castellanos
University of California, Irvine

Setting

Traditional University is a predominately White research institution serving diverse communities in a western state. The university is known for its seamless learning environment and its quality of baccalaureate, master, and doctoral programs. It has a commitment to standards of merit and its function is to prepare students to be effective in greater society. The university's academic programs expose students to theoretical and practical learning in a variety of fields. It strives to direct the future leaders of tomorrow into the next millennium by reinforcing academic excellence through research, teaching, and service. A student-centered environment is fostered and student involvement is highly encouraged. There are over 200 student organizations on the campus and a multitude of opportunities for students to learn both inside and outside of the classroom.

The student population is comprised of 30,000 students with approximately 10% of ethnic minority descent. Fifty-one percent of the students are females, 5% are openly gay, lesbian, bisexual or transsexual, and 3% are physically or mentally challenged. Enrolled students are [collectively] reported to speak over 30 different languages and convene to share personal insights from diverse cultural, social, and economic backgrounds.

Traditional University has approximately 2,800 faculty members all dispersed in the departments and programs of the nine academic schools. Women make up 980 of the academic faculty with a total of 168 ethnic minority scholars.

Characters

Barbara Horowitz is a university student and a member of a Latina sorority. She is a senior majoring in political science and is president and cofounder of the Political Science Scholars.

Ana Maria Lopez is a member of the Latina sorority. She is a sophomore and an English major. She is also a writer for the school newspaper.

Eugene Hernandez is a student in the brother fraternity to the Latina sorority. He is a senior majoring in environmental engineering.

Daniel Sterling is coordinator of Student Activities and is responsible for Clubs and Organizations and Greek Life. He reports to the associate dean of Students and has been in the university for ten years. Daniel has a good relationship with active student leaders and is considered a tad laissez faire. Furthermore, Daniel is close to the vice president of Student Affairs and knows her on a personal basis.

Francesca Gomez is the advisor to the Latina sorority. She just joined the institution a year ago as assistant professor in the Education Department. She came from a research institute which focused on the ethnic minority economic situation in the United States.

Charity Mayers, vice president for Student Affairs, has served the institution for 15 years. She is known to be charismatic and active with the student community. Mayers conducts multiple presentations across the nation to increase student enrollment at Traditional University and addresses the importance of cultural sensitivity and a tension free environment.

Joan Cranberry is a counselor for the Counseling Services of the university.

Facts

1. Traditional University's Code of Student Ethics does not include any clause barring student/faculty/staff relationships.
2. Traditional University's Code of Student Ethics does not address the expectation for students with the HIV virus.
3. The American Psychological Association Ethics requires counselors to identify and report any client who is a danger to him/herself and/or others.
4. The campus maintains a Multicultural Student Center, Health Center, Women's Center, and Gay, Lesbian, and Bisexual Center.

Case

Tuesday 11:30 a.m. Ana Maria Lopez has just gotten out of her class, Introduction to Psychology, and is visiting the Student Multicultural Center. Ana Maria is invited by a chapter sister to a party organized by the sorority she recently joined. She is told the brother fraternity will be the "honored guest."

Tuesday 10:30 p.m. Ana Maria attends the party and begins to socialize with her sorority sisters and fraternity brothers. Everybody is drinking and having a good time. Three beers later, Ana Maria beings to flirt with Eugene Hernandez, a senior in the university and fraternity brother. By midnight, the sophomore finds herself kissing Eugene and has sexual intercourse with him.

Three Months Later. Ana Maria continues to ruminate regretfully about her encounter with Eugene Hernandez.

Wednesday 12:00 p.m. Ana Maria visits the faculty advisor (Francesca) of the sorority group. The student expresses her fear of having had intercourse with an almost stranger in the beginning of the semester. The professor suggests that she and the student take an AIDS test or visit the Health Center.

Wednesday 3:00 p.m. Ana Maria goes to the university Health Center and takes an HIV test. The results will be ready Thursday.

Thursday 8:30 a.m. A concerned student from the Latina sorority visits student activities coordinator Daniel Sterling and reports hearing rumors that Eugene is an HIV carrier and is carelessly involving himself sexually with women.

Thursday 11:00 a.m. Daniel Sterling gathers the fraternity leaders and alerts the students about the possible circumstance. A fraternity brother admits to knowing about Eugene's condition but pleads with Daniel not to spread the word because he is concerned about the fraternity's reputation. Furthermore, the president of the fraternity goes on to admit that Eugene is bisexual and has multiple partners. In fact, he heard that Eugene told another brother he deliberately practices unsafe sex with his partners in order to infect them.

Thursday 12:30 p.m. After the meeting, Daniel calls the president of the Latina sorority, Barbara, and alerts her of Eugene's condition. Daniel justifies this notification due to the close interaction the women have with the fraternity and the risk of their health. Ten minutes later, a group of the sorority sisters visit the Coordinator's office expressing their concerns.

Thursday 2:00 p.m. Daniel calls a counselor at the Counseling Center and the vice president of Student Affairs. The counselor discusses the importance of confidentiality and the protected right of the student not to be identified as an HIV carrier. Furthermore, Charity Mayers, vice president of Student Affairs and good friend of Daniel, is not available for consultation. *Note*: Eugene has still not been contacted.

Thursday 5:00 p.m. Ana Maria gets her tests results and learns that she is HIV positive. She seeks assistance from her sorority sisters; however, before she tells them her situation they tell her about Eugene and his condition. Ana Maria asks who provided such delicate information and is informed that it was the coordinator of Student Activities. Without asking any further questions, Ana Maria becomes angry thinking that her situation could have been prevented had the university acted sooner.

Friday 8:00 a.m. The school newspaper comes out and on the front page is an anonymous article by Ana Maria publicizing her situation. She identified Eugene Hernandez, accused the coordinator of Student Activities with knowledge of

Eugene's HIV status prior to their encounter, and expressed dissatisfaction with the university's lack of attention to the situation.

Friday 12:00 p.m. Students gather at the Chicano/Latino center to discuss the situation and have an emergency meeting. Other ethnic minority organizations and the gay and lesbian student organization have been invited. The focus of the gathering is the lack of action the university took with the incident at hand. More specifically, students expressed their concern about the university not addressing Eugene's high risk behavior even after being informed.

You are the dean of Students and you just received information regarding this matter. There is an incoming phone call from the community newspaper to interview you on the topic and a colleague alerts you that the local TV channel is on the premises.

Chapter 6

Cases in Residence Life

The heartbeat of the campus might be felt in the residence halls. Twenty-four hours a day the residence center teems with activity. Typically it represents a microcosm of campus life—classes are offered, lectures delivered, movies shown, and art exhibited. Unfortunately, the residence center can also showcase some of the negative aspects of campus life—personalities, cultures, and customs clash when people from many areas of the country and the world attempt to create a "home away from home."

"Challenges of the New Frontier: The Internet and Student Affairs Practice" by Adrianna Kezar describes problems faced when a student sends a threatening e-mail to one of his floormates. A dorm room practical joke results in suspension for two students in "The Morning After" by Patricia Volp. Aaron Anderson's "Violence and Romance: A Case Study" highlights problems that can arise as college students struggle to develop mature interpersonal relationships. Fine shades of difference in what constitutes "Fighting Words" creates a dilemma in John Downey's case. Finally, in Julie Nelson and Flo Hamrick's "Hatred in the Heartland: Anywhere College Responds" debates spark over the rights of campus gay, lesbian, bisexual, and transgendered students.

As you read these cases let yourself take on the role of residence hall director, director of Residence Life or other residence life staff. Try to envision the perspectives and feel the emotions of the people involved.

Challenges of the New Frontier: The Internet and Student Affairs Practice
Adrianna Kezar
George Washington University

Setting

Liberal U. is a suburban campus of 40,000 students located in the southern United States in an affluent community. It is a state-supported institution with a reputation for outspoken students and faculty. The campus is known for its efforts to create a multicultural, safe, nonhostile environment for all students. Liberal U. has been trying to institute a speech code for two years with limited success. The courts have just struck down the most recent version as being too broad and vague.

Characters

Tom Jones is a sophomore living in Moore residence hall. His major is communications. He is very quiet, keeps to himself, and has a few close friends, but is generally perceived as an outcast. He has not had any disciplinary problems.

Becky Timmons is a sophomore also living in Moore hall, just a few doors down from Tom. She is very popular and is known by students throughout the hall. She is in a sorority and is an active member of Panhellenic. Her parents live a few miles from the university and are prominent members of the community.

Ted Donough is the area coordinator and is fairly new to the campus. He is also new to the profession, having recently completed a Master's degree in student life administration from another university in the state.

Tami Marshman is the RA in Moore Hall on Becky and Tom's floor. This is her first year as an RA and she has developed a friendship with Becky. Several students have complained to her that Tom is weird.

Janet Headington is the dean of Student Affairs and has been at Liberal U. for 20 years in various student affairs positions. She is a member of many national organizations and is well regarded in the profession.

Steven Notting is president of Liberal U. He has been president for six years and has furthered Liberal U.'s excellent reputation. During his tenure, he has been responsible for addressing many major issues including threats to affirmative action, managing the changing needs of the university hospital, renegotiating athletic agreements, and organizing a major capital campaign. Although he has been successful, state legislators think he acts too independently and they criticize the university for not addressing the needs of the local community.

Case

November 9. An alumna contacts the Office of the dean of Student Affairs saying she has seen a message from a student over the Internet that she thinks is highly inappropriate and she wants to notify someone on campus about the issue. The alumna is living in South America, so the message has been sent internationally. The dean's assistant pulls up the e-mail message and sees that it expresses a student's intention to rape and mutilate a fellow student at Liberal U., Becky Timmons. The dean's assistant is concerned about the vulgarity of the message, but is not sure how seriously to take the threat. She realizes that several people should be notified. She forwards the message to Ted Donough, the area coordinator where the student lives, and leaves a note for the dean to review the message when she returns from an out of town conference.

November 10. Ted Donough opens his e-mail the next morning and receives the message from Janet Headington's office. Ted looks at the roster for the hall and sees that the student who sent the e-mail, Tom Jones, does indeed live in the hall. While going down the roster he also notices the name of the other student in the e-mail. He wonders if the dean's office is aware that the other student lives in Moore. He calls in Tami Marshman, the hall RA, to find out about Tom Jones, who he does not know. He asks Tami about Tom but does not tell her about the e-mail. She describes Tom as quiet, shy, and studious. Ted also wants to know if Becky and Tom know each other. Tami says, no, not that she knows of. She asks what is going on. Ted describes the situation to Tami, but tells her not to say anything.

November 11, morning. Janet Headington returns from her trip and calls Ted Donough. He explains that Becky and Tom live on the same floor, but thinks they do not know each other. Janet expresses concern about the extremely threatening nature of the note. It was extremely threatening. It detailed a plan for kidnaping, rapping, abusing, and killing Becky and asked for other people to join in on the plan. According to the note, Tom had communicated his plans to other people and attempted to find interested accomplices. It seemed so implausible that this could happen on their campus, but the risk was too great to not take the threat seriously. Janet said she would talk to the president and get back to Ted.

November 11, afternoon. Janet stops by President Notting's office and asks to talk with him for a minute about an unusual situation with a student. She says she would normally not bother him with a situation like this but that there are several unusual characteristics. She describes what Tom Jones has done and then outlines five issues that need to be taken into account.

1. The mental and physical health of two students is at stake. A protective and supportive environment must be maintained.
2. The campus is still defining policies related to technology.

3. The campus speech code has been challenged several times.
4. The sexual harassment policy does specifically address messages such as this, but only in situations where the message is sent directly to the student.
5. Because the Internet crosses international borders, they may have to bring in federal agents to investigate.

As far as Janet knows, Becky is not aware of the threats. President Notting contacts legal counsel and then asks Janet to work with them to prepare recommendations on each of her five issues by the end of the week.

November 12. Legal counsel recommends suspending Tom Jones, saying that his threat is unprotected by free speech because it names a real person and demonstrates intent as well as planning. In the meantime, Tami tells Becky about the threatening note. Becky calls her parents crying, saying she is afraid. Becky's parents call Dean Headington and President Notting, threatening to sue the university if Tom Jones is not expelled. Students in the hall are talking about the situation. Becky's friends begin to threaten Tom. Tom Jones gets an attorney who says that Tom's free speech rights have not been protected and that he is going to sue the university for creating a threatening environment for Tom. Tom calls local papers telling them that Liberal U. is once again trying to limit students' rights to free speech. He says that the e-mail was a joke and that he is now facing being expelled for sending a harmless note.

November 13. Dean Headington calls Ted Donough into her office to discuss the situation. Legal counsel is talking with Tom Jones's attorney. Federal agents have been called and will arrive on the campus on November 14th. However, several issues need immediate attention. They have a recommendation from the legal counsel to suspend Tom; a mandate from the president to stop the chaos in the residence halls and to deal with Becky's parents who want Tom expelled permanently; and media all over campus that need to be handled.

Develop a plan of action for the dean and area coordinator to manage these various crises. Feel free to draw on any campus or external resources.

The Morning After
Patricia M. Volp
The College of William and Mary

Setting

West Audubon University is a state-assisted institution located in a town of 50,000 precisely in the middle of a large industrial state. With 13,000 students, primarily undergraduate, West Audubon traces its roots to a Teachers College. Approximately 5,500 students live in on-campus resident halls. The institution has approximately 9% African Americans, 83% European Americans, 3% other American minorities, and 5% International students.

Characters

Kathleen O'Grady has been assistant dean of Students at West Audubon for four years.

Milton Marley is the dean of Students at West Audubon and has been there for nine years.

Marchella Matberry and **Darcy Dee** are African Americans, juniors, and roommates on the third floor of the Martin Luther King, Jr. Residence Hall.

Terry Leonard and **Barbara Johnson** are European Americans, sophomores, and roommates on the King third floor.

Kelly Brown and **Pam Simpson** are European American freshmen living on the third floor of King Hall.

James K. Smith, Jr. is a 24-year-old African American senior at the university. He commutes from his family home.

Facts

1. The assistant dean of Students is responsible for administration of the judicial system. Judicial Procedures allow students to resolve their cases informally by a university hearing officer (where there is no dispute of fact and/or the student accepts responsibility for the violation) or to ask for their cases to be heard by an all-student University Judicial Board which is advised by the assistant dean. Hearing officers include residence hall directors and the assistant dean. All hearing officers and Judicial Board justices are trained regularly by the assistant dean and follow a manual describing judicial procedure in detail. Students have one level of appeal: The assistant dean reviews appeals from

cases heard by the residence hall directors and the dean of Students reviews cases heard by the assistant dean or the University Judicial Board. The Judicial system was the subject of a program review the previous year and outside evaluators commended the program for its fairness and consistency.

2. West Audubon University has a standard judicial sanction of suspension for violations of the college's drug policy. Students may be given a "suspension held in abeyance" in cases where they were consuming or possessing a small amount of marijuana. A student whose suspension is held in abeyance is required to sign a contract indicating that the student understands he or she has been suspended and that it will be held in abeyance so long as no further violations of any kind occur during the suspension period. If there is another finding of responsibility, the student will be suspended.

3. WAU has had several racially charged conflicts this semester. Minority student leaders have been complaining that they are held to a higher standard than other students are on the West Audubon campus. They have vowed to keep an eye on the administration. James K. Smith, Jr. established a watchdog club that meets regularly on campus to increase communication within the African American student body and with the university administration.

4. The dean of Students recently met with his staff to encourage everyone to continue to follow protocol, treating everyone fairly and referring problems to him.

Case

Monday, November 3. Kathleen O'Grady receives an Incident Report from the director of King Hall reporting a possible violation on Sunday afternoon. According to the Resident Assistant's report, a group of five Black and White female residents are accused of invading the room of Terry and Barb, unpopular students on the floor, spraying the room with deodorant, Silly String, whipped cream, hair spray, and Halloween Spider-Web-in-a-Can. While three women held the residents of the room down on their beds, the fourth and fifth invading women squirted Hershey's chocolate syrup and whipped cream on them, which dripped on the bedding and carpet in the process. Laughing all the time, the invading women then retreated. Kathleen immediately recognizes Marchella and Darcy's names on the list of accused students because of their current disciplinary standing. Darcy and Marchella each were found responsible in informal hearings with Dean O'Grady for sharing a marijuana joint in their room earlier this semester and sanctioned with "suspension held in abeyance." The abeyance period is for the rest of this semester and next semester. Each woman signed a contract acknowledging that if she had another violation this year she would be suspended. The other three accused students, one African American and two European Americans, have no prior history in the judicial system.

Tuesday, November 4. Kathleen meets with Terry and Barb to discuss the invasion of their room. The women are angry and want to have all five of the women who attacked them thrown out of the university. "I was never so frightened in my life as when they burst through the door without knocking. Someone could have been hurt," says Terry. "I can't get the deodorant and chocolate stains out of my comforter and my carpet," says Barb. According to their testimony, the five women were equally to blame for the assault. Letters from the office of the dean of Students are personally delivered to the five women accused of entering Terry and Barb's room, uninvited, and assaulting the residents. Each is given an appointment this week to meet with the assistant dean to discuss the Sunday incident.

Friday, November 7. Kathleen completed her investigation, having met with the victims, the five accused, and several other witnesses on the floor. Kathleen meets with Dean Marley to update him on the case. She tells him that there is sufficient evidence to support a charge of "behavior which infringes on the rights of others" for all five of the accused women. She points out that Marchella and Darcy are on "suspensions held in abeyance" and a finding of responsibility for these two would result in separation from the university. The dean and Kathleen agree that the case needs to go forward. Kathleen prepares letters with official charges and information about the judicial process. They are hand delivered by the hall director.

Monday, November 17, 3:00 p.m. The hearing is scheduled tonight at 7:00 for Marchella and Darcy. They have opted for a joint hearing in front of the University Judicial Board due to the seriousness of the sanction if they are found responsible. The other three women involved have settled their charges informally and confidentially and will be witnesses for Marchella and Darcy at the hearing. Kathleen has heard from two of the nonaccused witnesses, Kelly Brown and Pam Simpson, that Marchella and Darcy told them there would be hell to pay if they are suspended. Kelly is very frightened and doesn't want to testify. Pam says she believes the accused students mean what they say and she is afraid of being hurt. Dean O'Grady assures Kelly and Pam that the university will take steps to protect them if necessary.

4:30 p.m. Kathleen meets with Marchella and Darcy to question them about Kelly and Pam's report. Marchella and Darcy deny making such statements and say they know it would be dumb if they did anything like that; Kathleen remains uneasy.

5:00 p.m. Kathleen O'Grady updates Dean Marley, who advises her to take precautions if she believes they are necessary.

7:00 p.m. The hearing is held as planned in front of the University Judicial Board. Six student justices make up the Board, two African Americans, three Whites, one international student; three of the student justices are females, and three are males. A female African American withdraws from the panel, due to her familiarity with the case, and the students involved. Five panel members still meets the quorum required.

9:35 p.m. The hearing takes about two hours and after a short deliberation, Marchella and Darcy are found responsible. During the sanctions phase, the student justices open the envelope that describes the disciplinary history of the accused students. Because the accused students were on "suspensions held in abeyance," and because separation from campus is required in such a case, the student Judicial Board votes to suspend Marchella and Darcy. They reconvene the hearing to announce the decision. Dean O'Grady meets with Marchella and Darcy after the hearing is over to explain what suspension involves and the appeals process. She also explains to the two women that, because they have been accused of making threats directly related to the outcome of suspension, she has arranged for them to stay in a guestroom on the other side of campus from King Hall through the appeals process. This evening, Dean O'Grady has arranged for them to be escorted by a campus police officer to their rooms to get what they need. She also tells them that the hall director and resident assistant will be given instructions to call the police if Marchella or Darcy returns to the building without permission from the dean's office. Pam and Kelly will be informed about this precaution as well.

Tuesday, November 18, 7:00 a.m. You are Aassistant Dean Kathleen O'Grady and you have just opened the city newspaper's morning edition. A headline on the front page reads "University Accused of Racism in Discipline Case." The story cites James K. Smith, Jr., who reports that "two black women were thrown out of school for the same incident that two white women were given probation." The article also reports a demonstration will be held in front of the Administration Building at 10:00 a.m. this morning.

7:10 a.m. Your telephone rings and Dean Marley informs you that the president wants to see both of you at 8:00 a.m. sharp. The president wants to hear a brief report of the facts, followed by recommendations. As you prepare for work, you think about what you will say.

Violence and Romance: A Case Study
Aaron D. Anderson
University of Michigan

Setting

Sommerville State University (SSU) is located in a rural community north of San Francisco. A part of the California State University System, SSU was founded in the mid-sixties. SSU began as a small public liberal arts college and has since expanded to meet increased demand. Today SSU has a population of 18,000 full-time students, most of whom are traditionally aged. Approximately 8,000 students live on campus.

Characters

Paul S. Worth, coordinator for Hillary Hall, is beginning his third year at SSU and previously held a Hall Director position at a smaller New England College. He reports directly to an associate director of Residence Life and meets weekly with the central office leadership team. This team is comprised of the director, three associate directors, and the five coordinators for residence life. Paul will be completing his Ph.D. course work this year.

Sandra Harrington, associate director of Residence Life, is responsible for supervising Paul. She is also chair of the staff recruitment and training committees. She has worked in this position for 20 years and is thinking of taking advantage of the early retirement plan commonly known as the "Golden Handshake." Sandra is perceived as being ineffective, preoccupied, and no longer invested in SSU's Residence Life Program.

Theodore (Ted) Billings, associate director of Residence Life, is responsible for supervising Brenda and Sean. He was hired this year, immediately after earning his Master's degree, to focus specifically on diversity issues and needs of the nonwhite students. Ted is energetic and excited to be at SSU. As a novice, however, he is viewed as someone who needs to gain some real life experience.

Alexandrina (Alex) Smith, director of Residence Life, is responsible for the smooth running of the residence halls system. She reports directly to the dean of Students and serves on several university wide committees. Alex has been at SSU for ten years and is very well connected in the campus community. Yet, outside commitments leave her little time to spend in the office.

Robert Smilie, resident advisor on floor two of Hillary Hall, is a senior Sociology major and took the RA job to gain some "real people" experience. Robert is one of the more competent RAs on staff and is an independent worker.

Brenda and Sean, assistant coordinators for Hillary Hall, are working toward their Master's degrees. In addition to the two standard weeks of RA training, both have received an additional two weeks of training. Each has been an RA at a previous institution. This is Brenda's first year and Sean's second year at SSU.

Phil is an English major living on floor two of Hillary Hall. This is Phil's second year at SSU. Phil is a white male from an upper middle class divorced family. Since living with his mother, he has not associated with his father. Yet, he does appreciate that his dad foots the SSU bill. Phil lives in a single (or rather his roommate moved out) and has a reputation as a partier and drug user.

Yon-Wha is a Business major living in Wilkie Hall. This is Yon-Wha's second year at SSU. She is a Korean-American female and a first generation college student. Her parents run a small market in San Francisco and manage to get by. Yon-Wha is on scholarship at SSU. She has a few friends and is quite studious.

Facts

1. Phil and Yon-Wha have been dating since they met in English 101 last year.
2. Hillary Hall has 1,000 residents living in two towers. Each floor has one resident advisor. Living at the base of each tower is an assistant coordinator. The hall alternates gender by floor. The towers are connected by a common recreation, lounge, and dining area. The coordinator lives behind the lounge area and maintains office hours in an office located at the front of the building.
3. SSU Residence Halls maintain a "substance-free environment." Alcohol and drugs are prohibited at all times.

Case

You are Paul S. Worth, returning for your third year as coordinator of Hillary Hall. Far along in your Ph.D. program, you are beginning to worry about the dissertation. Fall semester went by quickly and you are starting to feel stress about making decisions for the future. Should you continue as coordinator for a fourth year or move off campus for the dissertation work?

January 23. Robert Smilie files an incident report implicating Phil, a male on his floor. Apparently the incident involved alcohol.

January 25, 1:00 p.m. You see Robert in the Dining Commons, pull him aside, and talk about the report. Robert indicates that he never saw Phil during the fall semester. Lately, however, Phil has been spending more time in the Hall. Up until now, Robert has not had any issues with Phil.

January 28, 7:00 p.m. You ask Brenda, assistant coordinator, to do the judicial hearing with Phil. He shows up ten minutes late and a bit out of breath. Brenda talks with him for a few minutes about why he was late and then moves onto the incident. At first Phil denies the whole incident, but Brenda catches him on contradictory statements. Reluctantly he admits to "having a few beers to let off some steam." Brenda continues the dialogue and Phil asks "Is there anything wrong with havin' a couple a brews to let off some steam after having an argument with my girlfriend?" Brenda continues the dialogue and places Phil on disciplinary probation for three months.

January 29,10:00 a.m. In your weekly meeting with Brenda you talk about staff recruitment for next year, the next staff meeting, the judicial case load, and several other topics. Brenda indicates that she placed Phil on disciplinary probation for the rest of the term. You approve of the sanction.

February 15, 10:00 p.m. Returning home from a night class, Robert hears some loud banging and crashing noises up in Phil's room. He rushes up to knock on the door and gets no response. Announcing that he is going to get the master key to enter, Robert goes to his room and calls Sean, the assistant coordinator on duty. Meeting in the stairwell, Robert and Sean proceed to Phil's room. They knock and ask to be let in. No response. Knocking again they announce that they will enter the room. Phil slowly opens the door. Scanning the room Robert and Sean notice glass shattered on the floor, a chair turned over, and Yon-Wha sitting on the bed fully dressed and in tears. Sean inquires as to what was going on. Phil attempts to explain it away as a mutual quarrel. Sean separates Yon-Wha and Phil and talks with them individually. Phil again provides a shaky explanation and assures Sean that "it will never happen again." In talking with Yon-Wha, Sean discovers that they had been arguing about an abortion. Apparently, Yon-Wha is pregnant. Yon-Wha cries and mumbles something about "life not worth living." Sean dissipates the situation by calling Kendra, a coordinator of Wilkie Hall, and letting her know what happened and tells her to expect them in a bit. Sean walks Yon-Wha back to Wilkie Hall.

February 16, 3:00 p.m. Sean and Robert meet with you and explain the situation. You decide that some action needs to be taken. After Sean and Robert leave you call Sandra and explain. She agrees with you that both parties would benefit from some counseling. You resolve to attempt to get Yon-Wha and Phil to go to the Health Center for an appointment.

March 19, 2:15 a.m. You are awakened by Robert. He says, "Phil and Yon-Wha are at it again. You'd better get over here fast!" Arriving at Robert's room, you find Brenda and Robert talking about the campus police. You query as to the situation. Robert replies "Listen for yourself." All three of you go down the hall to Phil's room and hear a large crash, a lot of yelling, and the sound of whimpering. You knock on the door and announce yourself and that you will enter the room. The door swings open, pungent smoke billows into the hall and Phil runs out. Yon-Wha dashes after him and grabs his shorts at the waist screaming "You're not leaving me! You're not leaving me now!"
What do you do next?

Fighting Words
John P. Downey
University at Albany

Setting

State University is a large, public institution located in the Northeast. Founded in 1948, State University has a diverse undergraduate population of 15,000 students. The University has a large on-campus population, with 5,000 students residing in the residence halls and 2,500 upper division students living in on-campus apartments. State University prides itself on the diversity of its student body, with over 25% of students coming from minority backgrounds and 5% from other countries. The majority of students come from large metropolitan areas, although State University is located in a rural part of the state.

State University is a comprehensive college, offering over 60 majors, and has always maintained above average academic standards. Average SAT scores are 1180 and 80% of students graduated in the top 30% of their class. In addition to academics there is a long history of student activism and involvement in out-of-class activities.

Characters

Carl Peters is a junior who had been written up by his RA on two occasions last year for consumption of alcohol and disruptive behavior. Carl is also an alleged member of an underground hate group in his hometown. He is currently involved in another incident where he claims to be "an innocent victim of a vicious verbal attack by a radical Islamic terrorist."

Jane and **Tammy** are friends of Carl who claim to have been with Carl the entire night in question at a party. They are seniors in good academic standing and have no prior disciplinary records on file.

Khalid Abdullah, a junior from Saudi Arabia, is in good academic standing and has no prior disciplinary record. He was recently elected to SGA Senate. He is accused of calling Carl a "racist redneck" and "skinhead."

Joe Jackson is the RA for the 2nd floor of Chaplinsky Hall, where both Carl and Khalid reside. Joe is an African American junior and this is his second year on staff. He also serves as a senator on SGA and is attending State University on a full academic scholarship. He considers the terms attributed to Khalid to be "fighting words" and thus documented the incident as a violation of the university's fighting words policy.

Professor Miles Coltraine has been the faculty-in-residence for Chaplinsky Hall for four years. He is a full professor of Music and has been at State University for 20 years. He lives in the apartment with his wife, a professor of law at another institution and part-time consultant to State University. Professor Coltraine is African American and is noted for his commitment to students. He is well known for holding "jamming" sessions in Chaplinsky lounge until late in the evening. He encourages students to bring their instruments and engages them in music playing and discussion, at times contentious, of current events. He has won several awards for his teaching and scholarship. He has heard about the incident in his hall and is concerned that such harsh words were used but is equally concerned that "the archaic speech policy has been used again."

Barbara Garcia is in her first year as the director of Residence Life. She is Hispanic and feels she has found a home at State University. The dean, who was impressed with her administrative and management skills, heavily recruited her. She has met with Joe Jackson, the RA, and supports his decision to document the incident using the fighting words policy.

Jerry Hart has been the dean of Students at State University for ten years. Dean Hart is extremely popular with students. He is known for his sense of humor and commitment to students. As a White administrator, he has worked very hard to bring a diverse staff to State University, a fact that has not gone unnoticed by the minority community. Dean Hart is concerned to hear the fighting words policy has been implemented and has called a meeting with Barbara Garcia.

Facts

1. On October 1 Carl Peters was returning from an apartment party at approximately 12:30 a.m. when he was confronted by Khalid Abdullah, who accused him of writing racist graffiti on his door in black magic marker. The note was scribbled in large print and read, "Terrorist go back to your own country." Carl said "I agree with the sentiment but that is not my writing." Khalid said he was "sick of the racist crap" he got from Carl. An argument erupted and Joe Jackson, the RA, came out to break up what he thought was about to become a fistfight. As Joe approached them he heard Khalid call Carl a "racist redneck" and "skinhead." At this time Carl became furious and turned to Joe and said, "I am tired of this crap being said about me, you better get this guy out of my face." Joe separated Carl and Khalid and met first with Carl and then with Khalid.

2. In his meeting with Carl, Joe listened carefully as Carl denied writing on Khalid's door and was outraged at being referred to as a "redneck racist" and

"skinhead." He claimed others on the floor, including Khalid, had called him these names before because he had "more conservative opinions." Carl claims he and Khalid did not get along because his father had fought in the Gulf War and "my family does not like radical Islamic terrorists." Joe rebuked Carl for referring to Khalid in this manner but allowed him to continue. Carl said he had been avoiding Khalid since their latest argument two weeks ago following one of Dr. Coltraine's jamming sessions.

3. Joe left his meeting with Carl and went to his room to review the Code of Conduct he had received as part of his RA training. He read the fighting words policy, which reads as follows:

"Any verbal or physical behavior, such as a disparaging comment, epithet, slur, insult, or other expressive behavior, that is directed at a particular person or group of persons, and which creates an environment wherein the verbal or physical behavior is inherently likely to provoke a violent reaction whether or not it actually does so. Such words include, but are not limited to, those terms widely recognized to be derogatory references to race, ethnicity, religion, sex, sexual orientation, disability, and other personal characteristics."

4. Joe met with Khalid, who had calmed down considerably and apologized for shouting in the hall. Khalid claimed, "I know Carl did this to my door and I am not going to take it." Joe listened as Khalid described how Carl had made statements against foreigners and affirmative action during one of Dr. Coltraine's jamming sessions in the lounge. Khalid said when he tried to talk with Carl he was belligerent. Joe had heard from other students about Carl's comments but he had always had friendly relations with Carl so he did not give it any further thought. Joe expressed sympathy for what happened to Khalid's door, told him he would document it and have it investigated by police, but he would also have to document Khalid for his use of fighting words against Carl. Khalid became outraged that he was being written up when it was his door that had been vandalized. His final words to Joe were "I can not believe you, of all people, are protecting this skinhead."

5. The next morning Joe met with Barbara Garcia, director of Residence Life. Joe described the vandalism to Khalid's door, explained how he had contacted the police, who were investigating the incident, and then described the argument between Khalid and Carl. He explained that he does not agree with Carl's politics but "if we allow Khalid to use verbally harassing terms against Carl, what will stop someone else from using them against me?" Barbara agreed with Joe's analysis and his decision to document the vandalism and Khalid's use of fighting words. She promised to call Khalid in as soon as possible to discuss the vandalism and would tell the area coordinator for Chaplinsky Hall to handle the judicial case with Khalid.

6. At 1:00 p.m. Dean Hart met with Barbara Garcia and expressed frustration that she had not contacted him prior to agreeing to pursue the incident through the judicial system. She indicated that she had many years of experience and did not consider this to be an incident she needed to clear with her supervisor. Dean Hart told her that the fighting words policy had not been used in ten years, his first year on campus, because the faculty were united against it. In fact, he had already received a call from Dr. Coltraine, who expressed concern that this policy is "once again being used as a tool against free speech."

The previous incident occurred ten years ago during one of Dr. Coltraine's jamming sessions when two students, one White and the other Black, engaged in a heated verbal exchange. At one point the Black student referred to the White student using a racial slur and the White student retaliated with his own racial slur. Everyone present agreed that Dr. Coltraine handled the incident very well, although the next day both students were brought before Dean Hart for using fighting words. Dr. Coltraine was outraged that someone had reported the incident. He asked that the charges be dropped and that this policy be abandoned because "it has no place on a college campus." Dean Hart did drop the charges and agreed to a more strict interpretation of the policy, but refused to remove it from the Code of Conduct. Upon hearing this history Barbara Garcia agreed the incident would have to be handled sensitively, but insisted that the fighting words policy be enforced because "otherwise it is useless to have it in our Code of Conduct."

7. Dr. Coltraine made an appointment with Dean Hart for 9:00 a.m. the next morning. He made it clear he is frustrated to hear this policy is again being used on campus and wants an explanation. He demands that it not be used in this incident and threatens to go to the faculty to finally have it removed from the Code of Conduct.

8. The *SUN (State University News) Times* called the Dean's Office to ask for a statement concerning "the racial incident that took place last night." The editor plans to run a front-page story on the incident and has been interviewing students from Chaplinsky Hall. She wants a statement by 5:00 p.m. the next day.

Case

You are Jerry Hart, the dean of Students. In the next 24 hours you must prepare for your meeting with Dr. Coltraine and respond to the request from the *SUN Times*. You begin to formulate a strategy for responding to these two important campus constituents. Then, you decide to develop a plan for how you will address the issue of the fighting words policy and its place on campus.

Hatred in the Heartland: Anywhere College Responds
Julie R. Nelson and Florence A. Hamrick
Iowa State University

Setting

Anywhere College is a small liberal arts college in the Midwest. Anywhere College began as a Lutheran Seminary in 1883. In 1927, the Seminary received a 3 million dollar donation from the estate of a wealthy alumnus, which stipulated that the Seminary reincorporate as a four-year private liberal arts college. The then-Board of Trustees readily agreed.

Over time, the former Seminary began to attract a much more diverse student body. Anywhere College became known for its art, drama, and creative writing programs, and was highly respected for providing an excellent education in the liberal arts and humanities. Today about 5,000 undergraduate students attend Anywhere College.

Ten years ago, a group of lesbian, gay, bisexual, and transgender (LGBT) undergraduate students became active at Anywhere. Among the group were some of the school's brightest and best-loved student leaders, who transformed the college and the town by creating a series of educational programs, dramatic performances, and political rallies aimed at illuminating and celebrating LGBT culture and life. The positive political and social actions of the students led many faculty and administrators, including those in Residential Life, to evaluate and reassess how to meet the needs of LGBT students. Some key faculty members even came out of the closet. Many wonderful programs were put in place to support and celebrate LGBT people. As a result, Anywhere has been successful in recruiting more LGBT students to campus and retaining them once they arrive.

At the same time, by the very nature of political action, the increased visibility of LGBT students, faculty, and staff has created tremendous dissonance for many other students (and their parents) on campus, particularly those who associated Anywhere with its Lutheran tradition and history. Initially stunned by the supportive reception given to LGBT students by the administration, some of these Lutheran students have organized to protest against LGBT people on campus, especially in the residence halls.

Characters

Madeleine Conley, director of Residence Life, reports directly to the dean of Students. Madeleine has served as dean of Residence Life for 20 years and was extremely supportive and instrumental in establishing LGBT programming in the residence halls.

Cornelia Hudson, dean of Students, reports directly to the president's office.

Gary Welsh is a sophomore who is gay. Gary lives in the residence halls and serves as an officer to the LGBT Alliance on campus.

Reverend Arthur Cass, an ecumenical campus minister, staunchly supports the gay community at Anywhere. Rev. Cass has had many run-ins with the Lutheran clergy, but, in spite of opposition, he continues to be a vocal and active supporter of gay students.

Terry Carson, director of Development and Alumni Affairs, wants Homecoming to run smoothly and wants to increase donations from alumni to the annual development campaign.

Emily Anywhere is a contemporary descendant and heir of the Anywhere family, who made the endowment to establish Anywhere College in 1927.

Paula Amblin is an alumnus of Anywhere and LGBT activist who fought to establish LGBT programming on campus and in the residence halls.

Gordon Felton, Faculty Senator, is an openly gay faculty member who publicly supports the LGBT community.

Howard Chittenden is the new president of Anywhere College. He was not present when the LGBT programming began ten years ago.

Members of the Board of Trustees, including **Lillian Held,** a closeted lesbian, and **Reverend Milton Adams,** a Lutheran Bishop, who staunchly opposes gays and gay rights. He serves as Emily Anywhere's minister.

Barbara Hanley, a worried mother who threatens to pull her daughter from Anywhere.

Case

Gary Welsh, a sophomore who is gay, recently found hateful epitaphs spray painted on his residence hall door. The vandals had blacked out all his gay-positive messages with marker and tied a used condom on his doorknob. Also, a muffled male voice left messages such as "die fag" and "gays make good road kill" on Gary's answering machine. The following day Gary came home to a flyer over his door announcing a bounty on his head. Gary suspects several men on his residence hall floor of these incidents. Gary is an openly active member of the LGBT Alliance on campus and has heard and seen ugly things before, although he never had his life threatened until now.

You are Madeleine Conley, director of Residence Life. Gary—accompanied by his RA—came to you this morning to report the incidents, complete with Polaroid snapshots of the used condom, defaced door, and bounty poster. Irate and terrified, Gary demands that swift and public action be taken to find those responsible for the actions. You readily agree. You call the Department of Public Safety to inform them and assure Gary that all steps will be taken to ensure his safety.

The following day the school paper, *The Anywhere Globe*, publishes Gary's photographs and story on the front page. During the next week, the hate-motivated incidents spark intense debate in the school paper. While many students deplore the violent threats against Gary, it becomes apparent that a groundswell of opposition to LGBT people in general exists on campus—or so it appears from editorials in the paper. Members of Lutheran Light, a Lutheran bible study student group, held a rally to protest the LGBT programs in residence halls and invited leaders in the Lutheran church to speak at their event.

LGBT student activists responded to the Lutheran Light student group by staging daily rallies in front of Gary's residence hall, which in turn have created new incidents of verbal harassment and threats of physical violence. This week five gay men were physically attacked on campus and in the residence halls. Reverend Arthur Cass, an ecumenical campus minister, and Gordon Felton, professor of biology and member of the Faculty Senate, are organizing a candlelight vigil in support of gay rights to be held next week at the clock tower.

The debate on the editorial pages of the *Globe* has drawn state-wide and even national attention. With the media attention, all of the Residential Life LGBT programs and services have been highlighted in a very positive light. But a few inflammatory articles in some conservative and religious magazines have fretted that Anywhere College will become known as "The Gay University." Their unfounded fears have struck a chord with worried parents. Some parents and students have threatened to withdraw from Anywhere if the administration does not change its policies toward LGBT students. The Admissions Office reported last week that applications are down by 4% compared to last year. Barbara Hanley, whose daughter Elizabeth is currently enrolled as a junior, spoke to a reporter in Chicago about the incidents at Anywhere College. Mrs. Hanley told the reporter that she has seriously considered having her daughter transfer to a school where "my child won't have to live with lesbians."

Since Anywhere College is not tuition driven (it is a privately-endowed institution), the drop in enrollment is not necessarily a crisis. However, in addition to the drop in enrollments you also learned the other day at a staff meeting that Emily Anywhere, a contemporary descendent and heir of the family who endowed the college in 1927, hinted at a Board of Trustees meeting that her grandparents

would be appalled to see how the college had evolved. "Hale and Betty Anywhere, my grandparents, devoted their lives to public service and the Lutheran
church" Emily said. "They had wanted to enable Anywhere to be financially independent, but had certainly never wanted the college to stray from the church's
teachings in this way. I may need to reevaluate my own planned donation to Anywhere in light of recent events."

Even as you hear this from your staff, Terry Carson, director of Development
and Alumni Affairs e-mails you. After the meeting, you find her message, which
reads: "Madeleine, please read this morning's paper with Emily Anywhere's comments to the press. As you know, I support your programs in Residential Life, and
I am not a prejudiced person. But what are we going to do? I am in the middle of
my development campaign, and if Emily Anywhere so much as hints that she will
pull her financial support, other powerful alums likely will do the same. I would
like you to reconsider maintaining current LGBT programming in the residence
halls."

Terry's message goes on to tell you that she has received an overwhelming
number of phone calls, faxes and e-mails running two to one against the LGBT
programming in the residence halls and elsewhere on campus. Many alums have
threatened to withdraw financial support from Anywhere if those programs are
not abolished, and Terry worries about the timing of events in light of the development campaign—especially now with Homecoming just around the corner.

That night, Reverend Cass and Gordon Felton lead a candlelight vigil in
support of gay rights. At the event, which begins at the clock tower and end in
front of Gary Welch's residence hall, a lesbian student is knocked unconscious by
an anti-gay protester, who threw a rock at her head. A near-riot ensued as the
Lutheran Lights engaged in hateful speech aimed at those marching in the candlelight vigil. Fortunately, the lesbian student appears to be okay, but the next morning the press and the national media plaster the story all over the front pages. You
have just finished reading newspapers and are about to read the Department of
Public Safety incident report when you hear a knock on your door. "Come in,"
you say.

Reverend Milton Adams enters. He implores you to abolish policies that
encourage homosexuality in the residence halls. He appears shaken. He reminds
you of the Lutheran roots of Anywhere, he reads passages from the Holy Bible on
the subject of homosexuality, and he demands that the Residence Hall policies
reflect the high moral standards of the church. You remind Reverend Adams that
a gay student has had his life threatened and that a lesbian student had a rock
thrown at her head. You mention that the educational programs have helped create
a positive environment for gay and lesbian students at Anywhere College and that
it appears that more, not less, programming seems to be necessary. "Then how do

you explain recent incidents?" he retorts. "It seems to me these principled young men have had to resort to violence in order to cast out evil influences and sinful behavior in the residence halls." In the midst of this conversation, your phone rings. Reverend Adams gets up as you answer the phone. "I will not stop until these policies are abolished," Reverend Adams says as he leaves your office.

The telephone rings. "Madeleine, this is Paula Amblin. How are you?" After exchanging news and some brief hellos (you worked with Paula to establish gay-friendly policies and practices in the residence halls ten years ago), Paula gets to the heart of the matter. "How are we going to protect the gains we've made in recent years given this crisis? It isn't ethical to attract LGBT students to Anywhere, telling them that they will be accepted for who they are, and then, poof, now that the going gets tough, abandon them to the hateful people. If we can't protect these policies we worked so hard to create, these students surely won't be able to stay at Anywhere. And I refuse to donate money to the development campaign until I am convinced the policies will remain in place."

Paula tells you that she and other LGBT alums have organized a counter-response and plan to disrupt Homecoming activities with an orchestrated and well-organized protest. She also hints that if Lillian Held, a Board of Trustees member, does not publicly support the LGBT community in this crisis, the Gay and Lesbian Alliance (GALA) Alumni group may choose to publicly out her as a lesbian. You encourage Paula to rethink outing Lillian, who has been very helpful in supporting gays and lesbians behind the scenes, but Paula cannot promise anything at this point.

The next day, the new president of Anywhere, Howard Chittenden, who was not present when the LGBT programming was first initiated and does not fully appreciate the historical development of or need for those programs, calls you into his office to express his views on homosexuality; they are not favorable. Without demanding an immediate end to current LGBT programming, although not supporting these programs either, President Chittenden reminds you that Anywhere is in the middle of its annual development campaign to raise ten million dollars. Further, in his view, after speaking at length with Bishop Adams, President Chittenden is beginning to feel that gay-friendly programs in the residence halls may promote homosexuality and the presence of the LGBT Alliance as a student organization may run counter to the mission of the college, which is, after all, he reminds you, the paramount consideration.

You have been the director of Residential Life for 20 years. You know that LGBT programming in residence halls has created a tremendous difference not only in the lives of LGBT students, but in the positive growth, development, and education of a majority of non-LGBT students as well, the current crisis notwithstanding. Just last year two lesbian students and five gay men told you that, had it not been for the educational programs in the residence halls, they would have dropped out of school. You know, too, that one student tried to take his life before finding friends in the Alliance and talking to a sympathetic RA. Further, many straight students have commented on the positive experience they had in the residence halls learning about gay issues and making gay and lesbian friends. The programming was particularly helpful to one young woman whose mother was just coming out of the closet; this student wrote an award-winning essay describing her mother's self-revelation and how the LGBT programs in the residence halls helped her to support her mother during the process. You know the overall climate for LGBT *and* non-LGBT students improved remarkably from the 1970s when you first became director of Residence Life.

What do you do?

Chapter 7

Cases in Student Activities

Student activities in some ways are some of the stickiest areas of student affairs. These are the areas that "belong" to the students. Yet, students do not always have the information nor the experience to wield their responsibility wisely. Somehow, administrators and advisors must find a way to guide and educate students while allowing them the freedom to make their own decisions. This chapter presents some problems that can arise with such attempts.

Jillian Kinzie and Patricia Muller's "Take Back the Night: A Gauge of the Climate for Women on Campus" outlines conflict both across and within gender groups regarding campus violence. In "Hazing is Prohibited: It Sounds so Simple" Catherine McHugh Engstrom and Suzy Nelson describe hazing incidents that implicate more than just the brothers. Campus officials in Christopher Brown and Steven Thomas's "Breakfast at Tara" find that one campus group's efforts at honoring tradition hold racial overtones. Campus conflicts over student organization funding spark racial conflict in Guadalupe Anaya and Lillian Casillas's "Tortillas with Dinner: An Excuse for Racial Harassment." In Robert DeBard's "Who's on First? What's on Second? Managing Projects in Students Affairs" a young professional faces the realities of doing more with less because of budget cuts. "Conflict in the Union: Whose Rights are Right?" by Florence A. Hamrick and W. Houston Dougharty describes problems when there is a mismatch between campus visitors' and their academic hosts' values. Students' efforts to bring in a big name also bring in big problems in Cathy McHugh Engstrom and Michael Elmore's "'Controversy Sells Tickets!' What Else Does Controversy Bring?"

Cases within this chapter demonstrate the range of issues faced by the student activities professional as students become more sophisticated about their "rights" to manage certain resources. Hopefully, they will help you expand your own repertoire of administrative response to similar campus problems.

Take Back the Night: A Gauge of the Climate for Women on Campus
Jillian Kinzie
Patricia Muller
Indiana University-Bloomington

Setting

Arlington University is a mid-sized, predominantly White, public university located in a traditional college town in the Northeast with an enrollment of approximately 15,000 undergraduates. Arlington University is primarily a residential campus with 10,000 students living on campus. Fraternities and sororities actively involve about 30% of the student population.

The ivy covered buildings and beautifully maintained grounds, surrounded by a quaint college town projects the image of an idyllic college community. Indeed, part of Arlington's allure for prospective students and their parents are the feelings of comfort and protection that the campus evokes. The occasional bike and unattended backpack thefts are the most frequently reported crimes. However, since Campus Crime Report Statistics have been made public, some students and their parents were surprised to learn that last year 11 rapes were reported on campus.

In an effort to educate students about safety issues for women, the Women Students Association has sponsored a number of events designed to heighten awareness. One such event, that occurs annually at Arlington, is the nationally recognized Take Back The Night march, to protest rape and violence against women.

Characters

Molly Tait and **Sonia Jenkins,** both juniors, are co-coordinators of the Take Back The Night event. They have been active in the Women Students Association since their first year at Arlington.

Pam Donlan is a senior and president of the Women Students Association.

Letrece Brown is president of the Black Student Union.

Rick Baldwin is a member of a fraternity.

Clare Vass is an untenured assistant professor in the Chemistry department.

Robin Chan is the dean of Students.

Joan Wainwright is faculty adviser to the Women Students Association.

Claude Penn is the director of Campus Police.

Case

On a warm evening in late September, more than 300 women students gather at Lincoln Quad for the annual Take Back The Night march. Most of these students have just walked over from the nearby Pratt lounge where the Take Back The Night speak out was held. The speak out provided women the opportunity to speak publicly about their experiences with rape, sexual assault, or harassment. The accounts of date rape and sexual assault told by women during the speak out were powerful. As the students assemble for the Take Back The Night march, flyers with protest chants and details of the march route, and candles are distributed. The dark quad is gradually illuminated as each candle is lit. Pam, the president of the Women Student Association addresses the group, stressing the importance of Take Back The Night to symbolically reclaim the night for women and promote women's empowerment. Molly, a co-coordinator of the event, informs the group of the national statistics regarding women's safety on campus. She then leads the group in a rehearsal of a few of the chants. By the second round of, "2-4-6-8, no more violence, no more rape!" the marchers' voices reverberate off the neighboring buildings.

The marchers move out to their first stop point, the site of an August campus assault on a first year female student. They form a circle around the site and then a woman reads aloud the police report that depicts the incident and describes the attacker. The speaker leads the chant, "women unite, take back the night." As the group marches to their next stop, a fraternity house where a woman was raped by an acquaintance last spring semester, the crowd is assaulted by bottle rockets fired and obscenities shouted from the windows of a nearby residence hall. The marchers were told to ignore such encounters and to drown out the distraction by increasing the volume of their chants. However, some marchers scatter as the bottle rockets begin to pop. The marchers stop in front of the fraternity house and a woman stands bravely on top of a stone pillar. She begins by reading the statistic that 1 in 4 college women have the chance of being a victim of date rape and ends with an empowering poem about women's safety. The march continues across campus, with two more stops at sites where assaults against women were attempted, and to various danger spots for women where lighting is particularly poor. These sites serve both as a somber reminder of women's victimization and, in the case of an unsuccessful assault, demonstrate women's ability to fight back.

You are the director of Student Activities. On Monday, the day after the march, Molly enters your office. She excitedly tells you about the successful march. However, her enthusiasm is dampened by the flyer she found this morning on campus kiosks and on a bulletin board in the Political Science building. The flyer reads: "Arlington men, who really deserves the night? Keep it for yourselves. Let's put those Take Back The Night feminazis in their place! March and rally—Bell Tower, 8 p.m. Tuesday." This flyer only adds to the anger she already feels in reaction to the obscenities and bottle rocket encounter of last night. Molly wants to know what action will be taken against the residence hall from which the bottle rockets were fired, and also wants to know how the administration will respond to the Tuesday rally given Arlington University's policies barring gender discrimination, sexual harassment, and hate speech. Molly promises to return later in the day to find out what the university's official response will be to these incidents.

Meanwhile, Claude Penn reads over the police report of a few bottle rockets being fired out of a residence hall window last night. No persons were cited for the incident. After reviewing the report, Penn places it in his "out box" to send over to residence life.

As Sonia heads out of her residence hall, she is stopped by one of the Resident Assistants. The RA shows her the police sketch flyer of the alleged perpetrator of the August assault on a new student. The flyer has been defaced with the words "give it up bitches," and "our hero." "It is no big deal," says the RA, "probably just some guy threatened by the march last night."

By Monday afternoon, one of the sororities delivers a petition with more than 200 signatures to the dean of Students Office demanding increased lighting and a safety escort service on campus. Dean Chan adds the petition to a pile of papers on the corner of his desk.

Over lunch, Pam and Molly read the report of the march in the daily *Arlington University News*. They agree that the reporter did an accurate job covering the event but they feel that the article downplayed the intensity of attacks on the marchers. On her way to her next class, Pam sees Rick Baldwin. She thanks him for honoring the request that men not participate in the march, adding "I liked your fraternity's display of candles on the porch as a sign of support. I only wish more fraternities took such an active stance in educating their members."

Clare Vass notices the flyer announcing the Bell Tower rally on her way into her office. As one of three female faculty members in a 25 person chemistry department, Clare has been acutely aware of gender issues during her tenure at Arlington University. She believes that some areas of campus are not safe for women at night and knows that some women students in her class are concerned about walking home since the class ends at 8:30 p.m. Because this section has fewer women enrolled than her morning section she believes that women may avoid her section because they fear for their safety. Knowing how her own activities in the lab are restricted to when there are others in the building, Clare decides to talk with her department chair about the ways that fear of rape or assault limit women's educational opportunities.

Concerned about the rally advertised for Tuesday evening, Molly also contacts Joan Wainwright, faculty advisor to the Women Students Association to discuss how to respond.

Still angered by the incident during Freshman Welcome Week, in which a scavenger hunt list required students to collect racially and sexually offensive items such as "a photo of a fat chick sitting on a toilet," and "impression of a girl's nipple in peanut butter," Professor Wainwright calls the dean of Students to discuss what she sees as the latest in a series of incidents that are abusive to women. Professor Wainwright also discusses with Dean Chan the circumstances surrounding a student with excellent grades and stellar recommendations who was recently turned down for a campus scholarship because her grades dropped dramatically one semester. The predominantly male scholarship committee was aware that the student had been raped that semester but felt that she should have been able to handle it and maintain her academic status.

Dean Chan calls you concerned about the call he has received from Professor Wainwright. The recent scavenger hunt incident resulted in a lot of negative national publicity for Arlington University, and Dean Chan wants to avoid further incidents that reflect poorly on the institution. The dean asks you to prepare a report detailing the current campus climate for women that can be used for public relations purposes and next week's Board of Trustees meeting to ease their concerns. Before ending the phone call, Dean Chan tells you to make sure that "some men's rally" he heard about does not interfere with the campus tour activities occurring that evening for potential students, or "give the girls the wrong idea about Arlington."

During your phone conversation with Dean Chan your computer notifies you that you have received an e-mail message from Letrece Brown, president of the Black Student Union. You check the message after ending your phone conversation with the dean. The e-mail message reads:

> Last night while walking across campus I heard women chanting "women unite, take back the night." After asking around I found out it was from the Take Back the Night March. It bothers me that the Black Student Union was not included in this event. So the event was in reality "Take Back the Night for White Women." As Black women on this campus our numbers may be small, but our issues should still be addressed. Women's issues are not just White women's issues.

Molly, Sonia, and Pam return to your office later on Monday. Molly asks what action will be taken against the residence hall from which the bottle rockets were fired, and how the university will respond to the Tuesday rally. Molly presses for swift and deliberate action. However, Pam interrupts Molly to state that she believes there is more at stake here than just the men's rally and the bottle rocket incident. Pam advocates focusing on the larger picture rather than on these two incidents, stating that these incidents are just a small part of a more general problem on campus that needs to be addressed. In fact, Pam thinks that responding to the men's rally will just unnecessarily add fuel to their fire. Molly and Sonia both strongly disagree. After presenting each of their perspectives, the three students wait for your response.

Hazing is Prohibited: It Sounds so Simple
Catherine McHugh Engstrom
Syracuse University
and
Suzy Nelson
Cornell University

Setting

Thomas University is a comprehensive research institution in the Northeast. It is located in a suburban area near several large cities. Twenty thousand students attend the institution which is comprised of eight colleges and schools. The institution takes pride in its ability to attract students of color. Twelve percent of the students are African Americans, 8% of the students are of Latino or Hispanic descent, and 2% are Native Americans. In the past five years, the number of Latino and Hispanic students has risen consistently. Three years ago, two new Latino Greek organizations were formed and recognized by the university. These two groups are local Greek organizations only. They do not have national affiliations.

Characters

Terry Small, director of Greek Life, has worked in student affairs for over 20 years. She has good relationships with students, Greek advisors, house corporation members, and Board of Trustee members who served on the Board of Trustee Student Affairs Council. Over the years, the director has done a super job working with the historically African American and Latino Greek chapters to understand their needs, cultures and practices. She has established a great deal of trust with members of these groups. She and the Board of Trustee Student Affairs Council members have had concerns about the perception among students that hazing activities are occurring "underground" and are still widespread in the Greek system despite clear policies that prohibit such behaviors. Terry has become cognizant of the cultural and historical significance of pledging in fraternities and sororities and the role hazing has played in this process. Last spring, two historically African American sororities and one predominately Caucasian fraternity were suspended for hazing activities. Terry has made several public appearances at Greek forums to communicate that hazing will not be tolerated.

Chris Miles is a first year, African American, graduate student in the Master's program in college student affairs. His graduate assistantship is as a resident director in Kimball Hall. In a very short period of time, he has contributed in many significant ways to the Thomas University community. Under his initiative, he worked with a group of diverse undergraduate residence hall students to host an "I have a dream" week consisting of a week long series of diversity programs and workshops. This past spring, in his current practicum experience, he developed an African American Congress, an intensive leadership and mentoring program for a select group of 30 African American men.

For his practicum in the fall, he will work with student organizations to sponsor, plan, and implement a Latino Heritage month. Chris also provides informal support and advice to two African Americans and two Latino men, RAs, he met during RA training. Finally, Chris has remarked to his peers and graduate faculty that he is amazed at how many stories he hears from his mentees about hazing, particularly hazing in the historically African American and Latino Greek groups. He believed that hazing was not tolerated at his undergraduate institution; at this institution, he perceives students to blatantly disregard university hazing policies and the university administration must have "their heads in the sand if they don't recognize how regularly these activities occur."

Robert Baez is a Puerto Rican American, second year student from New York City. This spring, he is pledging Xi Alpha fraternity, one of the Latino Greek organizations. Chris frequently asks Robert if he is being hazed; Robert consistently denies that hazing activities occur.

Eric Gutierrez, a Cuban American second year student from Miami, is a communication major with a concentration in media and journalism. He works at the desk at Kimball Hall and considers Chris Miles to be his mentor. He is well connected and involved in the Latino and Hispanic communities but has no interest in joining Xi Alpha or any other fraternity. He is well aware of the hazing activities that occur at Thomas University and local campuses. He wants nothing to do with the long-standing traditions that have characterized many of the Latino Greek groups.

Luis Fernandez is the director of Multicultural Affairs. He is quite respected on campus and well liked by students, administrators, and faculty. Students trust Luis and find him empathic and responsive to their concerns. He is perceived as someone who holds students accountable, expecting them to contribute to the campus community and society at large. He serves as a leader on campus to develop a curriculum and campus policies that are inclusive and supportive of students from diverse racial and ethnic groups and backgrounds. He supported the decisions last spring to suspend the African American women groups for hazing violations. This spring, he is Chris Miles's practicum supervisor.

Cynthia Johnson, an African American second year graduate student, works in Greek Life. Her primary responsibility is to work with the eight historically African American and Latino Greek groups on campus. She is in the same academic program as Chris. Several times, Cynthia has commented to Terry that she finds the loyalty to protect one another is more rigid and absolute in the Latino Greek groups than in the historically African American and Caucasian groups.

Jose Martinez is a Latino male who is a member of the Board of Trustees. He also serves on the Board of Trustee Student Affairs Council, a group that provides direction and consultation to the Division of Student Affairs. He also advises the newly recognized first male Latino Greek organization, Xi Alpha.

Case

March 4. Eric Guiterrez comes by Chris Miles's apartment and shares with Chris that he was over at North Campus and saw over 20 men in line bound arm to arm, with masks over their heads. He happened to have his instant camera with him from class and took several pictures of the scene. He shows Chris the pictures. Chris recognizes Robert, his mentee, outside the line watching the activity. Chris figured these were pledges from another campus. He knew it was typical of a pledge class to be required to visit numerous local campuses and to be hazed by the pledge leaders at that college or university.

Chris asks Eric if he can keep the pictures. Reluctantly, Eric agrees to give him copies of the pictures but only if Chris agrees not to tell anyone that he took the pictures. Eric shares that he is concerned about his safety if the Latino community found out he "ratted" on his peers.

March 5. Chris shares the pictures with Cynthia. He insists that the group be suspended immediately, with the final outcome pending the results of an investigation. Cynthia asks if she could keep the pictures. Chris says "yes." She explains that she will talk to Terry, her supervisor, and they will call the group leaders in promptly. She asks Chris to talk to the student who took and supplied the pictures and ask if he would come talk to Cynthia or Terry directly. Chris said he would talk to the picture taker but shares that he was not hopeful that Eric would willingly come to see the Greek office staff.

March 5, that afternoon. Cynthia fills Terry in about the situation and shares the pictures. In reviewing the pictures, Terry groans. She explains to Cynthia that she recognizes Jose Martinez in the picture. Terry puts in a call to Marsha Hallock, the vice president of Student Affairs, so Terry can fill her in on this evolving situation. Terry asks Cynthia to keep the information about Jose Martinez confidential (although she did intend to share this information with Marsha, her boss).

Cynthia calls the President of Xi Alpha and tells her that she and Terry need to talk to him the next day. She shares over the phone that they have pictures of alleged hazing activities. He asks Cynthia who gave her the pictures; she responds that the name of the source is not relevant. What is relevant is what the snapshots depict.

March 6. Terry and Cynthia receive an e-mail from a very angry, scared Chris Miles. Chris wrote:

I have had it. Xi Alpha is out of control and needs to be suspended immediately. Last night, at least 10 Latino male students were at my apartment door, yelling at me to "watch my step" and they would get back at me for "turning them in." How did they know I turned in the pictures? Did you tell them? I told them to leave immediately because they were not residents of the building and had no right to be up on the floors. They left in about 10 minutes after we shouted some words to each other. Then, to make matters worse, Robert Baez, one of my mentees, came to visit me late last night. He was terrified. He is pledging Xi Alpha and they came to see him last night. Clearly no studying is being done in this chapter! They drilled him to find out if he or I had taken any pictures of their activities last week. He denied taking any pictures and said he knew nothing of me even being at the event. They know that Robert and I are friends and that I am also friends with many of the underclass male Latino students. They told him to go talk to me and find out what I knew. Robert is very scared and wants to pull out of the pledge process. However, he is also frightened about acts of retaliation. I did tell him about the pictures although I did not disclose who gave them to me. I also told him about the visit I received from some of the men from Xi Alpha and that he should feel scared. Clearly, this incident demonstrates threats to Robert's and my safety. Can you inform me ASAP about what action will be taken? Thank you for your anticipated immediate attention to this serious situation. Chris Miles.

Terry instructs Cynthia to advise Chris that they recognize his fears and concerns. Terry is rather put off by Chris's demands and is concerned that his reactions might threaten to undo all of the work she has done to establish trust with the Latino Greek community. Terry asks Cynthia to instruct Chris to document the events of last evening in a residential life incident report and tell him that without that report, formally, the Greek office cannot move forward on his concerns. Terry puts a call into the director of Residence Life. She had heard nothing about the event and assured Terry that she would follow up to make sure protocol was being followed. Terry waits to hear from her boss about what to do with the Board of Trustee member who appeared in the pictures. She is confident that her boss will ask her advice about how to proceed on this issue.

March 6. Cynthia and Terry meet with two leaders of Xi Alpha. The women point out that they had an informal report about threats being made to Chris Miles the previous evening. The students do not deny the hazing event or the visit to Chris Miles. However, they emphasize that their advisor was well informed about the hazing event and these events happen on every large campus within a 300 mile radius of Thomas University. In addition, they think Chris Miles should be reprimanded for his racist comments. As a university official, in his resident director role, they think he should lose his job for his inappropriate comments to the students last evening. Cynthia and Terry ask for clarification. They explained that Chris lost his temper with them and shouted "Go away. I don't care anything about your fraternity anyway. You are not even recognized nationally like the African American chapters. I have no interest in your group's business."

Meanwhile, in confidence, Chris shares the events of the last few days with Luis Fernandez, his practicum supervisor. Actually, Luis had already heard about the events, including Chris's remark to the group about his lack of concern for this Greek group. Luis explained that the group perceives Chris as a racist since all he cared about were African American chapters. Chris is dumbfounded about how his comment was misconstrued. He basically meant that he knew very little about other Greek chapters except his own. Although Luis explains that he disagrees with the students' perceptions and that he shared with the students how supportive Chris has been to many Latino students, the students were not interested in considering new perspectives. Luis also shares that he did think it was unfortunate that Eric betrayed his brothers by bringing those pictures to Chris. That group had worked hard to establish itself on campus and in the local area. To report this activity was, in all likelihood, going to lead to the chapter's demise. Luis also points out that Chris should be concerned about his ability to advise students on Latino and Hispanic Heritage month because he has violated the trust of many student leaders in this community.

Chris leaves Luis's office in a state of shock. How can this advisor condone hazing activities? "Hazing cannot be tolerated," Chris remarks to himself. And now I know how some of my White colleagues feel when they are misunderstood and labeled as a racist. "Me, a racist?" Chris is in disbelief and pain. He feels hurt, misunderstood, and helpless about how to proceed. He heads back to his room to write the incident report so administrators can take action, and thereby hurt his relationship with the Latino community even further. First, he calls Cynthia and tells her about his conversation with his practicum supervisor. Cynthia remarks that she was not overly surprised. Luis's response was consistent with her observation that absolute loyalty to one another was deeply entrenched in the Latino culture on this campus. Chris told Cynthia that it was fine with him if she shares this reaction with Terry, in confidence, so she was not blind-sided if she was looking for support from the director of Multicultural Affairs to take severe action on this group.

Terry is particularly concerned about how her relationships might be strained with this Latino chapter after years of working to gain its trust. She comments to Cynthia that it is time to talk to Chris and chat about alternative ways he might look at this situation and deal with these students. And of course, she needs to follow up with the Latino groups immediately. "I can tell I am not going to have a lot of friends after this week!" she mutters to Cynthia as she goes to call Chris on the phone.

Breakfast at Tara
M. Christopher Brown II
Steven P. Thomas
University of Illinois at Urbana-Champaign

Setting

Smith Durham College is a small northern college located outside Boston, Massachusetts. The student population of 6,500 students has recently experienced an increase in its minority student percentages. Over the past ten years the enrollment pattern at Smith Durham has become predominantly nonwhite. Smith Durham College is the primary organization in Meadsville, Massachusetts that employs many community members.

The Federalists Society student organization is the most active and community oriented student organization at Smith Durham College. They have an active membership of approximately 110 students.

Characters

Dean Matting Whittaker has been the dean of Students for Smith Durham College for 12 years, and he has served as the advisor to the Federalists Society for the past four years. He is known for being student centered and an advocate for student organizations.

Dr. Debra Thomas is the newly hired vice president for Student Affairs at Smith Durham College. She has only been with the college for one month. She has made it quite clear to the college community and the town community that she is committed and dedicated to supporting the changing student population and the surrounding community that mimics the campus demographics.

The Federalists Society was formed 126 years ago by an active group of young students who wanted to express their political concerns and issues in an environment that would encourage and support their platform. Today, the Federalists Society continues to uphold those same principles and values as their founding members.

Lauren Brightley is the vice president of the Federalists Society and a member of a sorority on campus. She is known for being verbose and obstinate in her decisions.

Palmer Elliott is the president of the Federalists Society. He has served as president for two years. This is his senior year of college and his final term as president. Throughout his terms, Palmer Elliott has led many rallies and protests and sponsored, through the organization, controversial programs that have made their way to the front page of the campus newspaper.

Chad Matthews is chair of Programs and Activities for the Federalists Society and a junior in college. Chad is responsible for all programs that are sponsored by the Federalists Society. He is assigned with assuring that all programming adheres to campus policies and guidelines.

Facts

1. The Federalists Society received a warning three years ago after sponsoring a Slave Auction program during the month of February, Black History Month. Several student groups became outraged at this act and went directly to the dean of Students for action.
2. The Federalists Society sponsored a fund raiser eight years ago and invited D'Gisha D'Koona to deliver the keynote address entitled, "Remember the Good School," an address that focused on education in the U.S. prior to the 1960s.
3. All advertisements—flyers, posters, press releases—must be approved to post by the Public Information Office on campus. Once approved, the advertisement will be stamped with an "O.K. to Post" stamp.
4. The new vice president of Student Affairs has charged student organizations to provide more cultural and educational programs; this charge has been given to the dean of Students for implementation.
5. All student organizations can only be considered an official organization if, and only if, their constitution has been approved by the office of Registered Student Organizations (RSO).

Case

Monday, February 12. The Federalists Society has decided to sponsor a fund raiser to support the Hope House during the month of February (typically devoted to black history). The Hope House is a Boston based program that trains homeless and indigent individuals how to provide custodial and/or domestic household services (e.g., janitors, maids, babysitting). Under the leadership and guidance of Chad Matthews, chair of programs and activities, the group has decided to host a breakfast fund raiser on the last Saturday of the month. The breakfast will consist of food and a keynote speaker.

Wednesday, February 21. Plans are underway and final preparations are being made for this Saturday's fund raiser, "Breakfast at Tara." The name and theme of the fund raiser was decided upon by some of the members of the Federalists Society.

Breakfast at Tara will be a morning breakfast that will not soon be forgotten by Smith Durham College. This is the vision that was created by the Federalists Society for this Saturday's fund raiser:

The name, Breakfast at Tara, was used to create a plantation theme where the executive board members of the Federalists Society would dress in plantation servant style clothing and black-face while serving a southern style breakfast. A flyer was made, approved to post, and duplicated for advertising around campus with the following information: Breakfast at Tara is being sponsored by the Federalists Society on Saturday, February 24, in the Student Union Ballroom. The event, scheduled from 8:00 am–10:00 a.m., would feature keynote speaker Donald Pike—a former congressional candidate and former white supremacy advocate. According to the flyer, the breakfast menu would consist of "gitts, sokeye gravy, biskits, ham, sawsig, and bak'n, eggs, panicakes, frute, cofey, juce, and tea. Sorry y'all, chitlins and colored greens is only 'vailable at dinna." The cost for Breakfast at Tara is $12.00 per person or $20.00 per couple.

Saturday, February 24. The Student Union Ballroom is crowded with attendees. The Federalists Society members are dressed in plantation and servant clothing and serving the guests who have come for Breakfast at Tara.

Monday, February 26. 9:00 a.m. The phones are ringing constantly in the dean of Students office with outraged students calling and complaining from the Black Student Union, Latino and Latina Student Union, and other student organizations. Students are disgusted and offended by the Federalists Society's Breakfast at Tara fund raiser on Saturday.

The vice president of Student Affairs has even received phone calls from community leaders and students demanding action against the Federalists Society.

Dr. Debra Thomas has called a meeting with the dean of Students, Matting Whittaker, to take action.

As Dean Whittaker, what course of action do you take?

Tortillas with Dinner: An Excuse for Racial Harassment
Guadalupe Anaya and M. Lillian Casillas
Indiana University

Setting

State University is a midsize residential public university of approximately 11,000 undergraduates and 3,000 graduate students. It is located in a small college town and is approximately 175 miles from State Capital, the largest city in the state. The majority of the undergraduate students come from cities with populations under 40,000 or from small towns and rural areas. However, most of the minority students come from the greater metro area of the state capital. At State University 89% of the students are White, 7% are Black, 3% are Latina or Latino, and 1% are foreign students. The campus has a rich history of supporting student life and activities through the Student Programming and Student Activities Offices. Student clubs and organizations contribute to the variety of activities and the quality of life at State University.

Characters

Doug is the assistant to the dean of Students for Student Activities and advisor for the Campus Student Government; he is White. Doug has worked at State University for two years. He is responsible for overseeing the activities of all campus student clubs and organizations and he serves as advisor for Campus Student Government. In his role as advisor, he attends Campus Student Government Senate meetings and the Programming and Budgeting Committee meetings. Doug describes his supervisory style as hands off and gives students free reign. But, he also likes to feel like one of the gang and enjoys working with students. This has made him generally popular with the Campus Student Government and most student groups; however, minority student organizations perceive him as apathetic. In spite of his position at SU, Doug seldom comes into contact with African American and Latino students and staff. He is generally uneasy when approached about minority students and the attention he gives to their concerns is at best superficial. He tries to avoid sensitive situations and has expressed that the director of Minority Student Services is better prepared to handle minority student issues.

Natalia is the assistant dean of Students for Student Programming and the director of Minority Student Services; she is Chicana. Natalia has worked at State University for eight years reporting to the dean of Students. She supervises educational and developmental programs on campus and in the residence halls, and is responsible for student judicial affairs and minority student services programming. She is often called upon to address campus climate issues, racial incidents, and represent minority perspectives on campus committees. Natalia takes a big sister approach in working with students and adjusts the level of supervision and guidance she provides to her staff and to students as she sees fit. She is proactive and tries to provide developmental and adaptive opportunities for students. As an advocate for minority students, she has developed an assertive and engaging style in working with campus units and committees. Natalia is adept at adjusting her approach and behaviors to reflect the expectations that the university has for staff and students and she is able to interpret these expectations while considering the appropriate cultural modalities of minority staff and students.

Martha is dean of Students and has worked at State University for almost 20 years. Prior to taking the position of dean, Martha served as assistant dean of Students for 11 years. She oversees student activities and services (residence halls, health center, scholarship, and financial services) and is on the faculty of the College of Education. Martha has a strong public image, an outgoing personality, and a strong and visible presence on campus. She serves on key administrative and faculty committees. Her commitments to her staff and students, and her integrity have earned her the respect of her colleagues. Her regular presence at key student functions has made her popular with all students. She is Doug and Natalia's immediate supervisor and is aware that they have distinctly different ways of working with students in general and with minority students in particular.

Esteban, a sophomore, is Puerto Rican. He had been very active in various clubs and organizations in high school, thus he took to campus life during his freshman year like a duck to water. Esteban is a member of the college chess club, has a daily Latin-Pop music hour on the campus radio station, and is vice president for La Raza. While in high school he worked weekends as a sales clerk for a department store in an affluent White area of the city. He discovered that while he was popular among his classmates and his peers in his Puerto Rican neighborhood, he also did quite well interacting with White customers. Esteban's sales bonuses were proof of that. However, that was only a weekend job, now at SU he is in a predominantly White environment all day, every day. At SU Esteban encounters an environment in which he can hone what he called his chameleon talents. He has his radio show, has been elected to a student office, and is improving his status as a chess player. He feels like he is on top of the world. Thus, Esteban feels confident presenting the case for La Raza's request for funds for the ninth annual family weekend. He sees family weekend as an opportunity to showcase college life for Latino families. He has been looking forward to attending the Campus Student Government's Programming Committee meeting to make the case for La Raza's funding request.

The Committee had partially funded the activity since its inception; thus he saw this as an opportunity to practice his public speaking skills.

Scott is a senior and a White student. Scott is a Student Government senator and chair of the Campus Student Government Programming and Budgeting Committee. He is one of a few Campus Student Government Senators serving a second term and the only 2nd year senator on the Programming and Budgeting Committee. Scott is self-assured and enjoys a great deal of satisfaction when things go his way. Scott believes he has had enough leadership experiences and decided not to attend the mandatory leadership retreat for Campus Student Government senators and officers of student clubs and organizations. In fact, he has made it clear that he avoids any training sessions because they put too much emphasis on racism. Scott feels that these programs try to make him feel guilty and he is tired of it. He is angry with minority students because they are always bringing race into everything and knocking the university. Scott loves student life and SU and feels that minority students should change their ways, get some school spirit, and learn how to deal with the world as it is today. He tries to avoid minority students in order to minimize conflict with them.

Ken is a sophomore and is White. Ken and the other committee members are 1st year senators and, as such, often turn to Scott for direction and guidance during committee meetings. He attended a predominantly White high school in a suburb of the greater metro area of the state capital. Although his contact with minority students is minimal, his experiences at SU have made him aware of prejudice, discrimination, and social inequalities. As a freshman Ken was active in residence hall governance and a regular participant in the Student Programming workshops on race and gender issues implemented in the residence halls. However, he is at a loss at how to address day to day issues such as the one called to his attention by fellow senator, Kymbriel.

Kymbriel is a junior, and African American. Kymbriel and the other committee members are 1st year senators. She is majoring in marketing and is interested in crosscultural communication. She takes classes and attends all workshops that help her develop crosscultural knowledge and understanding and tries to share her insights and knowledge with her peers. Kymbriel has been active in several student groups and campus committees. Through these experiences she has come to see Scott and Esteban as loyal SU students, diligent in fulfilling their responsibilities as students and as student leaders. However, Kymbriel has noticed that Scott always manages to divert attention from minority-related topics and issues. Although she and Ken attended the same high school they didn't meet until he matriculated at SU. In addition to working with him on Campus Student Government business, she has been in Student Programming workshops with Ken.

Case

Campus Student Government Programming and Budgeting Committee. The university policy regarding funding for Student Programming and Student Activities was adopted by the Campus Student Government. Funding is made available to support the educational and developmental mission of the university. Although funding is not generally allocated for food, exceptions are made to fund activities that the institution does not typically sponsor as part of its normal operations. The Campus Student Government Programming and Budgeting Committee follows this policy.

The Campus Student Government senators conduct information meetings, provide guidelines for fund allocation, and a checklist to registered student groups. Qualified student organizations are chartered, registered, and given an account with the University Business Office. Budget requests are submitted by student organizations to the Campus Student Government Programming and Budgeting Committee and each organization is given a hearing appointment.

Weekly meetings and hearings for budget requests are held. Each student organization presents their case and addresses questions posed by the committee. The committee asks the organization representative(s) to leave the room, takes five to ten minutes to discuss the requests, makes a decision and calls in the representative to give her or him a verbal notification of the committee's decision. A memo is prepared and made available the following day to each group including the amount of funds to be disbursed. In cases where funding is denied, the memo includes the reasons funding is not made available. A student organization has the option to redraw and resubmit their request.

La Raza at SU. The Mexican American and mainland Puerto Rican students at State University established La Raza about 30 years ago. The student organization is comprised of undergraduates and is a primary sponsor at SU of Latino oriented activities and programming. La Raza has taken on multiple roles through the course of its history. Latino students have established outreach (recruitment), social-cultural and educational activities, as well as, intra- and extramural activities as part of their regular programming. One of the annual events sponsored by La Raza is Family Appreciation Weekend. The weekend includes class visits, a campus tour, a student-faculty-staff panel presentation, student talent show, and a parent appreciation dinner. A significant number of parents have limited English fluency and La Raza attempts to provide bilingual programming. This year the students plan to hold a reception and dinner at Casa Maya, a local Mexican restaurant. The organization has an annual budget based on a nominal membership fee, donations, and fundraising activities. The budget is supplemented with funds from the Student Programming and Activities Office and the Campus Student Government. The students raise funds by holding monthly arrachera and tamal dinners and occasional car washes. La Raza members have historically created a vibrant Latino community within the campus community, distinct yet integral to the campus environment.

The Campus Student Government Programming and Budgeting Committee Meeting. The meeting was held in the student union on Thursday evening. Present at the meeting was the Campus Student Government committee (comprised of five senators) and Doug (advisor to Campus Student Government). Esteban is asked to enter the meeting room to present the budget request for La Raza's Family Weekend.

Scott takes the lead during the question and answer session, expressing concern over the duplication of services already provided by SU's Parent's Weekend. Esteban informs the committee that the needs of all parents are not met by the university's Parent's Weekend. Esteban adds that in fact, this is not a parent's weekend but a family weekend. Scott reminds the committee that university policy prevents Campus Student Government from providing funds for food. He adds that SU student funds are not made available to support the development of minority businesses in town. Scott uses a derogatory phrase for the name of the restaurant and uses it throughout the discussion instead of the actual name. Another senator comments that the Mexican restaurant isn't very good, using the same derogatory name; this senator suggests that La Raza should have the event catered by the University Food Services. Following a barrage of derisive comments by her fellow senators, Kymbriel asks "is any of this appropriate?" Sensing tension in the room, Kymbriel attempts to focus on the task. She suggests that the committee has yet to assess the match between the program described and the funds requested. Esteban indicates that Casa Maya was selected primarily because the menu of the University Food Services is inadequate for cultural programming. He adds that the Student Activities Office and Campus Student Government have funded this program in the past under the exception clause. Scott closes discussion saying that this is not an educational program and that it in fact amounts to a free ride not only for the families of Latino students but for the Mexican restaurant. He asks Esteban to leave, conducts the committee's deliberations, takes a vote, and sends Ken to inform Esteban that funding was denied.

In the hallway Ken notifies Esteban that his request for funding was denied. Esteban asks Ken if the meetings are always conducted in this manner. Esteban makes it clear that he feels the funding should not have been denied. Ken explains that the committee was following established campus policy but does not remark about the meeting itself. Ken returns to the meeting. Esteban leaves to participate in a challenge chess match across campus.

After the Meeting. Kymbriel did not feel it was safe to stand up to Scott and the other senators during the meeting. Once the meeting adjourned, she expressed concern to Ken about the tone set by Scott and the inappropriateness of the mockery. Kymbriel believes that the committee was biased in making its decision and asks Ken to accompany her in speaking to Doug about this matter. Ken expresses agreement regarding the tone of the other three senators. However, he believes that the committee acted appropriately and that the decision should stand. Doug walks by the pair, Kymbriel calls him, and he steps over to her and Ken. Kymbriel asks Doug why he didn't say anything during the meeting to keep 'those guys in check.' Doug, looking at his watch, indicates that he thinks he didn't miss anything important. He looks at his watch again and excuses himself.

Esteban meets with Natalia the following week. He is clearly disconcerted about his experience with the Programming and Budgeting Committee meeting. Esteban felt angry, shocked, and distressed at the idea that his peers would behave so badly. He had reported the Thursday night events to La Raza membership. La Raza drew up a response statement expressing displeasure with Campus Student Government and its advisor. Esteban was given La Raza's three-part grievance document to support his own personal racial harassment case. First, La Raza charges that three committee members (names specified) engaged in the racial harassment of a student representative of La Raza. Second, La Raza charges that Doug, advisor, failed to stop the racial harassment of a student representative of La Raza. Third, as a result of racial bias on the part of the students and staff involved in this incident, an inappropriate budgeting decision was reached, therefore La Raza is demanding redress by the Campus Student Government.

Your are Natalia; how do you proceed?

Who's on First? What's on Second?
Managing Projects in Student Affairs
Robert DeBard
Bowling Green State University

Setting

Metro State University is a publicly supported institution of 17,000 students located in an urban southwestern area of 350,000 people. The institution is referred to as "Butterfly U" by both faculty and students who each feel that the behavior of the other is responsible for the name. Because of the continual increase in instructional fees, there has been increasing pressure for a moderation of general fees that have been used, among other things, to support student activities. Emphasis is on the generation of student credit hours that lead to formula funding from the state.

Dr. Lawrence Piper, the new president at Metro, is determined to improve the University's reputation by leading it to become a learning community with the theme "this is the time of your life that you became involved in learning." He brought in a new provost, Harvey Kitchel, to help build this learning community culture. Piper reorganized reporting lines and would stipulate that Bill Casper, the chief student affairs officer, will report directly to Kitchel in order to better coordinate the efforts of the offices of Academic and Student Affairs.

Characters

Lawrence Piper, in his second year as president, has the reputation of a gruff, no nonsense leader who displays encyclopedic knowledge and is a quick study on the issues. On the downside, it has been reported that he makes quick decisions without much consultation and can be dismissive if he judges that he is being asked to suffer a fool gladly.

Harvey Kitchel, the new provost, is a biologist who has generated hundreds of thousands of dollars in research grants before becoming an administrator. His ambition is to become a university president and sees his position at Metro State as a stepping stone. He has indicated to Bill Casper that, while he welcomed Student Affairs reporting to him in order to gain experience, he has little knowledge of specific operations.

Bill Casper, vice president for Student Affairs, formerly reported directly to the president but has been reassigned to report to Harvey Kitchel. He has been at Metro for 16 years, the last seven as the chief student affairs officer and is concerned about his job security under a new administration.

Jane Allton, director of Student Activities, is in her first year at Metro after spending three years as coordinator of Cultural Events at Thomas Jefferson College, a liberal arts college of 1,900 students. She has a Master's degree in College Student Personnel and has recently attended the American College Personnel Association's national conference where she went to several sessions on the Student Learning Imperative.

Richard DeFazio, director of the new Metro Student Center, has been given the task of making this facility self-supporting along with the payment of heavy debt service.

Ken Burns, associate professor of English, has been at Metro for 12 years. He is known as a maverick among his colleagues because of his emphasis on teaching and his willingness to get involved with students outside the classroom through the Metro Popular Culture Club.

Phil Bennett, general manager of one of the local radio stations, wants to build better relationships with Metro because he sees the institution as a significant advertising account.

Emily Beatty, president of the Adult Student Union, returned to college after her divorce. She became active in the Metro Popular Culture Club and is contemplating going to graduate school in order to prepare herself for a college teaching position.

Renee Rogers, director of the Multicultural Center at Metro State, spent six years at the institution trying to promote cultural diversity on campus. She is troubled that most Center activities are multicultural in content, but not attendance.

Case

Monday. Jane Allton goes into Bill Casper's office in an optimistic mood. She has several good ideas for the upcoming Parent's Day festivities that she wants to share with her supervisor. Casper greets her, but wastes little time in informing her that Harvey Kitchel has decided to change the priorities of some of the budget appropriations at Metro State in order to place greater emphasis on student retention through better academic advising in the individual academic departments. He is asking areas outside academic affairs to revert 5% of their operating budgets to his office to be redistributed to academic departments. President Piper has apparently approved this move without consultation with Casper.

Casper indicates that the traditional $12,000 subsidy of Parent's Day Weekend will need to be cut "as much as possible." He is genuinely distressed to break the news to Jane, who is handling this project for the first time. Jane realizes that it is not Casper's fault and says that she will do what she can to make ends meet. They briefly discuss the possibility of canceling the Weekend, but they agree that this would only perpetuate the "street car" campus mentality that is all too much a part of Metro State. Casper does not think Piper would like to receive complaints from parents. Jane concurs and returns to her office and thinks about what she can do.

She reviews the expenditure figures from the previous year, looking for areas that could be cut. She thinks about the theme that has been advanced for this year's Parent's Day Weekend: "Metro Pride." It gives her pause as to what certain cuts would mean in terms of perceived quality of the experience. She decides to try another approach.

Tuesday Morning. Jane receives a call from Renee Rogers, director of the Multicultural Center. Renee is upset about the news she has received from Bill Casper involving her budget. Jane tells Renee that she has been thinking about the problem and has a suggestion. Why not do some programs together that might generate revenues in excess of expenditures? While Renee is receptive, she expresses doubt. Jane responds that she has some of the same feelings, but the future at Metro seems to require that they try a new approach to programming. They agree to have lunch to discuss some possible joint programs.

Tuesday, Lunch. Richard DeFazio stops by the table where Jane and Renee are having lunch and mentions that he is counting on several events for Parent's Day taking place in the new Student Center. Renee complains about the amount of money being charged by the new Center for rooms, food, and instructional technology service. Richard responds that the days of "general support" are over and he has to recover his expenses through the sale of goods and services. Renee and Jane agree that the need for entrepreneurial activity seems to be a growing force on campus. They discuss various options after he leaves.

Tuesday, Later That Afternoon. Jane contacts Phil Bennett, general manager of one of the local radio stations where Metro has done extensive advertising— for the admissions office as well as Student Activities. This time, Jane asks his cooperation in co-sponsoring the Battle of the Blues Bands project that Renee suggested during lunch. Because it fits into the radio station's music format, Bennett shows some interest. He wants to keep his relations with the university sound and wants credit for supporting an event in conjunction with the Multicultural Center. Plus he assures Jane that he has confidence that she will "do things right."

Wednesday. Jane goes over to the office of Ken Burns, associate professor of English and an expert on popular culture. She introduces the idea to him to have the Parent's Day Weekend focused on the theme Urban Fun. The Battle of the

Blues Bands will be complemented by a Lindy Dance Day in the Student Center ballroom and City Food Festival on Campus Mall. She wants Ken to help organize an educational component with some of his humanities colleagues to make presentations about the music, literature, and storytelling of the city's cultural history. She talks to him about something called the Student Learning Imperative and wonders whether the Popular Culture Club could help support these activities. He says that he has been looking for a vehicle to organize the club's efforts and assures her that he will lend his expertise as long as she is willing to do the work of organizing the events. He stresses that he is not interested in "administration." He suggests that she attend the Popular Culture Club's next meeting on Thursday afternoon.

Thursday. Emily Beatty, president of the Popular Culture Club, introduces Jane and Renee, who explain their plans and what areas of cooperation they will need from members of the Club. The members look to Ken Burns for his support and he says that he really feels that some of the things he has been trying to teach in his Urban Culture and Entertainment course through the Popular Culture Department can be illustrated through these events. The Club votes to help with this project, but Emily asks Jane to explain what will be entailed in pulling it off.

The next day, Jane visits Casper and tells him of her plan. He is nervous about the possibility of losing money and not having the revenues to return to Kitchel. He tells Jane that before he approves the project he would like a report outlining the various tasks that will need to take place before, during, and after the events and how could they be done in such a way as to generate revenues in excess of expenditures. You are Jane. Write your report.

Conflict in the Union: Whose Rights are Right?
Florence A. Hamrick and W. Houston Dougharty
Iowa State University

Setting

Prairie State University (PSU) is a large public midwestern university enrolling almost 25,000 students, most of whom are state residents. Summer school enrollment is approximately 20% of PSU's academic year enrollment.

Characters

John Hemmings, PSU's Student Activities director, reports to the dean of Students.

Joyce Smith is a PSU undergraduate and current president of the Alliance.

Susan Adams is the director of the Summer Conferences Bureau, an office that reports to the vice president for Business Affairs.

Scott Miller is an officer in the scouting group that is holding its annual meeting at PSU this year.

Rasheed Martin, the Facilities coordinator of PSU's Student Union, reports to the director of the PSU Student Union who in turn reports jointly to the vice president for Student Affairs and the vice president for Business Affairs.

Bob Cassle, an assistant professor in Mathematics, has been the Alliance faculty advisor for one year.

Lynda Anderson is the Student Activities Office secretary and reports to you, John Hemmings.

Howard Williams is the chief assistant to PSU's president.

Timothy Frisch has been PSU's vice president for Student Affairs for 17 years.

Catherine Carlisle is PSU's dean of Students. She is currently on a week-long backpacking trip.

Case

As John Hemmings, you are responsible for monitoring student organizations, training faculty and staff advisors, coordinating student leadership development, advising PSU's student government, and establishing and enforcing policies relating to student activities and organizations. You also serve as the primary liaison to the Union staff. Over your six years at PSU, you have earned a reputation as a respected professional who has cultivated strong working relationships with other campus units and developed an impressive activities and organizations program for students.

One PSU student organization that has made tremendous strides recently is the PSU Lesbian, Gay, Bisexual, and Transgender (LGBT) Student Alliance, or simply, the Alliance. In addition to sponsoring educational programs and support groups on campus, the Alliance played a key role in advertising the SafePlace program and provided stickers to more than 2,000 people on campus and in the city who wished to display the sticker as a symbol of welcome to LGBT students. In late Spring, the Alliance also peacefully protested the visit of an anti-LGBT evangelical minister by visiting the site of his speech the following day with brooms and mops to "sweep up the hate." According to their organizational constitution, the Alliance is committed to "support, education, and work toward social change." Looking back over the past academic year, you are proud of the Alliance's accomplishments and conclude that the extra time you spent with the group's faculty advisor has really paid off.

On this Monday morning in early August, you work on revisions to the Fall Student Leadership Retreat and relish the large blocks of time available during the summer to think and plan. Your colleagues on the Student Union staff, however, are still in full swing with their busy summer conference schedule since the Union is the largest meeting venue on campus. In fact, just this morning, more than 7,000 representatives of an international scouting organization officially opened their four-day annual conference at PSU. Susan had personally worked hard to attract this conference, and it is regarded as a real coup for PSU. Revenue estimates from the conference are high, and many of the 5,500 high school-aged delegates hosted by PSU may well apply for admission.

Just before 10 a.m., Joyce Smith knocks on your open door and steps in, visibly shaken and angry.

She says, "Our display's been stolen! It had to have been the scouts. The Alliance reserved the main display case in the Student Union this week for the express purpose of documenting and protesting the exclusion of gay men and boys in scouting, and it didn't even last through the morning! The lock to the glass case was broken, and all of our posters and pictures are gone! They even took the badges and patches that two Alliance members who were former scouts loaned us to put in the case. I've already called the campus police and reported it."

Joyce then asks you to go upstairs with her to examine the display case. You first phone Susan Adams and ask her to meet you there. When you and Joyce get to the display case, six uniformed scouting delegates—all appearing to be between 50 and 60 years old—are standing nearby talking quietly.

Joyce shows you the case and the broken lock, and one of the delegates comes over, extends his hand, and addresses you: "Hello, are you on the staff here? I'm Scott Miller, and I'm an officer in the scouting group and a member of our conference planning committee. You'll want to know about this terribly insulting display that was in this case earlier. I couldn't find a staff member with a key this morning, but I just had to take it down since it was so disrespectful. Our members who saw this were really upset and angry." Scott nods toward the group of delegates nearby and continues, "We'll pay for the damage to the lock and return the display items, but we will not abide the display being put back up while we're meeting here."

You see that Joyce is getting visibly upset, and you ask her to wait for you in your office. As Joyce leaves, Susan arrives accompanied by Rasheed Martin. You introduce Susan and Rasheed to Scott, who continues: "You know, we didn't pay all of this money to PSU to pass by this offensiveness every time we go to or from a meeting in this building. We've called National Headquarters and our attorneys, but in the meantime, given the level of outrage among our delegates, I'm afraid that I can't assure the safety or well-being of anyone who is affiliated with the display if they try to put it back up. I'm just trying to be honest with you."

Susan and Rasheed continue a conversation with Scott while you return to your office where Joyce is waiting. She is very angry. "The nerve! Could you believe how matter-of-factly he admitted that he broke in and stole the display? Like there was nothing wrong with it. He's more concerned about them being comfortable than having the truth be out. I didn't tell you this before, but when we were putting up the display early this morning, two of the scouting delegates who looked about 15 or 16 came over to us and told us how grateful they were to see the display since they were gay but also committed to scouting. We've got to do this for us but most of all for them and others in their situation. This is exactly what the Alliance is here for. I'm going to call Bob and the rest of our officers now. We'll decide what to do." Joyce leaves your office.

A moment later, Susan knocks and ducks her head into your office. "Now, you know me, John. I'm all for students expressing their opinions, and Rasheed confirmed that the Alliance had gone through appropriate channels to reserve the display case. But this is our biggest conference this year, and we have a lot riding on them having a positive experience. Haven't the students made their point already? Can't they leave it be? This group will only be on campus for a few days. I need your help on this one, John, but now Rasheed and I have to put our heads together about all this."

The phone rings and Lynda calls out: "Howard Williams on Line 1 for you, John."

You pick up the phone and Howard says: "John, what's going on over there? The president of the scouting organization that's meeting on campus just brought by a petition signed by 2,000 of their members and all of the officers objecting to—what do they call it—the "slanderous display and the disrespectful treatment" they've received at PSU. What's happened? For heaven's sake, didn't they just get here yesterday?" You interrupt Howard because your direct line is ringing and the phone read-out tells you that the call is from the vice president for Student Affairs. Howard promises to fax a copy of the petition text, and you promise to call Howard back soon.

When you pick up the direct line, Timothy says, "John, what's happened? My assistant tells me that the Alliance has scheduled a press conference in our conference room for 2:00 this afternoon. They've invited the newspapers and television stations for a briefing on their stand against the policy of excluding gays from scouting, and then they're planning a trip over to the Union to show the vandalized display case. Is that going to be wise with the conference still in session this afternoon at the Union? I need for you to figure out what's going on and come up with a strategy. Call me back."

As you hang up the phone, Lynda comes in and hands you the fax from Howard. She also gives you a phone message from Bob Cassle informing you that the Alliance officers have scheduled a meeting with Summer Conference Bureau and Student Union staff at noon and inviting you to attend the press conference this afternoon. Lynda says, "A Mr. Scott Miller left this while you were on the phone," and hands you a stack of paper, pictures, and badges—the contents of the Alliance display case.

What do you do?

"Controversy Sells Tickets!" What Else Does Controversy Bring?
Cathy McHugh Engstrom and Michael Elmore
Syracuse University

Setting

Huntington University is a private research institution in the northeast. The 11,000 undergraduates and 8,000 graduate students are dispersed among the nine independent colleges. The Colleges of Arts and Sciences and Communications rank in the top 20 nationally. Admissions is selective to highly selective, depending on the college or school at the university. The institution has made a concerted effort over the past 10 years to increase the number of students from underrepresented groups. In the past five years, students of color have comprised over 20% of the incoming class.

The student organizations at Huntington University have, in the past decade, hosted a variety of cutting edge musical acts and speakers, on all sides of the sociopolitical spectrum. Examples include Marilyn Manson, the Wu Tang Clan, Khalid Mohammad, and Oliver North. Student fees have supported these high profile, controversial activities.

Characters

Kevin Flannery, director of Student Activities, Caucasian, is a seasoned student affairs professional. He, his assistant director, and four graduate students advise student government and the campus programming board, and provide advising support to all student organizations. He has been a director of student activities at two other large, state, research institutions. He believes his most central responsibility is to foster learning opportunities for students; the advice and consultation he and his staff provide students who are interested in planning and implementing programs are central to support student learning. He also believes that student activities professionals must be knowledgeable about student popular culture.

Marsha Terry, director of Greek Life, has worked in student affairs for over 14 years in residence life, student activities, and most recently, Greek Life. She has provided tremendous leadership, in response to a Board of Trustee mandate to "clean up the act" and reputation of the Greeks, particularly related to grades, hazing, and drinking. She also is committed to increasing the numbers of students of color who are involved in historically Greek groups and works to strengthen the leadership in those groups.

Larry Gray, student events coordinator of Greek Freak Committee, is a junior African American, political science major. Larry has had no programming experience but is committed to host an event that will regain Huntington Hall's reputation as holding highly visible, well-attended events during Greek Freak.

Wachen Washington, Daria Thomas, and **Brianna Davis** are some of the students on this year's Greek Freak Committee.

Jim Marlowe, assistant vice president for Student Affairs, is Kevin and Marsha's supervisor. He oversees the two union buildings and recreation services, leadership, and orientation. He trusts the competencies of his two directors and offers counsel only when sought. He tends to intercede only to surface possible liability issues that may evolve.

Zacker Brown, director of Judicial Affairs, also has a law degree. He came to the university three years ago, straight from working in a downtown law office. He has worked hard to understand and appreciate the educational mission of this institution and integrate it into work with student discipline.

John Logan, director of Facilities Management in the Sports Arena, is responsible for any concerts held there. He reports to the Athletic Department and Business Services. He has excellent working relationships with Student Activities and tries to provide as much flexibility to meet student requests as long as safety issues are addressed. John is constantly amazed at how well informed Kevin is about the different groups, speakers, and performers that students invite to campus. John has found such knowledge to be indispensable as his staff tries to manage events and anticipate problems that might arise.

Stu Parker, assistant director of public safety, is the departmental liaison with student activities and negotiates security needs for large events. Parker has a good appreciation for Kevin's philosophy with working with student groups. Although he might not be as hands-off as he perceives Kevin to be, he values Kevin's predictability and rapport with a wide array of students.

Case

For over 20 years at Huntington University the historically African American groups have sponsored a Greekfest weekend sometime during the month of April. The central leadership for this program has come from the National Panhellenic Council (NPHC) which is comprised of representatives from all eight historically African American Greek student groups. In order to be eligible for student government association money, NPHC created a separate student organization "The Greekfest Committee" which includes representation from NPHC and other non-Greek student groups.

Initially Greekfest started as a popular, well attended "Step Show" competition. In the early '90s it evolved to be a day long combined Step Show and large scale concert. Most recently, these two events have occurred separately, but in one weekend. These activities have lured over 4,000 students of color from over 500 miles despite the fact that only a handful of people have actually planned the event.

In the past few years, Kevin has become increasingly concerned about the pressure on the coordinator(s) responsible for Greekfest. They are typically inexperienced programmers who are under enormous pressure to uphold the regional, and even national, reputation for Huntington University's concerts during Greekfest. The concerts have also lost money for the past five years. Kevin finds that the expectations on these students to host a concert or speaker that is "bigger, better, and more dazzling" than the last Greekfest are enormous, unfair, and unrealistic. Yet, these expectations do exist.

Kevin now believes that his office is not equipped to provide the enormous amount of time required to a novice group of student leaders to pull off a major concert event. Last spring he proposed to Jim, his supervisor, and to Marsha, the director of Greek Life to consider one of two options; he believed both plans addressed his concerns. The first recommendation was that his office continue to advise the Greekfest Committee but responsibility for the actual implementation of the concert event would be through the union programming board, the group routinely responsible for campus concerts. This group gets training and ongoing experience in putting on large concert events, unlike the Greekfest members.

The second recommendation was that the concert portion of the weekend be discontinued, as neither the student group or the Greek Life office was equipped to handle it.

He believed that the advising responsibilities for these events should lie with the Greek Life Office, since this event really is a NPHC sponsored program. Although Jim and Marsha empathized with his concerns, they did not support his recommendations. Marsha felt she did not have the staff to advise this major program and thought the group was not ready to turn over the implementation of this event to the mainstream concert board with which they had no history or trust. So Kevin shared with his staff that, once again, they would advise this event. They would do their best, despite limited time and resources, to assure the event was safe and that involved parties (e.g., public safety, sports arena staff) were well-informed about evolving plans.

In early spring, the Greekfest Committee succeeded in securing Mr. X, a big Hip-Hop rap group that was particularly popular with students in the urban north. They were very pleased with securing this talent and were convinced this group would draw big crowds. However, a month later, the group's agent explained that there was a mix up and this performer would not be able to attend. The agent for Mr. X realized he had screwed up and in good faith provided the university with a $15,000 settlement. The students were in a panic. The event was only 1 1/2 months away. Who could they bring to campus that would sell tickets and maintain their regional reputation at this late a date?

March 5. Larry Gray, coordinator for the concert, holds a meeting with Kevin. He shares that the committee met a couple of times and decided to invite Leo and his dancers. Leo had a club in an urban southern city and was noted for his raunchy, vulgar music and dancing. In the club, the dancing was often of an X-rated nature. Kevin was very aware of Leo's "work" and challenged the students to consider the impact of this performer on campus. He outlined management and logistical concerns when campus events generate controversy. However, he ended by saying that ultimately the decision rested with the students, although Kevin would include a statement in the contract that the artist would not incite any destructive or high risk behaviors. Larry responded to Kevin's concerns by explaining that everyone was well aware of what Leo represented and students could make informed decisions about whether or not to attend. Most importantly, Leo would be a big ticket draw and the pressure to meet their financial and visibility goals would be met. "Controversy sells tickets" he stated to Kevin.

Later that day. Wachen and Daria come to talk to Kevin. They express concerns about the Greekfest committee bringing Leo to campus. They found Leo's promotional tape repulsive and demeaning. They expressed their concerns in the last meeting but were laughed at by the men in the group and told not to take it so seriously. They were reprimanded for not recognizing how many tickets this performance could sell and told the group was dependent on such an outcome. The more sensational the better! Kevin encourages them to go back and assert their views again.

March 6. Larry informs Kevin that the group decided to bring Leo to campus. Kevin asks how the committee came to this decision and Larry shares that by a 5-3 vote, the committee agreed to secure Leo. Kevin asks who voted against the proposal and Larry comments, "The women, of course. But we reassured them that we would understand if they did not want to attend the event. We would not hold it against them." Kevin tries to appeal to Larry's sensibilities about how offended other women might feel about the act, but to no avail. Kevin successfully offers a bid and secures a contract for Leo to perform.

March 7–April 14. Kevin has several meetings with John, Stu, and the student sponsors. Kevin informs them about the nature of Leo's act.

April 23. Kevin and all of his staff, Jim Marlowe, John, and Stu are all in attendance at the concert, along with 3,500 students. At the beginning of the show,

Leo's manager stated to John, "I can give you anything from a PG to a Triple-X show. What do you want?" John clarified that "PG" would be just fine. He emphasized that nudity on stage was not permissible.

The warm up rap bands performed for a few hours followed by Leo. Leo's act consisted of short snippets of prerecorded music interspersed with talking to the audience. His dancers, part of the on-stage show, did get out of hand. Although they did not expose any private body parts, their dancing was highly suggestive. Two dancers engaged in a lap dance and another dancer imitated sexual activities as she faced her partner on his shoulders. They invited volunteers from the crowd. Three volunteers and dancers also participated in similar activities. After a while, John said to Stu "this is enough" and he ended the show. No one complained. The crowd dispersed quietly. Leo had been on-stage for approximately 20 minutes.

April 26 8 a.m. Kevin has a few quiet moments to himself in his office. He reads the student paper and there is no mention of Friday's Greekfest event. "Hmm," he says to himself, "If this had been an event sponsored by the union programming board, women and other groups would be livid. They would be demanding that financial resources be cut to this event. There would be rallies and protests on the mall." But there was not one word about the event in the paper.

10:00 a.m. The parade of visitors begins. First, arrives Marsha. She was not at Friday's event, however, she heard about it from Liz, her graduate assistant, this morning. Liz was there and was quite offended by the suggestive sex acts; Liz was also mortified about what kind of message this presentation made about the Greek community, particularly the historically Black Greek community. She was also concerned because there were no steps taken to assure minors were not in the audience.

Marsha insists that judicial charges be made toward members of the organizing committee. "What university charges have they violated?" inquires Kevin. Marsha thinks the artist and his dancers clearly violated university policies regarding obscenity; since the student group brought them to campus, the sponsoring group should be held responsible. Kevin is very uncomfortable with this line of reasoning and proposed intervention. He believes that all staff involved with the event had been given adequate information about Leo. In his mind, these concerns should have been raised before the show. Marsha shared that she had a call into Zacker Brown at Judicial Affairs to seek his support for initiating judicial action against the group.

10:30 a.m. Wachen, Brianna, and Daria step in and share their anger about the event. They felt that the event was an insult to African American women and the historically Black Greek community. Kevin asks if they were surprised about what happened. They said "not really" but added that it was different sitting there, watching their dignity being violated. They were furious that their previous concerns had been dismissed by their male colleagues on the Greekfest Committee. However, they feel uncomfortable sharing their reactions to the committee for fear of being silenced once again.

11:00 a.m. Kevin receives a phone message to call Zacker.

11:30 a.m. Kevin gets a voice mail from Larry commenting on how excited he was about Friday night's event. Larry shares how thrilled he was with the big crowd and the response from visitors and Huntington Greeks. He expresses pride in maintaining the honor and prestige of Huntington University.

1 p.m. Jim Marlowe comes down to see Kevin. He explains that the vice president for Student Affairs called a meeting at 7:30 a.m. the next morning to discuss the incident. Kevin asks Jim why this meeting was called and what the agenda is. Jim explains that the vice president had his biweekly meeting with Marsha that morning and was appalled that the Leo act was allowed to occur. He also wants to know what the plan is if bad press occurs as a result of this activity. The vice president also invited Jim, Zacker, Marsha, John, and Stu to this meeting.

Kevin sighs and comments to himself, "Geez, I have administrators *overre-acting* to this event and I wish students would just react! I guess I should look at this situation optimistically and recognize the potential teachable moments."

You are Kevin. How do you prepare for the meeting?

Chapter 8

Cases on Academic Issues

At first thought, academic issues may seem to fall outside the purview of the student affairs administrator. Nevertheless, there are many instances when those in student affairs must work in partnership with their academic colleagues for resolution of academic issues.

In Ruth Russell and Gail Londergan's "We Want Our Money Back" students dream up a creative solution for a dissatisfactory learning experience. In "A Song for Solomon" Jane Lambert describes a new dean's effort to struggle through a web of duplicity. Margaret Jennings's "The Seminar Papers" details a situation on a small campus where cheating has become standard practice for much of the student body. "A Failure in the System" by Sally Hood Cisar and Jillian Kinzie highlights the problems presented when a student overextends herself both academically and financially. In "When Grades Eclipse Learning" Ruth Russell provides insight into an academic conflict that can arise between Greeks and non-Greeks. Finally, Robert Schwartz's "A Stitch in Time," describes a professional who struggles with a student that learns about plagiarism the hard way.

The academic issues presented in this chapter affect a wide range of student affairs professionals.

We Want Our Money Back
Ruth V. Russell and Gail Londergan
Indiana University

Setting

Dripping in both Spanish Moss and centuries of tradition, Lafitte University presents the perfect picture of the American college campus. Situated in the deep south of the United States, a campus stroll is rewarded with the sounds of babbling brooks and chiming clock towers, and with the cooling gift of mature shade trees. Simply put, it is beautiful. Yet, Lafitte University's reputation does not rest on its good looks alone. It is a highly respected private university with several graduate programs that consistently rank among the nation's best. To top it off, Lafitte has recently received accolades for the excellent care it takes of its undergraduate student body, offering both comprehensive student services programs and a learning centered curriculum.

Characters

Professor Walter Marcuse is a tenured full professor in the Psychology Department. Professor Marcuse is known for his use of technology in the classroom. Over the course of the past 20 years he has been the department's pioneer in using new technologies in his teaching. Early in his career, Professor Marcuse won tenure and a promotion to the rank of full professor based on several important books on philosophical critiques on Freud and psychoanalysis. In the past three years, however, he seems to have lost all interest in his research.

The students of PSYCH 399 for the just-completed fall term numbered 23. That semester the course, which is for undergraduate majors only, was taught by Professor Marcuse. Professor Marcuse has taught the course before, but he is not its instructor in this spring term.

Kristin Miller is an academic advisor for the Psychology Department. This is a half-time position, and Kristin is the only advisor for the department. She is regarded across campus as an efficient and effective advisor—one to whom other academic advisors frequently turn for information on university academic requirements and policy. Even though she has bachelor's and Master's degrees in counseling, she views her career as "on hold" for the moment while she focuses on her three young children. It was mostly her own idea to work half-time while her children are young, but lately Kristin has been showing signs of eagerness to make progress with a career in "real" counseling.

Dean of Undergraduate Programs and Services, Anne Whitman has been a campus-level administrator for two years. Before this she had served as an associate dean for Undergraduate Studies in the College of Arts and Letters. She has been on the faculty at Lafitte for 15 years.

Case

One afternoon just after the spring term began Dean Whitman was visited in her office by a group of four students from the fall PSYCH 399 class. They had been sent as delegates for the whole class. Their purpose was to complain about Dr. Marcuse. Although they had neglected to make an appointment, they had prepared for this meeting in every other respect. They had e-mailed their fellow students over the semester break to collect comments, and from these created a master list of complaints and a demand addressed to Dean Whitman. They wanted to be clear that they liked Dr. Marcuse as a person and respected his accomplishments in the field of psychology, but their experience in his class last semester had been a disaster and his performance as a teacher deplorable. They told Dean Whitman that they had complained most of the semester to their academic advisor, Kristin Miller, and that she was in complete agreement with them. In fact, they delivered to Dean Whitman a memo from Ms. Miller that substantiated their complaints.

Specifically, their complaints were:

1. Dr. Marcuse did not show up for almost half of the class sessions.
2. When he did show up, he was usually late, unprepared, and distracted.
3. He took 3–4 weeks to grade their assignments and didn't offer much commentary on the quality of their work. (Dean Whitman interjected a question at this point and learned that the students did not wish to complain about Professor Marcuse's grading. Later, in checking their grades with the Registrar she learned that Marcuse had given all As.)
4. He got far behind on the topics, readings, and assignments promised in his syllabus.

Because of these problems, the students presented this demand to Dean Whitman: "We feel that Dr. Marcuse's performance as a professor at Lafitte University is completely unacceptable. We learned nothing in his course and therefore feel that we are at least entitled to a refund of its cost. We believe that the University did not live up to its obligation to us, as its customers, in this course. We pay for education; this course did not provide any." The students then presented to Dean Whitman a list of the names and student identification numbers of all those who had taken PSYCH 399 in the fall and indicated that they expected to hear from her soon about their "well-deserved refund."

You are Dean Whitman; what do you do?

A Song for Solomon
Jane L. Lambert
Indiana University

Setting

Metropolitan University (MU) is an urban institution located in the state capital of a northwestern state. The institution enrolls 27,000 students with 75% in undergraduate programs and 25% in graduate programs. MU's campus was established 25 years ago with a complex mission typical of many urban institutions: to establish a research center with a national reputation and to provide access to higher education for the surrounding metropolitan community. MU has fulfilled both missions with considerable success and still maintains a virtually open admissions policy. Although the surrounding community is highly diverse, African American students comprise only 10% of the student population at MU and Asian students represent just 3%. MU maintains a connection with the main campus 35 miles away which enrolls 35,000 primarily traditional students. In fact, the faculty in many schools and departments at MU, including the school of business, have dual membership on both campuses.

Characters

Song Liu has been a student at MU for just over a year. She is a refugee from Vietnam and a transfer student from another college in the same city as MU. Upon her arrival at MU, she shared a letter with everyone who had contact with her that described the dreadful experiences she had undergone including witnessing the execution of family members and spending time in refugee camps under harrowing circumstances. A business major and widely known throughout the school, Song refers to many of the faculty secretaries and the counseling staff as her "aunties." Song is officially designated as "disabled" by the university and is therefore allowed extra time to take exams. She displays no apparent physical disability and appears bright and vivacious.

Sam Williams is a part-time instructor for MU in the School of Business. He has taught for eight years and his student evaluations are well above average. Williams is employed in the city as an accountant for one of the major public accounting firms. He is currently teaching a section of A312 Intermediate Accounting II in summer session where Song is one of his students.

Dean Houseman has been dean of the School of Business at MU for ten years. Highly respected by faculty, staff, and students, he is decisive, energetic, pragmatic, and shrewd. He is credited with providing the leadership that brought the school through some tough times. The school now thrives and Dean Houseman will retire from his office at the end of the summer semester and resume his former position among the full-time faculty.

Professor Cain has served as the chair of the undergraduate business program at MU for two years. A tenured professor in the accounting department, he juggles his multiple responsibilities with patience and diligence. A person of intelligence and humor, he has a soft spot for students and is often asked to speak at events sponsored by the School of Business. He has been responsible for hiring and evaluating part-time faculty and other related issues but this responsibility is being transferred to the new director of student services.

Claire Finneran is the new director of student services for the School of Business at MU. She is a former full-time, nontenured instructor for the school who left MU four years ago to pursue a doctorate. She has returned and just started her new position this week. The director's position is configured as 50% administrative and 50% teaching in the undergraduate program. In her administrative capacity she will hire and evaluate part-time faculty, supervise the counselors and other office staff, provide support for scheduling classes, deal with student problems, and handle admissions.

Case

A312 Intermediate Accounting II is a required course in the accounting program at MU, the second course in a two-course financial accounting sequence. Several sections are taught each semester with part-time faculty teaching summer sections and full-time faculty teaching in the fall and spring semesters. Students generally regard A312 as an extremely difficult class.

Academic dishonesty at MU is not regarded as a wide-spread problem. While it is assumed to exist and several cases arise each year in nearly every school, these cases are generally handled quietly by the instructor of the class with no major repercussions. An official institutional structure exists for handling cases that are not resolved by the instructor. The School of Business has been involved in two cases during the last six years that were referred to this review board. One case involved a student who allegedly cheated during the administration of an exam, another involved a student who was accused of altering a graded exam. The School of Business lost both cases.

Week One, Day One. Before noon of the first day on her new job, Claire Finneran is beginning to wonder what she has gotten herself into. Professor Cain, who is briefing her on her new responsibilities, has alluded to a "strange ethics problem" that she will have to help him deal with very soon. He has been handling the case for several weeks and as he leaves for lunch, promises to stay involved until it is resolved and not simply drop the file in her lap. A passing secretary overhears and says "You're NOT going to give her that UPS problem on her first day of work, are you?"

At 11:00 that same morning, Claire receives a call from Sam Williams asking for some advice as he struggles to deal with an ethical situation in his A312 class. When Claire asks for the details of the situation, Williams tells the following story:

Song Liu is a student in Sam Williams's A312 class. Due to her disability, she takes her exams in the testing center, a facility used to administer placement and computer adaptive tests. While the first midterm exam was administered without incident, the second midterm was a disaster. Williams dropped off his exam at the testing center the evening before Song was scheduled to take the exam. She arrived the following morning and began the exam under the watchful eyes of the proctor. About half-way through the time allowed, Song asked to go to the restroom because she was experiencing menstrual cramps. The proctor excused her and she was gone for nearly 20 minutes. She returned and worked for a few minutes more before saying she had to leave the exam because she was too ill to finish. She said she would contact her instructor about finishing the exam. As the proctor collected her papers, he noticed that Song was holding back a sheet of paper. He asked for it and she reluctantly gave it to him. It was a copy of a page of the exam. Song explained that it was a duplicate page and must have been included by mistake when the exam was photocopied by the faculty secretary. The proctor called Sam Williams two days later to tell him that he believed Song had copied the page during her long absence and intended to look up the solution to the problem before finishing the exam later. However, Song had already made arrangements with Williams and had finished the exam in the faculty secretary's office. When Williams graded the exam, Song had scored 100% on the multiple choice section of the exam and 92% on the problems. With suspicions aroused but with nothing to go on except the phone call from the proctor, Williams returned the exam to Song with a grade of A.

On the day of the final exam, Amy, another student in Williams's class, approached after the exam was over. Amy told Williams that Song had called her several days before the final and asked for help in studying. Song had several accounting problems that she was trying unsuccessfully to solve. Amy helped her and they arrived at answers they believed to be correct. Amy was astonished when those same problems appeared on the A312 final exam. She told Williams that the problems were identical and believed that Song must have obtained a copy of the exam.

Williams tells Claire that he is struggling with giving Song an F for the course, giving her an A based on her performance on course exams, or giving her an

Incomplete while he sorts out the situation. He says that Song is the only student he has ever had who has gotten perfect scores on the multiple choice sections of his exams, a fact which he feels provides further evidence that she has cheated. Claire promises to consult with Professor Cain and Dean Houseman and call him back before the end of the day.

Later that Day. Professor Cain returns from lunch and says to Claire, "I'd better tell you about the UPS problem." He tells her that a UPS driver has reported a student for ordering desk copies and test manuals of text books used in four business courses taught at MU. Because the books are shrink-wrapped in clear plastic, the driver, who is also a business student at MU, immediately recognized the books and test manuals. A fresh shipment is sitting at UPS waiting to be delivered to the student and UPS is offering to video-tape the delivery. The student involved is Song Liu. From Claire's office, Professor Cain calls one of the publishers involved to ask what prompted the shipment. The publisher tells Professor Cain that someone who identified herself as Professor Johnson from Metropolitan University requested the books via a phone call to the publisher, asking them to be sent to her home. When the publisher gave the address of the shipment, it was verified as Song Liu's residence.

Claire asks Dean Houseman to step into her office to talk about this matter while Professor Cain is still there. He listens carefully to both stories and asks many questions to clarify details. He shakes his head and says that the instructor's cheating allegations might as well be dropped right now. He describes details of the cases he has pursued on behalf of the School of Business during his term as dean. "Twice before," he says, "I've gone to bat for cases that I KNEW we couldn't lose. We had faculty and student witnesses, evidence . . . credible evidence. We took them all the way to the top and we lost. The fact of the matter is, central administration is not willing to back the faculty and the schools in these cases against students. I think they are afraid of potential litigation. I'm not willing to back *this* case based on what you've told me today. You may, however, have a case with regard to her ordering books. Tell the instructor, if he's asking for our advice, to give her an Incomplete while you check out these other allegations with our campus police department. That's about the best you can do."

Claire calls Sam Williams and relates the dean's advice, tells him there is another matter being investigated, and asks Sam to write down all of the details while they are fresh in his memory. She also tells him to ask for statements from the proctor and Amy. Williams does not ask nor does Claire reveal the other matter under investigation. He turns in an Incomplete for Song for A312 stating that due to unresolved circumstances it is not possible to determine her grade at this time.

Week Two. Professor Cain drops by Claire's office to say that he has contacted the campus police about this case. He asked for advice about accepting the offer from UPS to tape the next delivery of books. The police told him they would get back with him and suggested that he call the university attorney. The attorney told Professor Cain that with regard to the phone call to the publisher requesting the books, it is illegal for anyone to misrepresent themselves as a university employee. Song has received her grades and calls the counseling staff daily to ask if Mr. Williams has turned in her final grade for A312 yet. At the end of the week, Professor Cain contacts the campus police again. They ask, "How would you like us to handle this?" Professor Cain replies, "That's what I asked you!"

Week Three. Claire's staff are getting restless. Song's daily phone calls have turned into hourly visits. One of the counselors tells Claire in confidence that this is not the first time faculty have insinuated that Song has cheated in a class. Another counselor has a family member on the faculty and rumors are beginning to quietly seep through the office. No one seems to know about the UPS problem but everyone appears to know that Song is accused of cheating. Song has also contacted several of the faculty secretaries in an effort to contact Sam Williams about her grade. Professor Cain hasn't answered Claire's latest queries about the status of the investigation. Claire tells the office staff to send Song to her the next time she calls or drops by.

Claire returns to her office and tries to figure out what to do, expecting to hear that Song is outside her door at any moment.

The Seminar Papers
Margaret P. Jennings
Dickinson College

Setting

Pine College is a small liberal arts college, founded in the mid 1800s. Pine enjoys a reputation as a selective private institution whose students came from upper middle class and well-to-do families. The curriculum is traditional, and while the faculty likes to think of its courses as demanding, even rigorous, the truth is that students who attend class regularly and maintain the illusion of "trying hard" rarely fail.

Pine was founded by one of the mainstream Protestant denominations, and retains some association with the church, largely through special scholarships for the children of clergy, and the presence of several ministers on the Board of Trustees. There is no required chapel, nor is a course in religion required of students.

The college's mission statement extols the virtues of the liberal arts. Students are challenged to liberate themselves from "superstition, prejudice, and whatever shackles tradition or society has imposed upon them." The liberal arts should enable students to "achieve a sense of their own identity, and to live close to the upper limits of their capacities."

The catalog carries the following statement about academic dishonesty: "If a case of dishonesty is handled by the faculty member, he or she may take whatever action is deemed appropriate. It is not unusual in such cases for the student to be dismissed from the course with a grade of F. If the case is referred to the dean, he or she may recommend dismissal or expulsion from the college."

In the past five to seven years, Pine College has found it increasingly difficult to maintain enrollments. Tuition increases have been necessary; more of the budget is going to institutional financial aid in order to close the "gap" between what Pine costs and what federal financial aid programs provide. Senior faculty members have begun to grumble about the poor quality of entering classes, convinced that the Admission Office is simply admitting warm bodies with the money to pay the price of tuition. Student Affairs staff are dealing with more disciplinary problems in residence halls, more underage drinking, and more damage. The president has, however, laid down the law: entering classes must be larger, and retention must be stronger.

Characters

Dr. William Canterbury, chair of the Department of English, has been on the faculty of Pine College for 23 years. He thinks the quality of students in his

English courses is alarmingly poor. He vehemently opposed the creation of developmental (remedial) course work in Composition, English, and Math. At any opportunity, he accuses the Student Affairs staff of "babying" the students, the Academic Support staff of "spoon-feeding," and the Admission staff of diluting the prestige of a Pine degree by admitting "any half-wit son of a physician who can fill out the application form."

As department chair, Dr. Canterbury is responsible for the required first year seminar courses. These are a series of small group seminars taught by members of the faculty and senior administrative staff. There are several required readings, with standard associated writing assignments.

The readings are traditional texts, and have been the same for at least ten years. Most students don't do the readings, preferring to buy commercial annotated synopses, and talk with upper division students about what the writing assignments are likely to cover.

Dr. Steven Danforth, dean of the Faculty, has held this position for only two years, coming to Pine after serving as History Department chair at a mid-sized comprehensive university. He is a graduate of Pine College himself, and remembers with fear and trembling, and a certain degree of awe, his Freshman Composition course with Dr. Canterbury, who in turn, enjoys reminding him that he received a C– in the course.

Dr. Danforth loves Pine College, and supports the president's tough stance on enrollments. However, he isn't sure exactly how the dean of the Faculty can influence retention efforts. If the students aren't happy here, he thinks, that's the dean of Students' problem.

Ms. Rosemary Selleck is the head Women's Volleyball coach and assistant professor of Physical Education. Pine College has a superior women's volleyball program, consistently competing in the top ten in Division III. Because of its winning teams, Pine finds it easy to recruit and retain volleyball players. Summer volleyball camps are a major source of admission inquiries, and a steady source of income for the college. Ms. Selleck, who is known nearly universally as "Rosie," carefully nurtures her players, beginning to recruit them in their sophomore years of high school, and establishing close relationships with them and their families throughout their careers at Pine. She is well liked by team members, and by the students in general.

She teaches one of the first year seminars, and encourages new players to choose her section so she can follow their academic progress and help them get their "feet on the ground" at Pine. Students know she'll always be willing to work with them individually on their projects, meet with them in the evenings or on weekends for assistance, and give them the benefit of the doubt.

Dr. Mary Gilligan, dean of Students, has just joined Pine College after completing her doctoral studies in Student Affairs Administration. She is pleased with the amount of personal attention students get at Pine, but is concerned about the increasing amount of damage in the residence halls, and the prevalence of underage, abusive drinking among the students.

Several of her colleagues have encouraged her to teach a section of the first year seminar next year, but she has reservations about the required readings. She feels that the readings should be more representative of nondominant cultures, and has voiced her concern that none of the works was written by a woman, an African American, Native American, or Hispanic author. The student body is changing, the world is changing, she reasons, and the required readings should be relevant to those changes, if students are to appreciate and learn from them.

Case

While sitting at her desk, just outside the locker room, Rosie overhears several of her first year players talking about the upcoming seminar writing assignment. An upper division student has told one of them that it has been "standard practice" for several years to collaborate with students in other seminar sections on these assignments. Since the assignments (which are the same for all sections) will be read by the individual seminar instructors, the same paper can be turned into several different instructors, and no one is the wiser. They all see the benefits of this plan, and the consensus seems to be, "Why not?"

Unfortunately, Rosie can't clearly identify the individual voices over the other noise in the locker room, and feels that there is little she can do because no dishonesty has yet occurred.

You are Dean Mary Gilligan. The day after the writing assignments have been graded and returned, Emily Haskell, a first year student, accompanied by her RA, makes an appointment to see you. Emily has received a B on her writing assignment, and swears she spent several days working on it, to the exclusion of all other assignments and social events. Her roommate, Melanie, got an A, and all she did was pay a student downstairs $50.00 for a copy of his. You promise to investigate this issue.

As you begin to talk with RAs and other upper division students, you are astonished to discover that the situation described by Emily is widespread. You phone Professor Canterbury, and advise him of what you have been told, withholding the names of the students with whom you spoke.

Professor Canterbury declares that this is just what one must expect when admission standards are so low, and when students are not held properly accountable for their behavior. He vows to get to the bottom of this, and to deal harshly with any and all offenders.

Without discussing his plan with any of the seminar instructors, he requires that the next writing assignments be forwarded directly to him before they are graded. Professor Canterbury spends the next 24 hours drinking gallons of coffee, reading all 350 essays, and getting angrier every moment. When he finishes reading, he bursts into Dean Danforth's office clutching a cardboard box full of papers. Dropping them on the desk, he declares, "Eighty-two of these papers are duplicates of other papers! In some cases, there are triplicates, and quadruplicates of the same paper, and I might add that, of the lot, only five or six of them would earn a passing grade in one of my courses! Even you, Mr. Danforth, were a better writer than these poor slobs. I want all 82 of these cheaters dismissed . . . TODAY!"

When the dust settles, there are indeed 82 students involved, including nearly every first year volleyball player. The granddaughter of a Board of Trustees member is implicated. Word quickly spreads that the faculty is on to the scheme and tearful students begin appearing in your office. Some want to confess; others claim they are innocent victims ("My roommate and I use the same computer. He must have copied my disk when I wasn't home."). All want to know what will happen next.

As dean of Students, what do you do?

A Failure in the System
Sally Hood Cisar and Jillian Kinzie
Indiana University

Setting

Originally founded as a regional campus of the larger state university, Madison State University (MSU) has spent the last 30 years establishing its autonomy. The institution, located in a metropolitan area, has advanced its mission as an urban university by acknowledging and responding to the nature and needs of its students and by promoting programs and service that address local, regional, and state needs. However, years of uncontrolled growth have produced an organization with fragmented departments, underdeveloped lines of communication and weak links between units and with the local community. The institution was recently reclassified from a Master's (Comprehensive) to a Doctoral I University; however, the president has expressed her commitment to retain an emphasis on undergraduate education, teaching, and service. Enrollments of full- and part-time students topped 27,000 last year. However, the "drop-in, drop-out" nature of student matriculation has been identified as a subject of concern. As with students at other urban institutions, MSU students are unlikely to be involved in typical college activities or to spend much time on campus. For most students, the MSU experience is sandwiched between work and family.

Characters

Jeff Levinson is an adjunct faculty member in the Management Department.

Heather Chambers is a sophomore who is a business major.

Rick Chavez, is the director of a community agency, Housing Solutions, and co-chair of University-Community Partnership Initiative.

Kayla Green, is a staff member at Housing Solutions.

Linda York, is the department chair of the Management Department.

Patrick Mulligan is the dean of Students and a representative to the University-Community Partnership Initiative.

Case

Jeff attempts to control his nervousness as he descends the stairs, reminding himself that his primary goal on this first class meeting is to evoke confidence, firmness, and seriousness regarding the course requirements and responsibilities. Jeff's anxiety is partly due to the fact that it is the beginning of the fall semester at Madison State University (MSU) where he is an adjunct professor. Of more concern is that although he taught W250–Management and Nonprofit Organizations last spring, this would be his first experience facilitating the service learning component. Jeff spent several weeks during the summer preparing the syllabus and assignments after meeting with the previous instructor. She assured him that even though the service learning component required the instructor's coordination with an outside agency, student enrollment had always been low, reducing the number of placements and grading load. Jeff was alarmed when he received his class roster and saw 30 students listed. His focus this morning is to make sure every student understands that work with the outside agency demands a high degree of professionalism and a 30 hour time commitment over the semester.

Jeff believes he succeeds in his attempt to retain only the most serious students. By the end of week two, five dropped out. The most difficult part of the coordination of the service learning is scheduling. Most undergraduates at MSU register for 15–18 credit hours per semester, and in addition, most hold more than part-time jobs. Jeff notes that a couple of students have trouble identifying time in their schedules to complete the required hours. Jeff spends the next few weeks trying to negotiate the students' schedules with mentors at the community agencies, as well as matching positions with career interests. At the end of the month, all students were placed, except one. Heather Chambers had still not fit any of the available positions into her schedule.

Jeff goes the extra mile to accommodate Heather's needs. He meets with her before class so that she doesn't have to return to campus for his office hours. He also contacts Rick Chavez, the director of one of the agencies, Housing Solutions, and asks for assistance. Rick is upbeat and assures Jeff that there is a position for Heather. Six weeks into the semester, Rick arranges a unique post for Heather involving their volunteer recruitment program. Heather expresses enthusiasm and interest in this opportunity. She tells Jeff that she wants work that is meaningful and is dedicated to serving the community. Heather recounts the volunteer work she participated in during high school and explains her future career will be committed to promoting positive change in a local milieu. During class discussions, Heather reveals her views regarding equity in the work place, eliminating social hierarchies, and a citizen's responsibility to stewardship. Jeff is pleased with her contributions, especially in lieu of the other students in class who seem rather skeptical and cynical about the philosophy and mission of nonprofit organizations.

As midterm draws near, Jeff reviews his grade book and realizes that Heather has not turned in any of the three assignments. At the next class session, he talks to Heather about her missing assignments. She insists they are in progress, but she is swamped with work from her other five classes. Heather almost bursts into tears as she recounts how she has taken some courses out of sequence and is now having a hard time catching up while juggling all of her commitments. Jeff reassures her, extends the deadlines, and reemphasizes the expectations for the class. They talk for quite a while afterwards about economic and social problems in the community. Jeff is impressed with Heather's ideas for improving the conditions of the local residents and their surrounding neighborhoods.

One week later, Rick Chavez contacts Jeff and informs him that Heather has not shown up at the agency for two weeks. Further, she had not notified the mentor she was working with about her absences. Jeff realizes that Heather has also missed three out of four classes. When he asks students in the class if they've seen Heather, no one even knows who she is. Jeff is concerned so he calls Heather at home. Her roommate answers and explains that Heather is at work.

Meanwhile Heather has been frustrated and overwhelmed by the financial assistance office. With no help or support from her family, she has taken out substantial loans to finance her undergraduate degree. She has just been informed that her request for reclassification as an independent student has not been considered because of some missing information. Her worry about whether she can continue to afford college intensifies.

When Heather shows up to the next class, Jeff speaks to her afterwards about her absenteeism at the agency and in class. Heather breaks down, and attributes her failure to maintain her responsibilities to her efforts to complete as many courses as possible while working as a waitress five nights a week on the graveyard shift. She insists that she will make up the hours she missed at Housing Solutions and not miss any more classes. She hands him one of the assignments due two weeks prior. When asked about her other assignments she explains she is working on them. Again, Jeff extends deadlines for Heather and shows understanding for her situation.

Jeff receives a phone call two days later at his office from the mentor Heather works with at Housing Solutions, Kayla Green. She was very upset as she retold an incident involving Heather. Heather did not agree with the way Kayla was handling a situation with a client. Heather told Kayla she was not living up to the responsibilities of her job and that she was contributing to the obstacles preventing effective change in the community. After the confrontation, Heather walked out. As soon as Jeff arrives home, he receives a phone call from Heather. She cries while blaming the brunt of the argument on Kayla. Heather feels offended that her mentor told her she was inexperienced, not facing the realities of the work place, and living in a dream world. Jeff agrees with Heather that employees in a nonprofit agency should uphold the organization's mission, but firmly explains that Heather must demonstrate respect and professionalism while working at the agency, even if it means compromising her values. Heather feels that Jeff is working against her and states that she did not deserve to be treated like this for a course she was paying for. Jeff asks her to meet with him and Kayla to try to work out the problems between them. Heather refuses. Jeff reminds Heather of her commitment to finishing out the service learning hours.

After the University-Community Partnership Initiative meting, Rick Chavez approaches Patrick Mulligan to discuss a problem with a student working in his agency. He explains that an incident like this could add credence to the belief held by some that students aren't sufficiently supervised in service learning projects. As the University representative to a committee sponsored by the Office of the President, Patrick is concerned about the negative effects of this sort of incident and is annoyed that he was unaware of any problems. He speaks to Jeff about the incident, who then explains Heather's incident.

The following week, Heather tells Jeff that she would prefer to work in a different community agency. Jeff stresses her commitment to Housing Solutions and asks her to return to this site. However, he is more concerned about Heather's missing assignments. He sends her an e-mail message, outlining the missing requirements and asking her if she would be able to complete them in time for a semester grade. Heather responds with the following e-mail note:

No problem Jeff! Three weeks are plenty of time to finish the assignments. I've already got a good start on all of them and I plan on dedicating all of my time to them. I got someone to cover my hours at the Cyber Café so I have plenty of time. Thanks for being so understanding with me and giving me extensions.

The last three weeks of the semester, Heather misses four out of six classes and is evasive about her work with Housing Solutions. On the last day of class, Heather does not turn in any assignments. In the meantime, Jeff grades the other students' work and assumes Heather will take an Incomplete. Jeff sees Heather in the computer lab the Saturday before he is required to turn in grades for the semester. She looks weary and explains she is completing the assignments at that very moment. She asks him about one of the assignments. Jeff tries to persuade her that he would prefer her to take an Incomplete and do high quality work, rather than try to finish everything within 24 hours. She insists that she does not want to take the Incomplete because she must make satisfactory academic progress or her financial aid is in jeopardy.

On Sunday morning, Jeff finds Heather's work in his mailbox. He begins grading it and immediately realizes that Heather rushed through the assignments just to get them done. The quality of work was poor and did not meet his expectations as outlined in the syllabus. At this point, Jeff gets angry and does not spend much time writing comments on her papers. He feels upset that Heather led him to believe she was committed to quality work and he had been gullible to what now seems like empty stories and excuses. Jeff has no alternative but to give her an 'F' for the course and an Incomplete for the service learning component.

The first week of the second semester, Jeff receives a call from Heather. Jeff tries to explain why she failed the course. Heather tells him she worked hard on the assignments, that she has always been committed to nonprofit work, and she did not understand what she had done wrong. He refuses to argue with her over the phone, instead offering to meet with her to go over the assignments together. Jeff is disturbed about his interaction with Heather and contacts his department chair, Linda York, for advice. Linda supports Jeff's appraisal of Heather's performance, but states that Heather has a right to a meeting to discuss her concerns.

Two weeks later, Heather calls Linda York and claims that Jeff was rude and impolite to her on the phone and that he did not grade her assignments fairly. She insists that because she did not ask him to extend the deadlines she should not be penalized for late papers. She demands a meeting with the two of them and wants to go through each assignment with a fine-toothed comb. Linda tells her that she will be in touch with Jeff and will send an e-mail message to both of them to set up an appointment. However, Linda's schedule gets backed up and she is forced to postpone the meeting on two occasions.

You are the dean of Students, Patrick Mulligan. After reviewing the student grievance policy, Heather calls and sets up a meeting with you. However, before the meeting she sends you an e-mail, detailing her side of the story, emphasizing her economic hardships and efforts to maintain her academic status. She feels she was treated unfairly at Housing Solutions and should not have to take an incomplete for the service learning component. She also believes she was unfairly failed for the course by Jeff Levinson, an instructor, who in her opinion was very unorganized and ill prepared for the course. Heather feels she should not have to pay for the course again, noting that retaking it will prolong receiving her degree. Furthermore, because of her grade in W250, the financial assistance office has refused to increase her budget to cover the 19 credit hours she is registered for this spring. Finally, she explains her efforts to meet with Linda York and how the chair brushed aside her complaint. She tells you that no one is on her side, that everyone in the university is in this together, and that her rights are not being recognized. You know that Jeff Levinson is a top-rated instructor and are concerned about repercussions for the University-Community Partnership Initiative. In fact, this afternoon you're meeting with Rick Chavez and the president to discuss the progress of the committee. How do you respond?

When Grades Eclipse Learning
Ruth V. Russell
Indiana University

Setting

Like a mirage the square concrete buildings of Road Runner University rise out of the desert landscape. Surrounded by low density, upscale track housing, this is the suburban campus for a southwestern state's university system. While the main campus is located in the state capital 25 miles away, Road Runner's mission is to serve the rapidly growing population to the city's northeast. Primarily an undergraduate campus, Road Runner University's enrollment this year is 12,320 and within the last five years has supported an annual enrollment growth rate of 7%. When the campus was established 12 years ago, the goal was to create a mini version of the main campus. Thus, except for several main campus specialty programs such as a water rights policy institute, academic curricula and campus services mirror the offerings downtown. This includes a sorority and fraternity system.

Characters

Louise Skaggs is a tenured associate professor in the Sociology Department. Professor Skaggs is widely recognized for her teaching excellence, particularly in the large Introduction to Sociology (Soc. 100) lecture course. She has an enthusiastic personality, is a dynamic lecturer, and is well liked by students.

Jane Wood is the coordinator for Sage Brush Residence Hall. Jane is a part-time Master's student in Special Education at Road Runner University and this is her second year working at Sage Brush. Last year she was one of the three assistant coordinators, but received the boost to coordinator over the summer when the former coordinator graduated. As an undergraduate at Road Runner University she had been a resident in Sage Brush Hall.

Mary, Karen, Alissa, and **Melanie** are undergraduate students who are members of Lambda Mu Nu sorority. Mary and Karen are sophomores and sociology majors while Alissa is a junior in chemistry and Melanie is a junior in mathematics. They share a two bedroom suite in their sorority's wing, or "house," which is located within Sage Brush Residence Hall. Alissa and Melanie are also sorority honor roll recipients and big sisters to Mary and Karen. They are all enrolled this term in Soc. 100.

Wallie, Kathy, and **Sue** are undergraduate students—sophomores—who are residents of Sage Brush Residence Hall. They are not members of a sorority, and are also enrolled this term in the Soc. 100 course. Wallie and Kathy are roommates.

Harold Freedman is the dean of Students at Road Runner University.

Facts

1. Due to the newness of the campus and size of the enrollment, only two of the ten Greek organizations maintain their own houses. Most occupy specific floors or sectors in Road Runner's five residence halls.
2. Sage Brush Residence Hall is a campus women's living area for approximately 300 undergraduate students. It also houses two sororities: Lambda Mu Nu and Alpha Alpha Beta. The other four campus residence halls, which also include Greek "houses," are coeducational.
3. Lambda Mu Nu was chartered at Road Runner University in 1988. It is one of four sororities on campus and currently has 45 members who all live in the Lambda Mu Nu "house" in a wing of Sage Brush Hall. Perhaps the most recognized sorority on campus, it is consistently recognized for the high academic achievements of its members and its civic minded service projects in the community.
4. Soc. 100 is an introduction to sociology course taught each semester by Professor Skaggs. Typically enrolling 100+ students it is a required course for sociology and other social science majors, but is an elective course for science majors.

Case

At the beginning of every semester it is Lambda Mu Nu's tradition to host a scholarship dinner. Reserving an alcove section of the Sage Brush dining room, the dinner program includes recognition of those members who have made the honor roll the previous semester and an "unveiling" of the sorority's overall GPA. This is an important statistic to the Nuies (as they are called) because the Greek organizations on campus compete for the highest GPA distinction. Customarily the members also invite favorite professors to be their guests for the evening.

September 15. Mary and Karen, students in the Soc. 100 course this semester, approach Dr. Louise Skaggs after class and invite her to this year's Lambda Mu Nu scholarship dinner. Dr. Skaggs is flattered and accepts the invitation.

September 26. When Dr. Skaggs arrives at Sage Brush Residence Hall she is greeted by Mary and led into the activities room used by the Nuies for a predinner reception. Quickly Karen joins them along with two other members who are not in Soc. 100 and a lively conversation about Dr. Skaggs's class takes shape. Karen and Mary enthusiastically tell their sorority sisters about the exciting class. Later, sorority members and their faculty guests adjourn to the alcove of the dining room for the meal. Again at the table the conversation is enjoyable for Dr. Skaggs as Karen and Mary persist in talking about the class. As the formal proceedings of the dinner begin each member stands and introduces their faculty guest. Mary's introduction of Dr. Skaggs is highly complimentary. During the recognition of honor roll members, Dr. Skaggs is surprised to see Alissa and Melanie come forward to receive the sorority president's congratulations. Alissa and Melanie are also in Dr. Skaggs's course this semester, but did not approach Dr. Skaggs during the reception so she did not know they were also members of the sorority. The evening concludes with Dr. Skaggs seeking out Alissa and Melanie to offer her congratulations. She comments on her delight at having such good students in her course.

September 28. Right before the Soc. 100 class meeting, Dr. Skaggs stops Mary and Karen as they take their seats and thanks them for the dinner, and again congratulates Alissa and Melanie for their honors.

October 12. Students hand in a major term paper for Soc. 100.

October 21. A mid-term examination is given in Soc. 100.

October 27. Graded exams and term papers are returned to students and midterm grades are posted.

October 28. You are Jane Wood. Late this night you answer a knock at your door. Wallie, Sue, and Kathy charge in and inform you that a special meeting has been called by them for concerned nonsorority residents of Sage Brush to discuss "unfair advantages given by the University to sororities and fraternities." You are invited to attend. When you arrive at the 3rd floor lounge about 8 students are sitting around with Wallie leading the discussion. The students are angry. Doing a little investigative work following the issuance of midterm grades, Wallie says she's discovered an "elite form of dishonesty" at Road Runner and she demands that the university take action. She claims that Lambda Mu Nu sorority and other Greeks on campus keep files of old course exams. She further tells everyone that Alissa, Melanie, Mary, and Karen had access to last semester's Soc. 100 midterm exam and that's why they are performing better in the course. "Plus, I personally observed Dr. Skaggs giving preferential treatment in class to those sorority bitches," screeches Kathy. "Either the Greeks are required to share their files with the rest of us or disciplinary action must be taken against Lambda Mu Nu and the others," Wallie concludes. A petition is drawn up to this effect and signed by the meeting participants, against your advice that more investigation and discussion take place first.

October 29. Wallie, Kathy, and Sue deliver the petition to Harold Freeman, the dean of Students, demanding a meeting between the dean and the concerned Sage Brush students.

October 30. You go to visit Melanie, Mary, Karen, and Alissa in their suite in the sorority's wing, but only Mary is there. You say to Mary "the other night a meeting was called by some students here in Sage Brush to talk about a problem of academic dishonesty by your sorority in Soc. 100 this semester." Mary flushes and then replies, "I can explain it. Alissa and Melanie are not sociology majors so it is more important for them to get the A in the class for the sorority GPA than to learn about sociology. Karen and I let them read our term papers, but we didn't think they would copy them so closely. We have been worried ever since we saw what they did." Mary tells you she wishes to take full responsibility for the dishonesty and hopes that Alissa and Melanie will not get in trouble. "I really don't want the sorority to know," Mary pleads. You do not tell Mary about the actual complaint of last night's meeting, deciding you need to think more about what you should do. When you return to your room a message to call Dean Freedman is on the telephone answering machine.

A Stitch in Time
Robert Schwartz
Florida State University

Setting

You are the assistant dean for Academic Affairs at I. C. Moore College, a midsize public institution in the south. Moore is a moderately strong school academically and serves a population of 70% in-state and 30% out-of-state students, most of whom come from nearby cities or regions.

In your position, you serve both faculty and students. As an administrator, you work with academic schedules, faculty related issues, such as requirements for admission, college and institutional committees, student records, and "other duties as assigned." You have also assumed a role as mediator between faculty and students when necessary and have proven to be quite good at it. Consequently, the dean has passed most academic issues such as academic dishonesty, personality conflicts, and other concerns to you on an ever-increasing basis.

Because you are a good listener and typically quite fair to all involved, you have developed a strong reputation among students as a person to see if they have a problem related to courses or a faculty member. For the most part, you value this reputation and enjoy the opportunity to see undergraduate students, even if they often come with problems.

Case

You are in your office one afternoon when someone gingerly knocks at the door. Looking up, you discover a relatively young student, probably a freshmen or sophomore from his hesitant approach. The student asks if you might have a moment to discuss a problem. You usher him into a chair and settle back to listen attentively.

The student explains that the instructor in a political science class has told him he is about to fail the course. As it is several weeks from the end of the semester, you challenge the student's assumption, asking if there isn't ample time to pull the grade up to at least a D or even a C? The student, now near tears, explains that the instructor has accused him of plagiarism, and is not only planning to give him an "F" but also to forward the student to the Academic dean or dean of Students for disciplinary action, maybe even suspension.

Given the gravity of the charge and the possible consequences, you stand up and walk around the desk to close the door, ensuring the student privacy and also giving yourself time to think. In the *Student Book*, a compilation of rules and regulations regarding student conduct and behavior, the penalties for plagiarism, if proven, include loss of the credit for the class and possible suspension. The student in your office has every right to be concerned *and* worried.

You ask the student to describe, in his words, the events that led up to the present circumstances, specifically what he is accused of plagiarizing and why. The student explains that he never knew what plagiarizing was before and he never meant to cheat. He had a paper due in his political science class and was running out of time so he wrote what he could and then, as he had done in high school, he copied some material from books and put it into his paper. Further, although it may have been wrong, he doesn't see why it is as big a deal as this professor is making it.

Clearly, you think to yourself, it would appear that there are several issues at hand already. The student is admitting, to some degree, his awareness that he has committed an error and a serious one. On the other hand, to what degree is the student culpable for the cherished notion of academic honesty if no one has held him accountable in the past, e.g., in high school? Is it fair to presume that students will have encountered such issues before? Obviously it is important to get the instructor's perspective as soon as possible.

You put in a call to the instructor of the class while the student is still in your office. It would be nice to get as much information from both of them as early as possible. Unfortunately, the phone rings in an empty office. You check the schedule and quickly discover that the instructor is in class for another 45 minutes.

Returning to the student in the office, you collect pertinent information, telephone number, class schedule, and the like for your office records. You explain that this is indeed a very serious matter. It is also quite possible that you, despite your position as assistant dean, may not be able to do much more than talk to the instructor for the course and then give him, as a student, the best advice you can regarding how to proceed. Because of the nature of the problem, you would only be able to talk to him about what to do, not resolve the problem. It is possible (actually, it is quite likely but you hold back on this information for now—no need to make the poor kid more scared than he is) that he, along with the instructor, will have to appear in front of a committee to discuss the matter.

Shaken and contrite, the student assures you that he will be back the same time the next day to check in with you on the progress of the case. You assume that you will have been in touch with the instructor for the course by then and will know more about the direction of the case. You shake hands with the student and return to the office.

Within an hour, you reach the instructor for the class. She is not surprised to hear from you but does have a different interpretation of the issue. She explains that she distributes, with her syllabus, a description of various academic dishonesties, including plagiarism, cheating on examinations, and so forth. And, she makes the point, because many of the students in her class are new to college, she goes over this information carefully in the first class session and offers to explain it further if necessary to individual students.

In response to your questions, she indicates that she was alerted to the student's paper because although he tries hard, he is not a brilliant student. Therefore she noticed that certain sections of his paper were written in a much more polished, sophisticated style than he has used before and in one case, offered an interpretation which was very insightful, much more so than she expected he was capable of doing on his own.

Her next step had been to confront the student with the paper after class one day. At first he claimed the work as his own. Upon further questioning, however, he acknowledged that he had used portions of books he had found in the library for certain sections. She estimated that of the ten pages he had turned in, perhaps one-fourth to as much as one-third was taken directly from other sources without appropriate notation.

She tells you she fully intends to fail the student for the course because if she does not, other students will not see the gravity of the issue. Further, she argues, if the college does not pursue such matters to the fullest extent possible, what standards are other students to believe in, much less other faculty? Yes, she explains, she has discussed the matter with her department chair and has the support of the chair and other professors. For your part, you explain that while you agree with her principles and values, you wonder if the student in question isn't more of a victim of his own ineptitude than gross academic dishonesty? You agree to get back to her again tomorrow after you have had a chance to talk with the student one more time, now that you have her side of the story.

The next day, as promised, the student comes by your office. Seemingly fortified by the chance to collect his thoughts and regroup, and no doubt bolstered by a late night residence hall bull session, he is somewhat argumentative at first: How should he know that what was okay in high school would not be accepted in college? Wasn't this professor just out to get him to make herself look better to her colleagues in the department and in the college? Why couldn't he see the president of the college to complain that she was out to get him? What would he say to his mother and father who expected him to graduate and get a job, not be kicked out for some silly paper?

From experience, you wait patiently for the tirade to subside on its own before you answer. Yes, you explain, there are some valid points in what he has said but ultimately, the primary responsibility is still his, as will be the consequences of his actions. You return to the issue of the syllabus and the first day explanations. Did he have a copy of the syllabus? Yes, but nobody ever reads all that stuff except when papers and tests are scheduled. Did he not hear the instructor's description of plagiarism on the first day of class? No, he had a scheduling conflict and had been at the drop/add session trying to get into other classes and so had missed the first day of the political science class. Did he at least feel that something might be wrong with lifting someone else's work into his own without saying "I got this idea or interpretation from so-and-so?" No, not really. It seemed that if someone said it and it was in a book, it was in the public domain and could be used by anyone.

You dismiss the student and tell him that you will call him back within a day or two after you have investigated further. As you sit alone in your office, several questions float about in your head about the case of this individual student but also in regard to academic honesty in general. For some time now, you have been working on a position paper for the dean on the issue of academic honesty and plagiarism. Thinking of the paper and the case at hand, you move to the personal computer next to your desk and call up the file containing your notes for the paper. You begin to type the questions that you will have to answer for this case, knowing that you will have to address them in your paper as well.

Chapter 9

Cases Involving Legal
and Judicial Matters

In a reflection of American society in general, legal matters for student affairs professionals increased in salience through the 1980s and 1990s. In many of the cases discussed in previous chapters, there were legal considerations that could not be ignored. However, the cases in this chapter point to more obviously legal decisions faced by the administrators in question.

In "Free Speech and Sexual Harassment: Something's Not Computing" Becky Ropers-Huilman and Brian Ropers-Huilman describe an incident that seems to border on sexual harassment, but not quite. Teresa Hall's "The Bare Facts Post-Initiation Party" has a new administrator focused on sanctions when a celebration has gone too far. Kerry McKaig and Cheryl Lovell's "Sexual Harassment at All Saints College" presents a case in which a new professional may have acted too hastily. The fun of a "Scavenger Hunt" disappears when racism and sexism are the dominant themes in a case by M. Christopher Brown and Steven Thomas. Finally, administrators deliberating in "Safety at Arbor Hill: The Limits of Liability" by Michael Coomes weigh the pros and cons of arming the campus police force in the face of increasing violence.

The legal problems presented in this chapter are faced not only by college presidents, trustees, and attorneys. Rather, we see that deans and assistant deans of students, campus board members, and student life directors must increase their awareness of legal issues.

Free Speech and Sexual Harassment: Something's Not Computing
Becky Ropers-Huilman and Brian Ropers-Huilman
Louisiana State University

Setting

Set in the countryside of rural Wisconsin, Green River College (GRC) is an institution that prides itself on providing a liberal, well-rounded, and contemporary education to its 8,100 students. Almost exclusively an undergraduate campus, staff members, faculty members, and students are generally committed to developing a teaching and learning community in which all views are both heard and valued. Having enjoyed much success in recruiting, GRC has become a highly selective institution with a diverse group of students from all parts of the United States and other countries. GRC has a policy mandating that all first year students live in on-campus housing. This mandate is often unnecessary, though, since 75% of students remain in the residence halls throughout their entire college experience. Both for financial and educational reasons, GRC has gone to great lengths to ensure that students' experiences in the residence halls are positive.

Rockwell Residence Hall is home for approximately 225 students each year. Rockwell has earned a reputation on campus as being for serious students. Quiet hours are strictly maintained and enforced by residents, and hall programming often focuses on study skills and career development. Further, largely due to a very active hall government, Rockwell was one of the first halls to develop a large computer lab for resident usage. Each year, the hall government asks for—and often receives—additional resources to help them expand the computing capabilities of their lab. Because Rockwell is located furthest from other campus facilities, students who choose to live there often do so because of the exceptional computing tools.

Characters

Gaby is an undergraduate engineering student living in Rockwell Hall. Unlike most other students, Gaby does not come from a wealthy family and considers it a privilege to be getting her degree at an elite school like GRC. She buys into GRC's philosophy that education happens both in and out of the classroom, but believes that her class work has to come first.

Sam is the hall director for Rockwell Hall. This is her first year as a hall director, although she was a Resident Assistant (RA) for 3 years, so she feels that she knows the ropes. She believes strongly in freedom of speech on campus and has worked to develop forums where persons with various beliefs could be heard. She is completing her Master's degree in Women's Studies at a nearby university.

Erika is the dean of Students at GRC. Having received her doctorate nearly 25 years earlier, Erika has seen many changes in student affairs. She has been a strong proponent of student action, recently facilitating several trips to the state Capitol for students to lobby for environmental and educational issues. She is proud of the student body at GRC, and considers her job to be more pleasure than work.

Case

9:00 p.m., Rockwell Residence Hall. Gaby walked into the computer lab on the ground floor of her residence hall. She had a major engineering simulation to finish and was looking forward to using the quiet lab throughout the evening. As she headed to the back of the room, she thought to herself how nice it was to have a computer lab right here in her hall. It was especially great that her residence hall had finally equipped two of their lab computers with the capability to do her engineering work. She went to one of these machines in the back corner, pulled out her books and set to work.

It didn't take her long to notice that a student sitting at a machine in the row in front of her wasn't doing any real work. As a matter of fact, he was spending his time cruising the Internet. Gaby had a fleeting thought that it must be nice to have the time to do that. As the evening progressed, she noticed that the student had started looking at pornographic web sites and newsgroups. Full screen pictures of people in various sex acts filled the monitor. Gaby was shocked. She couldn't believe this person was sitting in a public access lab, where anybody could see, looking at porn.

She wasn't sure what to do. She got up and walked to the student worker seated at the front of the lab and said, "The guy sitting in front of me is looking at pornography on the computer. Could you please ask him to stop?" The lab monitor looked up and shook her head slowly, saying "I'm sorry, but I'm not supposed to monitor what people are doing on these computers—I'm just supposed to make sure the computers are working and no one steals anything. Besides, they have just as much right to do what they're doing as you do."

Frustrated, she walked back to her computer and tried to focus on her work. Yet as her frustration built, she couldn't get any work done; she kept seeing those images out of the corner of her eye. She finally decided to ask the person to use another computer, where she couldn't see what was on the screen, or to stop looking at pornography. The response was a self-assured "No."

She tried to stay at her computer and focus on the lab assignment, due the next day, but finally couldn't stand it anymore. She packed up her books and headed back to her room. As she was putting her coat and boots on she thought of how nice it would be if she only had a computer in her room, one with access to the campus network, too. Checking again that she had everything, she trudged through the snow and across campus to the engineering labs.

10:45, Engineering Hall. It took Gaby about 10 minutes to get to Engineering Hall and down into the computer lab. She knew the lab would be busy tonight, but grew concerned when she realized all the stations were full and she was fourth in the waiting line. It took her 53 minutes to finally get seated. It was past 11:30 and she still had hours of work to do. She knew that if she had been able to work in her residence hall, she would just about be finished now, rather than barely half-way into the assignment.

At 2:30 a.m. she finally finished and packed everything up. Sleepily, she headed back across campus following the specially lighted walkway. She passed by the computer lab in her hall as she headed to her room noticed the student from earlier was *still* there. She didn't bother to walk back and see what he was looking at. Instead, she marched past the elevator and proceeded to her hall director's room. There she left a note for Sam, saying: "I need to see you ASAP. Call me first thing in the morning! Gaby."

7:45 a.m., Rockwell Residence Hall. The next morning, Gaby woke up to the ringing phone. Since she was used to going to bed at least three hours earlier than she did last night, she had slept through her alarm. It was Sam inviting her to come and discuss whatever was so urgent. Gaby threw on some sweats and stormed down to Sam's office.

"Sam, somebody was down in our computer lab all night looking at pornography! I had to leave and finish my assignment in Engineering Hall because I couldn't stand it. What can we do so that this doesn't happen again?" Gaby asked.

"I'm not sure," Sam replied. "According to University policy, freedom of speech and expression is protected, even on computers. However, there is a policy regarding use of the campus network for academic or research purposes only. Maybe that could help us. I can talk with Erika, the dean of Students, about it in my meeting later today. If it fits in your schedule, you're welcome to join our discussion."

2:30 p.m., Dean of Students Office. Later that day, after Gaby attended her engineering class and turned in her assignment, she and Sam walked to Erika's office. Erika had an open door policy and knew Sam well, so the three quickly got down to business. Sam had Gaby recount the situation from the previous night and then asked what could be done.

Erika pulled a copy of the university's computer usage policy from her files. "I'm sorry," she said, "but it doesn't look like there's much you can do. The appropriate section of the policy reads:

Inappropriate use of the Internet and other networks to which this university is directly or indirectly connected will be deemed abuse of computer privileges. Examples of inappropriate use of the networks are participation in network activities that place a strain on limited computer resources including any type of network games, the sending of obscene and/or harassing messages to other individuals on the network, and the unauthorized access or attempted access of another network computer system from university computer resources.

They weren't sending you the images and the Internet surely isn't an unauthorized network."

"Well, what about harassment?" Gaby questioned. "I was very offended and felt like they were intruding on my private space." Again, Erika pulled the appropriate policy statement from her files. "Hmmm . . . I'm not sure if this will help either. Our definition of sexual harassment reads:

Sexual harassment is unwelcome verbal or physical behavior, related to sex or gender, the purpose or effect of which is to unreasonably interfere with the targeted individual's work or learning environment.

Gaby, do you feel like you were sexually harassed according to our definition?"

Gaby responded that she didn't want to label it "sexual harassment" she just wanted it to stop. She didn't want to have to walk across campus in the middle of the night ever again. After all, computer access was one of the main reasons she stayed in the residence halls.

You are Erika. Both Gaby and Sam are willing to take your direction and work with you to deal with the current situation. What are your recommendations? You know you need to address this individual incident, and work to develop a broader computer usage or sexual harassment policy at your institution to address similar situations that might occur in the future. What do you do?

The Bare Facts Post-Initiation Party
Teresa L. Hall
Towson University

Setting

South State University is a regional comprehensive state university, located in a town of 50,000 people. SSU began as a teachers college in 1878 and has evolved into an institution with seven colleges and 55 majors and 35 concentrations leading to a bachelor's degree. SSU enrolls approximately 10,000 students, 8,200 undergraduate and 1,700 graduate students. SSU houses 2,300 students on campus including 600 students in fraternity or sorority residences. As much as campus representatives would like it otherwise, many students go home or away from campus on the weekends with an exception being the members of Greek letter organizations. The SSU Greek system has 22 chapters and over 1,200 members. Several fraternities either rented or owned property in the city at which they held social functions.

SSU has a conduct system that includes a student judicial board, advised by the director of judicial affairs. The SSU Code of Student Conduct prohibits the usual types of on-campus violations but also includes a provision to sanction off-campus behavior that may have negative impact on student life or the academic reputation of the campus.

Characters

Steve Carr is the president of Lambda Lambda Lambda, a fraternity that has been on campus as a national fraternity for 50 years and as a local group for some 50 years prior to that. Steve has been highly involved on campus including serving as an officer of the Interfraternity Council and as a justice on the university judicial board.

Kerry Davis is the Greek Life coordinator at SSU and has held that position for four years. Kerry has completed a Master's degree in college student personnel and was an undergraduate sorority member.

Kelley Smith is an officer on the Panhellenic Council and a student assistant in the Greek Life Office.

Marie Patrick is the director of Judicial Affairs and advisor to the university judicial board.

Case

Monday, January 12. As always the first thing that Kerry Davis does on Monday mornings is to get a cup of coffee, then check her voice mail messages. The usual messages were there but there was one of a different nature. An anonymous female caller left a message that stated, "You should know that Lambda Lambda Lambda had a stripper at their post-initiation party and that she had sex with the members in attendance." Kerry immediately picked up the phone and attempted to reach Steve Carr, the chapter president and a student with whom Kerry was very close. Steve wasn't home.

Kerry called Marie Patrick, the director of Judicial Affairs, to inform her about the anonymous phone call she had received and to discuss what course of action Kerry should take. As Kerry was finishing up her conversation with Marie, Kelley, her student assistant came into the Greek Office to work. Kerry asked Kelley what she had heard about the Lambda Lambda Lambda post-initiation party. Kelley said that most of the sorority women knew that the Lambdas had strippers at their party and that most of the women were angry with their Lambda boyfriends. Kelley went onto say that she talked to her best friend who is also a Lambda and he said that even their advisor was present at the event. Now more than ever, Kerry wanted to talk to the chapter president.

Steve, the chapter president, strolled into Kerry's office later that afternoon. Kerry asked Steve how initiation went. Steve responded, "Real good!"

Kerry asked Steve if a stripper was present at the post-initiation party. Steve said, "Yes there was but it was a 'brothers only' party. Is there a problem?"

Kerry said, "I heard that not only was a stripper present but that she had sexual intercourse with your new members. I also heard that your advisor was present."

Steve said, "She did not have sex with our new initiates but what would it matter if she did?"

Kerry responded by saying, "Initiation should be the most sacred event any member ever experiences. You have cheapened that experience and that ceremony for your new members. Do you want the Lambda Lambda Lambda Fraternity to be synonymous with a strip joint?"

Steve walked out of the office.

Around 4:30 p.m. Kerry received a phone call from a mother of one of the Lambda new initiates. The mother was very upset. They had raised their son with Christian ideals and could not believe that he was forced to participate in such a despicable activity. She went on to say that her son was devastated. He felt pressured to participate so that he would not be excluded from the fraternity. She was shocked that this fraternity would do such a thing—they were just there for Parents' Weekend and there was such a nice presentation about the values of the fraternity. The mother said the fraternity went on and on about how much they would help her son grow and develop and be a good student. Never once did they mention that they did anything like this. She wanted to know what the university was going to do about this event.

Kerry called Marie, the judicial affairs director, to relay both of her conversations. Kerry and Marie decided to interview the officers and members of the new initiate group to try to get to the bottom of the situation.

Tuesday, January 13. Marie meets with Steve to inform him of the university decision to investigate the incident. Marie also informs Steve that he is placed on temporary leave from the university judicial board until the investigation is completed. Marie asks for Steve's assistance in scheduling members to be interviewed during the next two evenings. Marie asked Steve if he has informed anyone from his fraternity's national office about the event. Steve replied, "No, because we didn't do anything wrong." Marie suggested that he should make the call as soon as possible.

Wednesday, January 14 and Thursday, January 15. Interviews are scheduled with all the Lambda Lambda Lambda new initiates, members of the executive council, and any other men deemed to be connected with this event. The chapter advisor denied any involvement with the incident and refused to be interviewed. Kerry and Marie conducted the interviews together and Steve was the first to be interviewed. He explained that a number of seniors had begun going to a strip joint in November and during one of the visits, one member came up with the idea that it would be great if the strippers came to the post-initiation brothers' party. The prior week, they had finalized their plans and negotiated a contract with a stripper. "In fact," Steve said, "I skipped a values and ethics workshop in order to finalize these details last week." Marie asked Steve what kind of contract the stripper had with the men. Steve said that she could do this trick with her teeth and pull the waistband off of men's underpants. She then would tie the elastic around their heads so that by the end of the evening, a lot of guys were wearing their underwear waistbands as headbands. "She had no other contact with the men?" Kerry asked. "Not beyond the usual stripper contact such as lap dancing, and such," said Steve.

Marie and Kerry continued to interview the officers and were told the same information repeatedly. No one would corroborate the lone statement that an advisor had been present for the event. The members of the executive board, for the most part, did not think that having a stripper at a post-initiation party was a very big deal; they saw it as something fun and different to do for the new initiates. Several of the officers laughed when they were asked if the stripper was touched by any of the members or if she had intercourse with any of the men. They went on to say that in their opinions, the guns that the stripper's escorts carried with them discouraged any person from thinking about getting out of line. When asked to describe the men and guns, the officers said that both the men and the guns were big!

Marie and Kerry talked to 15 new initiates, all of whom were convinced that somehow they had done something wrong. They believed that the chapter was in trouble because one of them must have "talked." The new initiates told similar stories to the initiated members. However, from the new initiates Kerry and Marie learned that the older brothers supplied beverages of choice for the new initiates, mostly beer. The average amount of beer provided seemed to be a 12 pack per new member. Of the 15 new initiates, only one was 21 years of age. New members denied that the stripper had sexual relations with anyone; they did acknowledge that several of the new members were singled out for increased attention from the stripper. But aside from having the waistband removed from their underwear, the stripper did not touch most of the new initiates. In addition, the new members said that they did not see their chapter advisor that evening but many acknowledged that their attention was directed at places other than the door.

You are Marie. The last interview has been completed. Kerry calls you on Friday morning and tells you that the executive director of the fraternity is on his way to SSU. You start to wonder what action if any the university should take in response to this incident. You begin to prepare for your meeting with the fraternity director. As you work you mentally formulate recommendations for the university's response that will have to be included in the report you will make to the dean of Students. What are they?

Sexual Harassment at All Saints College
Kerry McCaig
Arapahoe Community College
Cheryl D. Lovell
University of Denver

Setting

All Saints College is a private college and enjoys a small traditional-aged student body. Admissions to the college are beginning to grow as its reputation for academic integrity has been highly touted. The president has enthusiastic support from local community leaders, faculty, staff, and students. He has recently been recognized in the higher education community as a dynamic and creative leader. The school has a comprehensive liberal arts core and ethical and moral values development is the cornerstone of the undergraduate curriculum. Due to the school's location near a larger city there has been an increased emphasis on business and management programs.

The student body consists of largely White upper-middle class students with 68% of the students from out-of-state.

All Saints College is a church-related institution but it promotes diversity in the religious backgrounds of its students. The mission statement of All Saints College clearly promotes the need for justice and equitable treatment for all. In keeping with its mission, All Saints has recently made a strong commitment to eradicate sexual harassment.

Characters

Tim Jones, the director of Student Life, is 26 years old and this is his first position since completing his bachelor's degree in management. He reports directly to the vice president for Student Affairs. Part of Tim's responsibilities include serving as the advisor for the student judicial board.

Sally Smith is a 19-year-old junior class member at All Saints College. She is an honors student and she has been elected as a residence hall governing board member and a member of the junior class leadership program. She chairs the student task force on sexual harassment. She also works part-time as a life-guard at the campus recreational center.

Bill Wright is a 22-year-old sophomore who entered All Saints College in a special program for academically at-risk students. Immediately out of high school he enlisted in the United States Marine Corps, completed his service, received an honorable discharge, and enrolled in All Saints, where he has been an excellent student. He is in the sophomore leadership program and acts as a "big brother" to the students in the special program he was in last year.

Facts

1. The student sexual harassment task force has received a great deal of attention during the past year largely because of Sally Smith's vocal role on this committee.
2. The school's judicial board consists of five junior and senior class students. These students are appointed by the student government executive board and must be approved by the director of Student Life, Tim Jones.
3. The judicial board procedures are clearly identified in the student handbook along with sanctions and possible remedies. However, definitions of certain infractions are wanting. For example, sexual harassment, as noted in the handbook, is clearly not tolerated but behaviors which could be considered sexual harassment are not specified.
4. The judicial board advisor is to be available during judicial board hearings for assistance with clarifications concerning college policies and possible sanctions. However, the manual states that the judicial board advisor is not to be involved in the deliberation process.
5. No formal training occurs for judicial board members in regard to weighing and evaluating testimony and evidence.

Case

January 15 3:00 p.m. Bill Wright is sitting on the side of the swimming pool at the campus recreation center along with three other friends. While his friends are swimming he talks with Sally Smith, the lifeguard on duty. These are the only five people at the pool. Sally and Bill talk about a school party which was held the night before and they joke and tease each other about their dates of the previous evening. Casual discussion leads to Bill's drive to show-off a little. During some swimming acrobatics and horseplay Sally accuses Bill of "mooning" her and showing disrespect for her gender and position of authority. She asks Bill to leave the pool area immediately. In dismay, Bill denies "mooning" her and says he did not mean to show disrespect toward her or her position. He gathers his towel and leaves the pool.

January 17 around noon. Bill is told by a close friend who serves on the executive board that Sally is filing a grievance against him which will be taken to the judicial board. The charges are "indecent exposure," tampering with pool safety equipment, and sexual harassment.

January 17 7:00 p.m. Bill approaches Sally who is having dinner with two resident assistants. He tells her what he has heard and asks her if this information is true. She refuses to discuss anything which further frustrates and angers Bill. He accuses her of slandering his name and character. In disgust Bill leaves the table and states, "Someday you're going to grow up, little girl!"

January 17 10:00 p.m. Bill Wright gets a knock at his residence hall room door. Tim Jones demands to speak with Bill in the resident assistant's room immediately. Bill refuses. Tim then forces his way into Bill's room and demands some form of explanation for Bill's behavior earlier that evening when talking with Sally Smith in the cafeteria. Bill refuses to discuss anything, tells Tim that he is invading his privacy, intimidating him, and harassing him. Bill asks Tim to leave. Tim leaves the room and slams the door on his way out.

January 18 8:00 a.m. Bill goes to his academic advisor regarding the course of events over the last few days. The advisor calls Tim for information about the incidents. Tim confirms the report that a formal grievance has been filed by Sally Smith charging Bill with indecent exposure, tampering with pool-side safety equipment, and sexual harassment. Tim states that a notice has been sent to Bill via campus mail.

January 18 2:00 p.m. Bill receives written notification of the charges and that his hearing date has been set for January 20. He has the responsibility to notify any witnesses and present evidence which supports his testimony.

January 20 4:00 p.m. The judicial board meets to hear the case. Bill presents his three witnesses from the pool incident. Sally claims that his friends are collaborating with Bill on his story and it is really his word against hers. Since she had the position of authority she claims there should be no question as to who is telling the truth. Sally maintains that Bill mooned her, tampered with pool equipment, and then harassed her.

Bill insists that he did none of these things and that she is overreacting, confusing horseplay with sexual harassment. Bill argues that Sally is too sensitive to sexual harassment issues because of her role as chair of the sexual harassment task force. He feels like she is slandering his name and character.

During a closed door deliberation, Tim subtly influences the judicial board members to consider facts which were not presented during the formal hearing. He refers to Bill's high school reputation and his initial admission status during his freshman year.

After three hours, the judicial board decides that Bill acted inappropriately at the pool and in the cafeteria and has been found guilty of two counts of verbal (not sexual) harassment and one count of interfering with the safety operations in the pool facility by distracting the lifeguard while she was on duty. Sanctions for these offenses include placing Bill on final notice (the last step in the disciplinary process before expulsion), forbidding him to use the pool facility for the remainder of the school year, and requiring Bill to visit the campus counseling center three times.

January 21 1:00 p.m. Bill Wright is approached by one of the members of the judicial board who tells him that she feels uncomfortable about what happened in the judicial board hearing. She tells Bill about the closed door deliberations. He now, more than ever before, feels that he has been unjustly punished.

You are Tim Jones. The vice president for Student Affairs calls you to tell you that she has been contacted by Bill Wright's lawyer and Bill is considering a lawsuit against the Residence Life staff and the school. The lawyer says the basis for the lawsuit is that the judicial board procedures were not followed properly. The lawsuit specifically states that you (Tim Jones) invaded Bill's privacy by forcing yourself into his room. Furthermore, the suit states that you overextended your involvement in the judicial process. The vice president wants to see you in her office in the morning. What explanations and justifications can you offer for your actions? Would you change the manner in which you handle similar incidents in the future?

Scavenger Hunt
M. Christopher Brown II
Steven P. Thomas
University of Illinois at Urbana-Champaign

Setting

Hampshire State Agricultural College and Polytechnic Institute (HSAC & PI) is a beautiful college located at the foot of the mountains in a town called Thrashing, New Hampshire, population approximately 100,000. Hampshire State Agricultural College and Polytechnic Institute's mission is to serve the agricultural and industrial needs of the state and surrounding areas. The current enrollment is 14,735 undergraduate students and approximately 1,800 graduate students. Since HSAC & PI was established over 120 years ago, there has been a long tradition of fraternities and sororities existing on campus.

Characters

Dr. Jannie Hewton is the dean of Students. She has a total of seven departments that are responsible for reporting to her.
Mr. Peter Sharon is the director of judicial affairs, a department that reports to the dean of Students,
Joseph Bremen is a member of Lambda Kappa Alpha Fraternity. He has a roommate that he considers to be one of his best friends.
George Charleston is an African American male who is majoring in Criminal Justice. He is vice president of the African American Student Union, a registered student organization.
Lambda Kappa Alpha is an all male fraternity with a current membership of approximately 45 members. The fraternity has existed on the campus for over 80 years with a long history of traditions that date back to its original members.

Facts

1. Lambda Kappa Alpha has never been suspended or placed on probation for any hazing or unlawful acts as a fraternity.
2. HSAC & PI has very strict and enforced policies outlined for all fraternities and sororities as it relates to their membership intake and pledging processes.
3. A majority of the students who attend HSAC & PI are from the surrounding cities and towns of Thrasher within a 150 mile radius. The minority student population is approximately 10%.

Case

During the second week of the first semester of each academic year, many of the sororities and fraternities have membership intake for potential members of their respective organizations. For Lambda Kappa Alpha, the tradition has long been established that the last week of the pledging process is strictly devoted to Hell Week. For the first time in the history of Lambda Kappa Alpha, Hell Week will have a closing activity, one that is called "Scavenger Hunt." The idea behind the scavenger hunt is to divide the pledges into two teams of five. Each team is responsible for completing their scavenger hunt list, a list that contains legal and illegal items such as stop signs, women's underwear, brochures and flyers, and a photo of team members assaulting a person of color or a homosexual.

Monday, September 15. Team A finds the photo requirement to be offensive, but realizes that they must complete the hunt in order to become members of Lambda Kappa Alpha.

Friday, September 19. The scavenger hunt is scheduled to begin at 6:30 p.m. at the house of Lambda Kappa Alpha. All pledges are with their teams and have received instructions and are ready to hunt. Joseph is on Team A and as the team is collecting its items, he realizes they can go to his roommate George for the photo.

Team A arrives at Joseph and George's residence hall and decide that Joseph should go in and persuade his roommate to stage the photo for the scavenger hunt. Joseph enters the room and explains the situation to George asking him if he will allow the team to take a photo of them holding him down with a baseball bat over his head. George is appalled and offended at the idea of such an act; therefore, he refuses to take the photo. Joseph and George argue back and forth for about 10 minutes.

Finally, Joseph decides to proceed with the hunt despite his roommate's decision and calls his team members in to hold George down with a baseball bat over his head while Joseph takes several instant-image photos. George was not beaten or physically injured in any way. George calls campus police to make a formal assault charge. Two campus security officers come and take his statement.

Saturday, September 20. News of the scavenger hunt and photos are spreading across the campus and local community. George contacts campus police to see what action will be taken. He is informed that the incident is not covered by any university or state laws; and as such is not an assault.

George contacts the African American Student Union, and begins to plan a campus demonstration. He also contacts local civil rights groups who pass it on to the media. By the end of the day several television stations have visited campus about the "alleged beating of an African American student with a baseball bat in a campus dorm room." The alleged event is recounted on the evening and late night news.

Sunday, September 21. The Thrashing morning newspaper includes a brief front page mention of an "alleged beating of an unnamed African American student on the HSAC & PI campus." The editorial page also features a half page essay by a local minister about the state of race relations on the university campus and the repeated attempts by administration to sweep racial incidents under the rug.

The African American Student Union sponsors a candlelight vigil outside the president's house. The vigil includes passionate speeches by both students and local civil rights leaders. The event is taped by local media. At the same time the vigil is occurring, the Lambda Kappa Alpha Fraternity is conducting its final oath and initiation ceremonies.

The university president receives midnight calls from members of the institution's Board of Trustees regarding statewide news reports of racial unrest on campus.

Monday, September 22. The student-run campus newspaper features the headline: "No Beating, Black Students Overreact." Beneath the headline are photos from the vigil, and one of the photos taken by Joseph. African American students, as well as other concerned students are outraged. There are discussions of taking over the administration building.

Dr. Jannie Hewton arrives on campus at 8:00 a.m. after a weekend out of town. She returned to Thrashing after midnight and is unaware of any of the weekend's events. She is greeted by a voice mail from the president requesting to see her at 9:30 a.m. to discuss a potential response to both the incident and student unrest. Dr. Hewton calls Peter Sharon for an update on the weekend's events. After a 30 minute phone call, Dr. Hewton requests Mr. Sharon provide her with a set of recommendations by 9:00 a.m.

What recommendations would you as Mr. Sharon make?

Safety at Arbor Hill: The Limits of Liability
Michael D. Coomes
Bowling Green State University

Setting

Arbor Hill College is a product of the 1960s. The founding Board of Overseers desired to start a college that would incorporate innovative and nontraditional approaches to teaching and learning. The following excerpt from the mission statement of the college captures the uniqueness that is Arbor Hill:

Arbor Hill College was founded in 1965 as an alternative to existing postsecondary opportunities in the State of Oregon. The Board of Overseers set three goals for Arbor Hill that have shaped its development:

1. Arbor Hill College is committed to teaching.
2. Students will be empowered.
3. Arbor Hill College will be a just and caring community.

"Arbor Hill College is committed to the establishment of a community of learners. Faculty, staff, administrators, and students cooperate in a spirit of mutual inquiry in the search for Truth. Toward that end, we strive to foster a sense of cooperation, respect, mutual support, and friendship. We do not utilize formal titles at Arbor Hill because it is our belief that titles infer status and status serves to set up barriers to equality. We treat all members of the Arbor Hill community with the respect due to all persons.

We firmly believe that critical thinking is developed and that content is mastered when students take responsibility for their own learning. The heart of the Arbor Hill curriculum is the learning project. These projects are designed as interdisciplinary experiences by teams of faculty and student colearners. Learning projects can grow out of an individual student's interests or a faculty member's desire to explore new areas of intellectual curiosity. By making learning projects interdisciplinary in focus we will help our students see the interrelatedness that exists within our College and the world." (Arbor Hill Bulletin, p. 1)

Arbor Hill College is located on the outskirts of a city of 25,750. The campus sits on 250 acres. The campus grounds are surrounded by an eight foot brick wall. During the day entrance to the campus is possible through one of four gates. At night, entrance to the campus is only possible through the main gate, which is monitored by a member of the campus security force.

The focal point of campus is The Quad, a large grassy area that is bordered by the Allen Library, classroom buildings, and the College Union Building (CUB).

The area is the scene of informal discussions, impromptu concerts, political rallies, and outdoor classes. Students and faculty use the portico of the CUB as a place to set up tables and distribute materials for a wide range of social and environmental causes.

Arbor Hill College enrolls 5,235 undergraduate students; 65% of the students are from the state of Oregon. Approximately 20% of the students are people of color. Eighty percent of all students live on campus in low-density "houses." There are no fraternities or sororities on campus. The typical Arbor Hill student is liberal, environmentally conscious, and actively involved in a number of social, political, and campus causes. The primary reasons new students cite for selecting Arbor Hill are its antiauthoritarian image and its innovative curriculum. Students, true to the wishes of the college's founders, actively participate in all levels of college governance and are perceived as equals by administrators and staff. Arbor Hill exudes feelings of cooperation, activism, and community.

Characters

Dr. Judith Pruitt is Arbor Hill's fourth president. A faculty member since the college was founded, she has also held the posts chair of the Department of Psychology, dean of the Faculty, and college provost. She has been the president for the past four years and is highly respected by the campus community. While she firmly supports the mission of the college and appreciates its informal atmosphere, she has been charged by the Board of Overseers to improve administrative functioning at the college. To realize those goals, she has formalized the college's mission statement and has called for the institution of a strategic plan. The latter action has met with some opposition by long standing members of the campus community.

Dr. Sarah Roth is the dean of Students at Arbor Hill College. She is a graduate of the college and has worked there for the past ten years. She is a tenured associate professor in the Department of Psychology. Sarah was hired by President Pruitt three years ago. She firmly believes in the mission of the institution and has worked effectively to integrate student life functions with the academic curriculum. Reporting to her are seven functional areas: Residential Service, Student Activities and Organizations, Counseling and Psychological Services, Orientation, Leadership Development, Co-operative Learning Experiences (a cosponsored program with Academic Life Division), and the Student Health Center.

Dr. Frank Lester, vice president for Business and Finance, is new to Arbor Hill. He was hired two years ago and brings with him considerable private industry experience. He was specifically hired to improve the college's investment portfolio. His division includes: The Bursars Office, Accounting, Campus Security, and Physical Plant.

Larry Wonderly, chief of Campus Security, is a former city policeman. He has been employed by Arbor Hill for three years. During that period, he has doubled the size of the security force at the college. Few serious crimes have occurred on campus during his tenure.

James Johnson, Campus Security officer, is, like his superior, a former city policeman. He was hired last year and is head of the Campus Security Officer's Association, a quasi-union.

Deborah Putnam, chair of the Student Congress, is an Arbor Hill senior planning a career in politics. Like most Arbor Hill students, she is highly active in political and social causes. As the chair of the Student Congress, she serves as a member of the president's Cabinet. She considers Judith to be both a co-worker and a mentor.

John Tasker, Sally Sokola, and **Wendy Rains** are all Arbor Hill students. All three students are members of the ad hoc committee on campus security. Wendy is also a member of the Women's Union, a group of female students and faculty who advocate for women's issues on the campus.

Case

August 20. During the first president's Cabinet meeting of the year, President Judith Pruitt distributes a letter from Larry Wonderly, chief of Campus Security. In his letter, Larry indicates that a number of his security officers question the security policies of the college. Most specifically, they question the institution's policy that prohibits security officers from carrying side arms. Campus security officers are currently armed only with nightsticks. While most members of the Cabinet support the current policy, Frank Lester, vice president for Business and Finance, raises the issues of the publicity surrounding increasing incidents of crime on the nation's campuses and the need for Arbor Hill to avoid negative publicity. After considerable discussion, President Pruitt asks Deborah Putnam, chair of the Student Congress, to head an ad hoc committee to examine the issue of campus safety and the request of the security officers.

September 15. The ad hoc committee on campus security meets for the first time to consider the issue of safety on the Arbor Hill campus. The committee consists of: Deborah Putnam, Larry Wonderly, Frank Lester, James Johnson, John Tasker, Sally Sokola, and Wendy Rains. During the meeting discussion centers on whether the security needs of the campus truly warrant arming the campus security force. The most vocal supporters of such an action are James Johnson, who is serving as the spokesperson for the campus security officers and Wendy Rains, a member of the Women's Union. James is concerned that the failure to authorize the carrying of side arms may jeopardize the safety of his fellow officers. Wendy supports the security officers' appeal by arguing that an armed security force would serve to deter attacks against women. After two hours of discussion, the committee decides to poll the campus on the issue of arming the security force.

October 1. All members of the Arbor Hill community (i.e., faculty, administrators, staff, and students) receive a survey concerning the issue of campus safety. The survey seeks information on how safe members of the community feel and whether campus security officers should be armed.

October 2. The lead editorial in the campus newspaper severely criticizes the idea of arming campus security officers. The editorial concludes with: "Armed police are antithetical to the sense of community that is Arbor Hill College. We would seriously hope that the college administration demonstrates its good sense by ditching the idea of arming the campus security officers. Please send a strong message to the decision makers by indicating that campus safety can only be endangered by allowing guns on campus. Don't turn Arbor Hill into a police state!"

October 3–9. Subsequent issues of the campus paper run numerous articles responding to the earlier editorial and the question of arming the security officers. Sentiment runs five to one against arming the officers. The most frequently cited response is that armed officers would violate the sense of community that exists at Arbor Hill.

October 15. The ad hoc committee on campus security meets for the second time and reviews the survey data. Completed surveys are returned by 72% of the campus community. An overwhelming majority (86.5%) of respondents oppose arming the campus security officers. Comments opposing arming the security officers frequently cite the sense of family that is fostered at Arbor Hill and the current safe conditions at the college (most specifically the night security guards and the limits on access to the campus at night).

During the meeting, Larry Wonderly presents the Arbor Hill crime statistics for the past three years. The majority of incidents at Arbor Hill have involved crimes against property (e.g., theft, vandalism) and disorderly conduct resulting from substance abuse. There have been no reported rapes and only one reported assault in the past three years, far below the national average. James Johnson once again pleads the case for arming campus security officers and asks that the committee not be swayed by the survey results, but consider the informed opinion of a professional security expert.

October 25. The lead article in the Portsmouth *Beacon* reports on security at Arbor Hill college. During the previous week, an investigative reporter with the *Beacon* was given a midnight tour of the campus by an unnamed member of the security force. In his story, the reporter claims that the guard house at the entrance of campus was left unattended for as long as 30 minutes at a time. He also reports on building entrances with poor or no lighting, students sleeping and studying in unlocked classroom buildings, residence hall doors propped open, and graffiti smeared walls. The article closes with a quote from the college's *Viewbook* that highlights the safe nature of the Arbor Hill campus.

October 29. The ad hoc committee meets for the final time to draft its recommendations to the president. While the committee is concerned about the adverse publicity generated by the *Beacon* article, the committee recommends against arming the security officers. The committee cites the relative lack of serious crime on campus, and a belief that the institution's culture would not support armed officers on campus. The latter conclusion is supported through reference to the data from the all-campus survey. Finally, the committee suggests that armed officers may present an image that would adversely affect the recruitment of students. James Johnson expresses extreme dissatisfaction with the Committee's decision and indicates that he will take his case elsewhere if necessary.

November 1. You are Sarah Roth, the dean of Students. You are notified by campus security that a female student was assaulted the previous night following a Halloween party in one of the houses. The attack occurred on a poorly lighted campus footpath. No one reported hearing any disturbance at the time. The student was admitted to a Portsmouth Hospital where she was treated, held for observation for a day, and released. She reported the attack to both Campus Security officers and to Portsmouth police. In her reports she indicated that she did not believe that the assailants were students. She also indicated to her roommate that she would not be returning to campus for an undetermined period of time.

News of the assault spreads swiftly through campus. The Women's Union has called for a "Take Back the Night" rally for the night of November 2.

You present the facts of the assault, as you know them, to the president during the regularly scheduled president's Cabinet meeting. On the agenda for that meeting is the report from the ad hoc committee on campus safety containing its recommendation not to arm campus security officers. Cabinet members are also handed a letter from James Johnson who indicates that if the Cabinet accepts the committee's recommendation, he will be forced to file a complaint with the Oregon Department of Labor and Industry. In the complaint he will charge the campus with unsafe working conditions for security officers on campus.

The president asks you to take the report, Johnson's threatened complaint, and the recent assault into consideration in drafting both short- and long-term recommendations for the college. She also asks you to identify any relevant case law should the victim of the assault choose to sue the college. What information would you include in your reports?

Case by Case Index*

*This case study index is intended to serve as a general guide for instructors and facilitators who wish to identify specific characteristics for their classes. It is not comprehensive, and in fact, nearly every case will involve additional constituents and issues that would need to be addressed for adequate resolution.

Case	Constituents	Issues	Page
First Generation College Students: Tension between Faculty and Staff	Students Student and academic affairs staff	Advising Academic support First-generation students	100
Culture Clash: International Student Incident at Middle Valley University	Students Faculty Parents	International students Diversity Classroom incivility Counseling	103
Aiding International Students: Whose Responsibility?	Faculty Student affairs staff International students	International students Campus climate Advising	109
Little Secrets and Chain Reactions: The Case of Ana Maria Lopez at Traditional University	Students Student affairs staff	Greek life HIV/AIDS Counseling	113
Challenges of the New Frontier: The Internet and Student Affairs Practice	Students Parents Student affairs staff Media	Technology Student conduct Legal issues Residence life	118
The Morning After	Students Student affairs staff Media	Diversity Judicial affairs Student conduct Residence life	121
Violence and Romance: A Case Study	Students Student affairs staff	Residence life Alcohol Judicial affairs Student conduct	125
Fighting Words	Students Faculty Student affairs staff Media	Diversity Judicial affairs Student conduct Residence life	128
Hatred in the Heartland: Anywhere College Responds	Students Faculty Board of Trustees External public	Diversity Student conduct Religious affiliation Residence life	132
Take Back the Night: A Gauge of the Climate for Women on Campus	Students Faculty Student affairs staff	Gender issues Diversity Student conduct Student activities	140
Hazing is Prohibited: It Sounds so Simple	Students Student affairs staff	Greek life Diversity Student conduct Student activities	144
Breakfast at Tara	Students Student affairs staff	Diversity Student activities Student conduct	149

Subject Index